The Extraordinary Life of *Helena Sztukowska*

AN AUTOBIOGRAPHY

THE CHOIR PRESS

First published in the United Kingdom in 2025 by
The Choir Press

ISBN 978-1-78963-533-1

English version: ArcusLink Małgorzata Kierska

The author as a young lawyer. Vilnius, 1929

HELENA SZTUKOWSKA NÉE FALEWICZ
Excerpts from the Memoirs of a Vilnius Defender
Toruń 1977 • Nieborów 1954

Contents

ACKNOWLEDGMENTS

Jan Sztukowski wishes to place on record his appreciation to all those who have assisted in bringing this project to fruition. In particular he wishes to thank:

Peter Birkett K.C. For his guidance support and advice. This project would not have succeeded without his help.

David and Rachel at the Choir Press for their support throughout.

Joshua Lambert who edited the book.

Malgorzata Kierska for the remarkable talents she exhibited in translating the memoir from the original Polish. Her skill in translating the poems written to Helena are deserving of particular praise.

Ewa Papis for her determination and drive in seeing the project through.

All those whose love and regard for Helena provided the inspiration for the book to be published in English.

*To my most beloved boys: son Jan, grandchildren Patrick and Dominik,
and great grandson William*

ABOUT THE AUTHOR

Helena Sztukowska, née Falewicz, was born in Vilnius on 1 April 1901, the second child of Jan Marcin Falewicz of the Pobóg nobility family and Wanda Więckowska of the Prus nobility (she had a brother, Kazimierz, two and a half years her elder, and two years younger a brother, Stanisław).

Helena grew up in a home with strong patriotic traditions. Her great-grandfather, Jan Felix, a philomath and friend of Zan and Czeczot, was involved in secret student organisations at Vilnius University. His son and Helena's grandfather, Karol Szczęsny, an agricultural engineer, landowner, social activist and publicist, took part in the January Uprising in Lithuania, was secretary to its leader, General Zygmunt Sierakowski, and a member of the Provisional Government of Lithuania. He was arrested and sentenced to death by Mikhail Nikolayevich Muravyov, and only by chance did he escape the death penalty and have his sentence changed to several years in the Dinaburg Fortress. Her father, Jan Marcin, graduated from St Petersburg Polytechnic and worked as a chemical engineer in sugar factories in Podolia.

Helena was educated first at home (taking her exams at a girls' boarding school in Warsaw), then in Kiev and at Mrs Arciszowa's girls' boarding school in Lublin, where she graduated in the spring of 1920. After the Battle of Radzymin (the Miracle on the Vistula), she volunteered for the sanitary service, worked as a surgical nurse in a field hospital in Warsaw and spent a few months at a field hospital close to the front line. After the armistice, Helena returned to her family estate, Balinpol near Vilnius. At the time, her father was the speaker of the Vilnius-Trakai District Assembly and a member (and even a deputy speaker) of the Central Lithuanian Parliament (Sejm). His signature appears on the Act of Incorporation of Central Lithuania into Poland, passed by that parliament.

From 1921 to 1924, she studied at the Faculty of Law and Social Sciences at Stefan Batory University in Vilnius. At the same time, she worked for the Social Insurance Company in Vilnius, preparing insurance records at home. Helena graduated from the Faculty of Law in 1924, her diploma bearing the number 1.

In 1924–1925 she stayed in Paris, where she studied at the Ecole des Sciences Politiques, at the same time working as a correspondent for the Vilnius daily *Słowo* (*Word*) and as an intern at the Polish embassy in Paris (where she prepared court requisitions).

In 1925 Helena married Józef Sztukowski of the Jelita coat of arms, a lieutenant in the 23rd Uhlan Regiment (cavalry unit), who worked in the military attaché's office at the Polish embassy in Moscow. She and her husband spent the end of the year in the Soviet Union. On her return, Helena resumed her judge and barrister training (her patron was the eminent civilian Walenty Parczewski). After completing her training and passing the Bar exam, she opened her own law office specialising in criminal cases. She also took part in numerous political trials, defending, together with the lawyer Mieczysław Szerer, the communist youth from the weekly paper *Po prostu (As Simple As That)*. Together with her friend, barrister Halina Sukiennicka, she served as a model for the character of the beautiful barrister in Jerzy Putrament's novel *Rzeczywistość (Reality)*.

Helena was also a prison probation officer and an active member of the Vilnius Prison Patronage. She contributed to the Vilnius daily newspaper *Słowo*, and co-edited the weekly women's supplement *Kobieta i Życie* (*Woman and Life*). She was an active member of the Union of Higher Educated Women, which fought for women's emancipation.

In the interwar period she gave birth to a son (in 1935). Helena was an active sportswoman, she played tennis, was an equestrian (taking part in hunters' races), hunted and flew (she was one of the first members of the Vilnius Aero Club, of which her husband, Józef Sztukowski, was the president).

The outbreak of the war found her in Vilnius. She stopped practising law and started working as a prompter at the Small Theatre of Vilnius. At the same time, Helena became involved in the underground movement in the Vilnius area. In 1940, her husband, a prisoner of war in the Kozelsk camp, was murdered in Katyń.

After the Germans entered Vilnius, she began to hide Jews and Poles wanted by the German authorities. She hid them both in her apartment in Vilnius and at the Balinpol family estate, and organised other hiding places. She was denounced and arrested twice, once for helping her sick niece Helena Falewiczówna in Warsaw, and the second time for hiding people of Jewish origin. She spent several months in a prison she knew well from her work for the Prison Patronage – Lukiškės Prison in Vilnius.

After her release, Helena returned to underground activities. Expelled from Vilnius, she moved to Toruń, where she practised law from 1946 to 1973. She continued to specialise in criminal cases, but also acted as a defence lawyer in political trials (against members of the Home Army [AK], the clergy, the Polish People's Party [PSL], etc.). Twice she was submitted to disciplinary action. In 1951 she was arrested on suspicion of failing to inform the authorities of the alleged conspiratorial activities of her fifteen-year-old niece, Wanda Falewiczówna, who lived with her. She spent seven months in prison in Bydgoszcz.

During the Stalinist period, Helena's home was subject to many forms of repression. Her fifteen-year-old niece spent three years in prison in Toruń, Fordon and Bojanowo. Her cousin, Jan Wierusz-Kowalski, with whom she grew up and whom she treated as a younger brother, was murdered by the Security Service (UB) in Bydgoszcz during an investigation.

After release from prison, she obtained a craftsman's diploma and began to practise arts and crafts. However, she returned to legal practice (with the help of the 'academic left' from Vilnius).

From 1957 to 1970, Helena was actively involved in motor sport. She made several trips abroad (England, France, Norway, Canada, Mexico), after which she gave lectures on her travels and the countries she visited at the General Knowledge Society (Towarzystwo Wiedzy Powszechnej, TWP) and the International Press and Book Club (Międzynarodowy Klub Prasy i Książki, MKPiK).

In Toruń, as in Vilnius, she was an active collector and ran an open house where representatives of Vilnius and Toruń artistic circles met. She was friends with many scholars and artists (including Tymon Niesiołowski). Her collections included valuable works of contemporary art.

When Antoni Bohdziewicz directed the film *Rzeczywistość* (based on the novel by J Putrament), Helena acted as a film consultant and made her beautiful, typical Vilnius apartment available for filming.

She retired in 1973, but continued to appear in court from time to time. In all, Helena made more than 8,000 court appearances. She also began organising her archive and writing her memoirs, which are included in this volume.

In 1978, Helena moved to Warsaw, where she lived for the rest of her life and died on 4 August 1985.

She was awarded the Poland to its Defender Medal for her actions in 1920, the Silver Cross of Merit with Swords for her activities in the Vilnius Home Army, and the Righteous Among the Nations medal for saving Jews; she has a tree dedicated to her in Jerusalem.

Helena's son Jan, a chemical engineer (born in 1935 in Vilnius), has two sons, Patrick (born 1980) and Dominik (born 1983), and lives permanently in the UK where he works as a consultant for large chemical companies.

The above notes are a substitute for the foreword to the excerpts from the memoirs of my aunt, a person who led a very colourful, interesting and rich life. These excerpts consist of twelve chapters of varying length. The first eight (with the exception of the short chapter on studies in Vilnius) were written in 1977 in Toruń, Chapters 9–11 were written between 1981 and 1982 in England, in Prestbury, while Helena stayed with her son, and the final chapter was written in Warsaw between 1983 and 1984.

Jan Karol Falewicz
Nieborów, April 1984

CHAPTER I
Childhood

꧁꧂

Going back to my earliest childhood, I see a large, single-storey house standing by the side of the road. You entered the house from the right gable side, up a flight of steps. From the hall you entered a large living room that spanned the whole width of the house and then a corridor that led to other rooms on the right side of the house.

Behind the house was a park, or rather a forest. At the end of it was an old moat, the opposite bank of which was very high. Behind the moat was a fence. As children we were not allowed to go near the moat, which was overgrown with grass and often filled with water.

It was a time of social unrest and 1905 was approaching. I was four years old and everyone called me 'Dolly'. I had scarlet fever and remembered the doctor's face as he bent over my bed. I had a brother, Kaj, who was two and a half years older than me, and Stach, who was two years younger and taking his first steps.

We did not go to the park behind the house very often. It was a gloomy place with no sunlight. With my nanny and older brother, however, we often went to the beautiful park that belonged to Mr Leszczyński, a Russian who owned the estate and the factory. My father worked as a director in his sugar factory. Those walks in the magical garden will always remain in the memory of the young child. It was in Ukraine, in the Kiev governorate, and the village was called Kijanica[1]. In this magnificent garden there was a palace which you entered through a long and high rose tunnel made of wooden rails overgrown with roses. It was a long walk through the rose tunnel, but I think I only entered the palace once, when I stepped up the red carpet-lined stairs. I remember one interesting feature – every few steps, once to the left and once to the right, there were large aquariums full of agile fish. I found it very interesting and impressive!

We probably went to the palace gardens every day. We travelled along

---

[1] My Father worked in Kijanica in the years 1903–1905.

1

long, wide paths in a two-wheeled pram on which you could sit both front and back, pulled by a pony led by our nanny. What I remember from those walks were the gazebos of various shapes and sizes and the part of the garden with the alpine garden: stones, rocks, flowers and a waterfall.

In my childhood imagination everything was huge, but I suppose the park of Leszczyński's grand residence must have been really beautiful and well kept. My father later told me that Mr Leszczyński fled to France after the revolution and ran a restaurant in Biarritz.

I remember visits with my parents to the sugar factory officials, where I played with other children with various new toys.

I remember watermelons in the fields of Podolia, gathered in heaps just like sugar beets at our estate. My mother used to buy a cart full of watermelons, there were a hundred of them, and she later said that it cost her one rouble – one watermelon cost one kopeck!

I also remember once pushing my younger brother in the hallway at home. He fell and cut his lip. As a punishment, I was locked in a junk room separated from the corridor by a partition wall – it was full of trunks and suitcases. Poor Dolly climbed on top of a pile of junk and fell asleep. When the prisoner was about to be released, she appeared to be asleep, and her otherwise stern mother, moved and contrite, took the poor, punished child in her arms.

The second sugar factory in the Seized Territories [*the eastern voivodships of the First Republic of Poland seized by the Russian Empire as a result of the Partition of Poland (1772–1795), constituting the area of Russian annexation, excluding the territory of the Kingdom of Poland established in 1815*] in Russia, where my father worked as a director, was Trostianets in Podolia[2]. The estate and the sugar factory belonged to the Pannenko family, well-known Polish sugar makers. In the interwar period Ludwik Pannenko was a member of the executive board of the Polish Sugar Association.

This must have been during or just after the Revolution of 1905, because the factory had its own guard. I was fascinated and impressed by their appearance. They were Circassians – tall, handsome men wearing high papakha hats on their heads, dressed in long frock coats with numerous diagonally arranged cartridge pockets on their chests.

---

[2] My father was director of the sugar factory in Trostianets for only one sugar campaign – in 1906.

We lived in a large single-storey house, not far from the factory and not far from the owners' house, which was hidden behind a large gate in a shady and mysterious garden. There was a lawn and a driveway in front of our house.

At that time we had a pointing dog who used to push us around in a two-wheeled pram, with a tasty snack strapped to his thill, which he tried in vain to reach by running forward.

One incident from Trostianets sticks in my mind. We were travelling with my parents in a carriage drawn by four horses. An old man fell under the speeding horses. I was horrified to see the man's head under the carriage. I was not told what happened to him ...

I have only vague memories of Trostianets. Part of the large house was occupied by our family, and the other part was used as guest rooms. Empty windows, gloomy inside, seemed frightening to the children. I never saw anyone living there, no visitors, no sign of life.

My father obviously liked change, because by the time I was eleven he had moved the whole family to the third sugar factory in Ukraine, in Blahodatne by the river Seym[3], which flowed very close to our house and on which the passenger ships *Hugo* and *Karol* operated. There was a path leading down to the river over its high bank. There was also a park near the house, bigger than in Kijanica and completely wild. We often found hedgehogs there. We would take them home and put them in an empty hall, where they would run around at night making such a noise that they would wake us up. Our parents would tell us to take them back to the park.

My father was a keen hunter and whenever he went out to hunt birds, he would take us with him. The river was full of bends and reeds. It was a breeding ground for mosquitoes. The place was infested with them! When we went hunting with our father, we used to wrap paper around our legs under our stockings to protect them from the mosquitoes.

What I remember from those days was a boat trip to get apples. We all walked down the path to the boat, in the middle of which was a large wicker basket with a lid, ready for the apples. The biggest attraction was a ride in that basket. Unfortunately, on the way back the basket was full of apples and we had to sit on the regular benches.

---

[3] Father worked there for only one campaign – in 1907. The Seym river joins the Desna, the right-bank tributary of the Dnieper River.

I remember our baths in the bathroom and then running around the children's rooms in long nightgowns and being herded into bed by our mother: a prayer, kisses and sleep!

Blahodatne was the third sugar factory in Podolia where my father was a director. But he had worked in the sugar industry before that, as a chemical engineer, a graduate of St. Petersburg Polytechnic. When he was still a bachelor, he took up the post of deputy director of the sugar factory in Shamraivka in the Kiev governorate in the so-called Branicki region, the estates and sugar mills of the Branicki family of Bila Tserkva. For thirty-five years, the director at the sugar factory of Shamraivka was Kazimierz Więckowski, who had two daughters, Wanda and Joanna. My father married the older one, Wanda. She was my mother. I will return to her more than once in my memoirs. Now I would like to say a few words about Kazimierz Więckowski's second daughter, Joanna. Aunt Joanna, a year younger than my mother, married Michał Wierusz-Kowalski, a native of Greater Poland region, who died tragically during the Bolshevik Revolution. He was pushed off the step of a carriage and fell under the wheels of an approaching train. The train decapitated him.

They had four children: Marychna, Antek, Wanda and Janek. After returning from Russia, all four of them came down with tuberculosis. My mother took care of the family and brought them to Balinpol. Wanda and Antek died from tuberculosis. Marychna, who was a very beautiful woman, married Colonel Ożyński. She was of delicate health and underwent years of climatic treatment for tuberculosis. She died in Toruń after the Second World War.

Aunt Joanna was seriously ill with liver cancer. I often visited her in hospital. She died in Balinpol and was buried next to my father in the village cemetery in Buivydžiai. The youngest of the siblings, Janek, grew up with us in Balinpol and we all treated him like a younger brother. Janek was active in the underground resistance movement as Lieutenant 'Frog'. After the war he returned to professional military service with the rank of major. He was a lecturer at the War College. During the Stalinist period he was murdered by the Security Service in Bydgoszcz.

After three jobs as a sugar factory director in the Seized Territories, my father eventually ended up in the Kingdom of Poland in 1908, in the Lublin governorate, at the sugar factory in Strzyżów by the Bug River, located at the border of Volhynia, close to the Austrian border. My father became the director of that sugar factory, which belonged to a joint-stock company (the main shareholders were Messrs Rulikowski, Chrzanowski and Moroczyna) and the administrator of the property associated with the sugar factory. Strzyżów had been formerly owned by the Starzeński family, and had a large stately one-storey palace standing on the banks of the Bug River.

On the ground floor of the palace were the offices of the sugar factory and father's large study. There were also four large guest rooms and servants' quarters. We lived upstairs. There were seven rooms, a kitchen, two pantries and a huge covered veranda. The dining room was oval and spanned the entire width of the house. Below it, on the ground floor, was father's huge study, once used as a ballroom.

The dining room over the eastern side of the palace overlooked a beautiful view of the Bug River, which surrounded the grounds, flowing slowly through the meadows, and in the distance, on the horizon, one could see the great forests of Volhynia.

Strzyżów was my childhood paradise. Everything a child could dream of was there.

From my father's study on the ground floor, you walked into a flower garden, fenced off from the Bug River meadows by a very high wall. There were beautiful old chestnut trees in the garden, which my brother and I used to climb, and in the hollows of which we would hide our treasures: pebbles, coins made of stones, etc. From these chestnut trees we could admire sweeping views of the Bug River, the surrounding meadows and forests of Volhynia. My father used to organise hunts in these forests. We, the children, always rode on sledges and then stood behind the hunters, waiting for the hunt to begin. It was very exciting for us. In winter, a long pole was put up on the palace balcony and the trophies from the hunt, such as hares or deer, were hung on it.

SWEDEN

Bornholm (Denmark)

Baltic Sea

GERMAN EMPIRE

Pomerania · West Prussia · East Prussia

Brandenburg · Posen · Silesia

RUSSIAN EMPIRE

Memel · Panevežys · Dyneburg
Kovno Gov. · Utena · Ukmerge · Švenčioneliai
Taurage · Kovno · Vilnius Gov. · Vilnius
Tilsit · Marijampole · Suwalki · Lida · Minsk
Königsberg · Grodno · Białystok · Baranavichy · Slutsk
Elbing · Allenstein · Lyck · Grodno Gov. · Minsk Gov.
Stolp · Köslin · Danzig · Ciechanow · Ostroleka · Brest · Pinsk
Kolberg · Neustettin · Thorn · Plock · Siedlce
Stettin · Schneidemühl · Bromberg · Konin · Warsaw · Lodz
Pyritz · Landsberg · Frankfurt · Posen · Leszno · Sieradz

Kingdom of Poland

Radom · Lublin · Kovel · Volhynia Gov. · Rivne
Glogau · Grünberg · Czestochowa · Kielce · Zamosc · Shepetivka
Bautzen · Görlitz · Breslau · Oppeln · Beuthen
Jablonec · Glatz · Krakau · Rzeszow · Jaroslaw · Lemberg (Lviv) · Ternopil · Podolia Gov.
Kingdom of Bohemia · Prague · Pardubice · Opava · Tešin · Przemysl · Kamianets-Podilskyi
Jihlava · Olomouc · Austrian Silesia · Nowy Sacz · Sanok · Drohobych · Boryslav · Stanislawow
Margraviate of Moravia · Brno · Trenčín · Ružomberok · Prešov · Cherniytsi · Duchy of Bukovina
Břeclav · Banska Bystrica · Košice · Sighetu · Suceava
AUSTRIAN EMPIRE · Lower Austria · VIENA · Pressburg
Kingdom of Galicia and Lodomeria
Kingdom of Hungary
Györ · Budapest · Debrecen · Satu Mare · ROMANIA

POLISH LANDS IN THE YEAR 1900

0 ——— 250 ——— 500 km

Map creation: Marcin J. Sobiech, www.exgeo.pl

——— State boundaries
— — — Provincial boundaries
○ cities
VIENA Name of state capitals
Lemberg Name of provincial capitals

6

In winter we used to slide on the pond near the entrance gate to the palace grounds. We went sledging down the hill, while in the forest we practised riding. We often played tennis.

In addition to the flower garden next to the palace, on the side of the meadows and the Bug River, we had a vegetable garden with a greenhouse, which was tended by a gardener, and further away an orchard with 400 trees. We loved the time when we could pick fruit and put it into large, two-handled baskets. The fruit was then stored in the cellars under the palace, and there was so much of it that they lasted until the following summer. The orchard was also full of walnut trees. I remember carrying huge baskets full of walnuts down to the cellar.

We studied at home. A tutor came from Warsaw and lived with us. In the mornings we had lessons in general subjects, while French was taught by another person, a Frenchwoman, with whom we spent our free time, went for walks or sat at the table during meals. First it was Mademoiselle Margueritte Chaselet, then Mademoiselle Berthe Diremger. Every year my mother and I went to Warsaw, where I took exams at Miss Kowalczy-kówna's boarding school and received a certificate allowing me to move on to the next grade. It was not until after the exile that I actually went to school, to the fifth grade of secondary school – in Kiev, where we had fled as war refugees. On my return to Poland in 1918, I entered the seventh grade of Mrs Arciszowa's girls' boarding school in Lublin and passed my matriculation examination in the spring of 1920.

I had a lot of free time in Strzyżów. I used to run around the gardens with my brothers, climb trees and look after the animals. We had a few dogs: pointing dogs for hunting and fox terriers as house dogs. There was also a deer enclosure next to the director's stables, and I took care of it.

There was also a domesticated squirrel called Crunchy, who had his cage on the balcony. In the summer, we would have meals and entertain on this large balcony, which was covered and closed at the sides, and this is where Crunchy had his cage. The cage was open most of the time so Crunchy was free to roam, and would obediently return to his cage after a walk. The inside of the cage was made of wood and divided into two parts. One was the bedroom, padded with cotton wool and a piece of fleece nailed over the opening to keep the wind out; the other end of the 'house', also with an opening, was his pantry.

At Christmas we made a Christmas tree for Crunchy by putting a spruce branch inside a large potato. Crunchy would come out of his bedroom sleepy and warm, walk up to the Christmas tree, knock it over with his paw, take all the goodies: sweets, dates, figs, etc., and carry them all back to his pantry.

Crunchy was very domesticated and always tried to get into the house, but when he did, he damaged the furniture with his teeth. He ran along the ledges of the ground floor of the palace, looking in all the windows, but the windows were protected with mesh, so he danced in front of it, leaning on the mesh with his front paws, and then ventured further. When he got into the house, he would climb all over the members of the household, over their clothes and onto their shoulders. One guest was particularly disturbed when, as he ate his dinner with his head bent over the plate, Crunchy noticed the gap between his neck and collar, popped a walnut behind the collar and began to bury it with his front paws.

Although walnuts were plentiful in Strzyżów and Crunchy had plenty of them, he jumped on the table, grabbed the nuts and buried them in flower pots. After a while, the walnut trees Crunchy had 'planted' sprouted from the soil. Crunchy was fond of perfume and when someone wearing perfume picked him up, he would stretch out on his back to have his white belly scratched[4]. He would often crawl into my pocket and fall asleep, and I would have to be very careful not to wake him up. Crunchy was not always so benign. I remember one, simple Grzela, trying to chase him out of the room with a rag in his hand. When he was finally caught, Crunchy bit Grzela's hand down to the bone. When we had to leave Strzyżów during the war, we left Crunchy in his cage. Later I learnt that he was killed by a soldier.

I also raised rabbits in a box room. The first Frenchwoman who came to us, Mademoiselle Margueritte, was also very fond of animals. We used to go to the meadow with her to pick the grass that the rabbits liked. Once, when we were giving them food, we noticed blood under the eye of one of the rabbits – the poor animal was injured. It turned out that the rabbit had been bitten by a rat. We took it back to treat it, and when the wound healed, no fur grew back where it had been bitten. We called the rabbit

---

[4] We were playing hide-and-seek with Crunchy in the park. Crunchy, seeing one of us coming, would hide at the other side of the tree. When you looked on the side where he was hidden, he would run to the other side of the trunk and so on.

'Was, was' at the time, as this poor thing was pretty on one side and was ugly on the other.

The rabbit settled in with us. He got used to living in our house, and slept in the living room on the carpet under an armchair. The rabbit always did its business at the same place in the hall, on the tin under the stove, so its presence in the house was not unpleasant. The rabbit was very tame. It would go into father's room when he was taking a nap and check if anyone was on the bed. If so, the rabbit would jump in and lie with them …

Dogs played an important part in my childhood. We had various hunting and domestic dogs. They were kept in the pantry beside the kitchen and in a kennel outside: pointers, setters and fox terriers. When the pointer bitch had puppies, I loved going into the big dog kennel and spending time with the little ones, picking them up, stroking them, watching them …

I remember once she raised a little piglet with her own puppies. The bitch and the sow gave birth almost at the same time. The sow, however, ate her own piglets. We took the one surviving piglet from the pigsty and put it in the dog kennel, where it was accepted and fed by the pointer bitch. It was very amusing to see a black pointer bitch with black puppies and a white piglet. We spent many hours watching this phenomenon. The piglet was lucky.

Sometimes the bitch would give birth in the attic, where there was also a kennel. The attic was huge, it ran the whole length and width of the palace. Planks were laid on the beams for the washerwomen to walk on while hanging out the laundry.

I was drawn to the attic to see the puppies, and I would also take the opportunity, unbeknownst to the adults, to crawl out through the opening in the roof to a place where it was covered with a slippery, metal sheet. I would sit on the metal sheet and slide all the way down to the balustrade that ran around the whole roof of the palace. The balustrade was old and dilapidated, but at the time it did not occur to me that sliding down the roof in this way could end in disaster, that the balustrade I was leaning against could fall off and take me with it.

I have a photograph of the palace where the balustrade is gone. Apparently it had to be removed for safety reasons, but not because of my mischief, because no one ever found out.

Near the palace, next to one of the outbuildings, was the director's stable with four horses for the carriage, two ponies for us children and two riding horses. One chestnut Hiawata was a purebred Arabian, and came from the stable of my uncle Wojciech Falewicz, my father's brother living in Marwa in the Kaunas region. Another, black horse, Łaska, was an English half-breed. Sometimes I was allowed to ride not a pony and only very rarely I could ride Łaska, each time making me very proud to ride a horse intended for adults. But most of the time I rode a pony. I remember once, when the Bug River flooded and the water came up all the way to the garden, I used to ride splashing through these flooded meadows. I had completely forgotten about a deep ditch that was used to discharge the wastewater from the sugar factory into the river. The ditch was deep and the banks steep. My pony and I fell into this ditch and I was up to my waist in water. Miraculously we managed to get out of the ditch and I quickly ran home to change before my parents saw me and gave me a well-deserved punishment.

I was brought up by my father to be a very independent girl. I grew up among boys (we had two, Uncle Wojciech had three) and they teased me, and sometimes hit me, so I had to defend myself. I had to do everything the boys did to avoid being called a 'wimp'.

My father got gout once a year and was bedridden. This happened several times during the sugar campaign. He would call me to him and send me to the factory with various orders that I had to pass on to the foreman, the chemists or the laboratory workers. Although I liked walking around the factory during the campaign because everything was interesting there, you could eat lumps of sugar while they were still warm, and the chemists made caramel in the laboratory, I did not like going with these orders and I would say to my father: 'Where can I find them?' Father would reply: 'On the tip of your tongue,' and so I had to go and do what he said. I would go to the sugar factory ...

The allowance in kind from the sugar factory was 24 poods of sugar per year (1 pood = 16 kilograms). Twelve poods were needed to make confiture (jam was not yet known in those days). Marmalade was made in the garden, in a huge cauldron that hung over the fire. It was made from plums and stirred for a long time until it was completely thickened.

In addition to the gardens, the director had six cows, pigs, poultry and a large farm that required many servants, all supported by the factory. The rooms were cleaned by a servant, who also waited at the table, and there was also a cook, a maid, a gardener, a coachman and a boy to help. On festive occasions the coachman, Józef Pachniewski, wore a black jacket with a red lining. He was good with the whip, and as he was bringing the carriage out of the stable, he knew how to make the front horses rear up on their hind legs. Then he rode elegantly around the gazebo two more times, not stopping directly in front of the porch, but slightly to the side, only approaching when people were coming out of the palace doors.

In Strzyżów, as I recall, there were several servants. I particularly remember one of them, who was not very bright – Grzela, the one who chased the furniture-chewing Crunchy with a rag in his hand. One of Grzela's duties was to keep the palace in order. He once tried to polish the floors – to no avail – and then complained to Mum: 'I even tried using sugar to make them shine better, but dammit, it's sticky.' Grzela left to work for one of our neighbours. When they were discussing the terms of his employment, he reportedly said: 'I don't eat dumplings without cream.' Despite these strict conditions, the neighbours hired him, as he was a good-hearted and hard-working man – albeit a bit simple. There was also a servant who was a ladies' man. He seduced our cook, Ewa, and got her pregnant with their daughter Hanka. Ewa spent the whole war with us, and after the war she came to Balinpol with her daughter and cooked for us for many years. Hanka, a pretty girl, married a Balinpol coachman.

Life in Strzyżów was exciting, comfortable and prosperous. We had everything our hearts desired, although the children were brought up rather strictly.

My mother sewed my clothes herself, mostly navy blue or festive white, pleated from the yoke down. The most important thing for me was that they had big pockets. Not much importance was attached to clothes, and any coquetry in girls was frowned upon. I remember once a teacher caught me looking at my nails, polished with chamois and chalk – and was visibly outraged. Usually I wore boots, overcoats and hats after my older brother, when he grew out of them. I wore boys' shirts that were striped, with a collar and a pocket on the left side. This was the pocket that Crunchy had used to take a nap.

Looking back, the years I spent in Strzyżów were very beneficial. I developed courage, resourcefulness and physical endurance. Admittedly,

Helena in her family home in Balinpol

I spent one winter in Zakopane because during medical consultation in Kraków (that included no less than two professors of medicine) that found enlarged lymph nodes in the upper part of my left lung my doctor recommended Zakopane. I lost a year of school but came back as fit as a fiddle.

I remember my stay in Zakopane very well. I underwent climatic treatment that involved a lot of sitting on a veranda to acclimatise, dressed in a sheepskin coat and muffled in a fur sack. I did not go on trips to the Tatra valleys or *Morskie Oko* [Eye of the Sea] with my mother, brother and the French lady because I had to avoid situations where I might catch a cold. At that time we lived in Sienkiewicza Street, in the Zacisze villa, in the house of Mrs Alfonsowa Parczewska. We had two rooms on the ground floor. When I lay on the veranda, I was often accompanied by Mademoiselle Bertha, who described vividly the books she had read. I enjoyed it very much, but it could not last long for it was freezing outside, and Mademoiselle Bertha would want to get inside. Then, unable to read because my hands were freezing, I would look out and, with houses, fences and streets in sight, I would count. I counted the windows, the pegs in the fence, the people walking along the street, and so on. I think that those long hours on the veranda of the Zacisze villa in Zakopane made it a lifelong habit of mine to count everything in sight almost automatically.

During that time I had to drink cream, which I did not like, but my mother started to pay me 10 hellers for each small glass, so I drank it to collect those hellers. That was also a learning experience …

Mrs Parczewska's cooking was excellent, but I enjoyed the sweet desserts the most. These included a variety of ice creams, chestnut creams, whipped cream and the like. As I was 'born in sugar', I always had (and still have today) a sweet tooth, something I do not advise for any of my fellow human beings nowadays, being aware of the harm that excess sugar in the body can do. Years ago, however, our knowledge of the subject was limited, and Melchior Wańkowicz's slogan 'Sugar makes you stronger', promoted before the Second World War, was blatantly contrary to the knowledge we have on the subject today.

I also remember a trip from Strzyżów via Kraków to Zakopane. We travelled in a carriage drawn by six horses: four in the shaft and two in the bridle. In Sokal we crossed the Austrian border to get to the railway station. As a child, and later in life, I was prone to travel sickness, which spoilt any journey. I would sit opposite Mlle Bertha, put my head in her lap and feel a little better. The carriage would get stuck in the mud and the horses would have a hard time pulling it out. The 55 km journey seemed like an eternity …

In the summer, relatives from Warsaw would come to stay with us in Strzyżów, and there would be a lot of hustle and bustle. At other times of the year, too, we never complained of a lack of company. The sugar factory in Nieledwia, 20 km from Strzyżów, was run by my grandfather's brother, Edward Więckowski. His daughter Maria married Nieledwia's neighbour, Mr Janiszewski, the owner of Nowosiółki. The Janiszewski family had two sons. Aunt Maria died in Gdynia after the Second World War. One of her sons took part in the battles of the Polish I Corps under General Maczek in France, Belgium and the Netherlands. He then settled in Belgium, where he still lives today.

Not far away, in the Wieniawka estate, near the famous Horodło, lived Mr Wierzbicki and Mrs Wierzbicka, who had three daughters about my age. We used to visit, to play with the girls.

We had many neighbours – sometimes interesting, sometimes strange.

I remember one of them, a Russian, the owner of the Uściług estate on the Austrian border. He was the owner of the first car in the area, which made him very proud. One of his favourite games was to stop the car in the countryside, put it into reverse and persuade the peasants to push it. The peasants, stuck in mud, could not believe how heavy the 'damn' car was.

The roads in the Hrubieszów area were terrible. Obviously there was no tarmac or asphalt. During the autumn rains and spring thaw, the black earth formed a bog in which the wheels of a vehicle would sink up to the axles. Four horses were needed to pull the carriage out of the mud. I loved sitting next to coachman Pachniewski, he would give me the reins and I would drive the four horses. I was good at this.

But sometimes, when we returned from visits at night, there were such holes and deep puddles on the side roads that the rein horses fell into them and struggled to crawl out, dragging the shaft horses behind them. The wheels up to the axles in mud and the steps of the carriage were covered with black earth. It was very difficult for the farmers to transport the beetroots by horse and cart, and the beetroots were covered in mud.

From Strzyżów it was 40 versts to the nearest railway station in Dorohusk. More than once a carriage was sent for me when I returned home. Józef Pachniewski, seeing that I was suffering from the travel sickness, would stop the horses and say: 'Maybe you should go for a walk, madam, maybe it'll pass.' It was even worse on sleigh rides. To this day I am afraid to travel by boat or ferry. But I suppose it was somehow related to my nervousness, because when I was a sports pilot flying an RWD-13 touring plane, I never got sick. I also tolerated travelling in large airliners quite well. I also found out that this ailment can be overcome and that singing is the best remedy.

The years we spent in Strzyżów were wonderful! My mother's favourite flower was the lily of the valley, and so in May we used to go by wagon to a forest beyond the Bug River in Volhynia. The Bug was crossed by ferry at the historic village of Horodło. The forest was beautiful! We spent the May weekend lying on the ground on blankets, eating a variety of delicacies and returned laden with bunches of lilies of the valley.

Horodło was our parish. Every Sunday, four horses would ride up to the palace, Pachniewski would crack the whip, and we would all ride to church. The horses, full of verve, would gallop up the only hill we passed on the way. Inside the church, opposite the pulpit, was our patron's pew.

We children found the mass long and terribly boring. We whispered to each other and our parents gave us stern looks of reproof. The sermon seemed to go on forever. After Mass we would visit the priest for breakfast. It was also possible – even though it was Sunday – to take care of certain matters in the Jewish shops in the market square in Horodło.

This is how the years of my childhood passed. The atmosphere at home was always cheerful, and my parents loved each other and lived in great harmony. My father was a very cheerful man, but he had a temper. His anger, however, was as quick to go away as it was to appear. My mother, on the other hand, was not easily upset. But when she did, she held a grudge for a long time.

It is difficult to describe your childhood in detail. Much of it is forgotten, and even the facts and feelings that are remembered are difficult to put down on paper. You are always left with understatement and the realisation that all the things that made those times so charming and valuable have not been remembered.

This is why I end the first part of my memoirs with the year 1914, when a world war broke out. A war that brought the independence we had all dreamed of.

CHAPTER II
Youth

❦

In the summer of 1914, my parents went to Vichy, France. It was then that the assassination in Sarajevo took place and war broke out. In Strzyżów, 55 km from the Austrian border, we heard cannon fire from the besieged fortress in Przemyśl. Everyone was terrified, especially us children, who stayed at home without our parents. There were three of us: Kaj, the eldest, me and my younger brother Stach. Our caring grandmother, Julia Karolowa Falewiczowa, who lived in Verkiai near Vilnius, knew that we were alone almost on the Austrian border and sent aunt Janina's stepson Luniek Niewodniczański[5] to pick us up and take us to Verkiai. But Kaj opposed that idea. We, the younger ones, saw him as an authority figure, and we all resolutely refused to go to our grandmother's with Luniek, saying that we would wait until our parents returned and then they would decide our fate. And that is what happened. My parents had not yet reached Vichy when the war broke out, but as Russian citizens they could not return via Germany. However, they were able to leave via England, Sweden and Finland, and my parents returned home before we were forced to leave Strzyżów.

However, the situation at the border was uncertain for a long time, and cannon fire could be heard all the time. Finally, the fortress was abandoned and the offensive began. News indicated that the Austrians could reach Strzyżów any day and our region would become a battlefield. We had to flee. At that time we never imagined that our fate would take us as far as Podolia. We were all convinced that the situation could change, that we would return to Strzyżów, that we only had to retreat a little beyond the dangerous front line and keep a certain distance from it.

The escape was organised in such a way that we left the furniture at home and walled up the more important things in the cellar (which, inci-

---

[5] My aunt Janina Falewiczówna married a tsarist general, Felicjan Niewodniczański, who had a son Luniek and a daughter Maja from his first marriage.

dentally, was completely looted after we left). We were left with only two vehicles: a carriage and a ladder cart. As none of the carters wanted to leave Strzyżów and their families behind, we – the children – took the reins as stewards. From Strzyżów we took our cook Ewa with her daughter Hania and, of course, our two dogs: a pointer and a fox terrier. My parents rode in the carriage, while we were changing places. We stopped on the way to eat and rest the horses, and set off towards Polesia. We reached the Raków estate, where we stopped for a while, hoping that the front would move back.

In Raków we met our aunt and uncle Janiszewski who, like us, had left their Nowosiółki estate near Hrubieszów. But the front was not retreating. On the contrary, the Austrian offensive continued, so we moved further east to the Borki estate of Mr and Mrs Parniewski's. There we waited for news of the war, but further developments forced us to move to Pińsk. I remember that the roads in the wilderness of those forests were terrible. It was a marshland. The roads across the bogs were covered with fascine, branches and reeds, so we drove the swaying vehicle with great caution. The horses stumbled over branches, occasionally sinking into the mud. Still, we breathed a sigh of relief. Fleas were a terrible plague in Borki. I had never seen anything like that in my life! Why there were so many, I have no idea. On the smooth blankets we covered ourselves in, the fleas looked like someone had spilled a bowl of poppy seeds. Sleeping was obviously out of the question. We were very tired when we arrived in Pińsk.

In Pińsk we met the deputy director of the sugar factory in Strzyżów, Mr Jan Piechowski. We decided to continue our journey by boat. A spontaneous description of our departure and journey written by Mr Piechowski[6] is still preserved in my family archive. He wrote:

We arrived at night to a dark and empty ship, as we wanted to be the first on board. Kaj stayed with our stuff, even though he was hungry. But he made a fuss that we'd left him hungry with inedible things. Around 12 o'clock, we all tried to get on the boat and as it was about to leave, I returned to get the things. When I came back, lot of young ladies were kissing one another, promising to write each day. They took

---

[6] He was my first love. To impress him, I used to climb tall trees in Strzyżów. I loved to stand next to him.

another passenger, packed some more goods, and then another passenger. We concluded that the boat was already crowded. They were whistling, ringing, and shouting – which meant we were leaving. The boat moved like a vicious goat with all the stuff. We ate lunch. There was a lovely view of the grey willow and marshland. The ladies were whispering. We were moving – there was a lovely view of reeds and rushes. We took wood, and the ladies went to get flowering weeds. The Jews argued and worried, and a stowaway went to sleep with no shoes on. In the face of protest from fellow passengers, he slept on, but with his shoes on this time. There was lovely view of the grey willow and reeds. We had dinner, a kid was going on the Pripyat to Riga. The rest of the passengers ventilated and disinfected the place of their nightly ordeal (in other words – a mattress on their baggage), the stowaway spat, the baby was coughing, the rest of the passengers were busy catching fleas and other bugs, keeping the light on and awaiting the morning. In the morning we passed under the bridge. We had breakfast. There was a lovely view of reeds and osiers, the temperature was three degrees Réaumur. I got to know the ladies. Their noses were all purple from the cold. We had breakfast: five bad eggs, which we did not eat. Ewa made some lunch. Mr Dąbkowski tried to persuade me to find a wife. There was a lovely view of the sands and grey willows. We had lunch. To the displeasure of the ladies, I fell asleep next to them on the deck. Dek's gluttony stopped me from getting any more sleep. We bought a fat hen. That was Mr Piechowski's account.

We left by boat, sailed down the Pina, the Pripyat to the Dnieper and arrived in Kiev. I remember that we passed by Narowlya, the Horwath's estate, where we bought the candied fruit produced there and offered it to the passengers of ships stopping on the riverbank. The daughter of the owner of Narowlya married Stanisław Wańkowicz, the future senator of the Republic of Poland. They both died tragically during the occupation, shot by the Germans at the massacre in Zbydniów, at the Horodyński manor[7].

For us children, the boat trip was pleasant and entertaining. We disembarked in Kiev and stayed at a hotel at the Dumskaya Square.

---

[7] The Germans murdered all the wedding guests. Only the bride, who went to the photographer, and the Horodyński brothers hiding in the attic survived.

My father started looking for a job and soon found one. He became the director of an estate and sugar factory owned by Mrs Sumowska – the owner of several thousand hectares and a sugar factory in Rubizhne.

My father rented a house for us in an unpaved street in Belgorod, a town on the border of the Kharkiv and Kursk governorates, not far from Rubizhne, and we lived there with all our 'clobber' and dogs. Father only came to visit us on Sundays. Belgorod was a small but beautiful town. There was a large Polish colony there which met in the Catholic church and after mass you made various acquaintances. It turned out that there was a teacher who could teach me the fourth-grade material.

Church meetings with other Poles were very important because the priest gave patriotic sermons. My mother found out by chance that there was also an Englishwoman in Belgorod who could give lessons, and she was engaged to teach me English. I learnt it quite quickly, because after six

Sztukowski family and rittmaster Żukowski visiting Parczewski family in Juzin estate

months our lessons were limited to conversation. It was, of course, a childish, poor language, but what I learnt then stayed with me and helped me a great deal in my later travels abroad, when I met the English or Scandinavians.

We lived comfortably and well in Belgorod, but our house was very modestly furnished. The trunks were covered with cloths and served as tables. We had a pointing dog Dek and a fox terrier Psotka, and our cook Ewa (with her daughter Hania) looked after the household. There was a cinema, shops and markets in the town, where wonderful fruit was sold. And so we lived, always waiting for my father to come home on Saturdays. After some time, my father took us to Rubizhne to see the village where he worked. I have photos from that time.

Kaj did not come with us. From the second year of secondary school Kaj went to school in St. Petersburg, where he stayed with his uncle, Colonel Wojciech Falewicz, father of three sons not much older than Kaj, and where the exclusive Prince Tenishev School, attended by Nak, Tak and Andrak Falewicz, guaranteed better education than other schools. Kaj came to Strzyżów for holidays and was away from home for the whole school year. I remember him telling me about his entrance exam for Prince Tenishev School. He was ten years old when he took the exam. He knew too much for the first grade and not enough for the second, but they decided that he was smart enough to be admitted to the second grade. He took the exam together with a Chinese boy who came with his professor, a man with a long braid that he put in his pocket. The boy was the son of a Chinese diplomat. When he came out of the exam, he was crying. The headmaster saw him and asked him why he was crying and he replied: 'Go to hell – you're not one of us.'

When we left Strzyżów, Kaj was already in St. Petersburg. The Tenishev School was very expensive, white-gloved butlers served hot lunches to the children. In the park next to the school there was an artificial ice rink and hills for sledging. Six boys (four Falewicz and two of their cousins Zawisza) lived with my uncle, the aunt was very strict, but at the same time there was a lot of cultural entertainment. My uncle had a box at the opera and ballet, where Kaj was taken with the other members of the household. This explains why my older brother is a great connoisseur of music and ballet. When he lived in London after the last war, he was invited by ballet schools near London to attend performances, and his opinion of the performers and students was much valued. Kaj also wrote articles on the subject for the London press.

After a year in Belgorod, my parents decided to move to Kiev. They were drawn to the west, closer to the Motherland: the war had to end eventually, so they needed to be closer to the country to be able to return. My father looked for a new job there and found one in an institution that worked for the army. It was a chemical plant in Kurenivka, about 8 km from Kiev, called Vsierosiyskiy Ziemskiy Soyuz.

We moved to Kiev. We settled at 72 Mariinskoblogovieshtianska Street, in a beautiful tenement house, in a large, elegant five-room apartment, but with almost no furniture. There was no point in buying it, as all we really needed was a place to sleep, and the trunks still served as furniture. There was a huge buffet in the dining room, but it was not ours either.

In Kiev we met acquaintances, Mr and Mrs Parniewski, the owners of Borek in Polesia, where the fleas had attacked us so badly, and Mrs Brzezińska, an acquaintance of my mother, whose daughter later married Mr Wilson, an English consul in Warsaw. In Solovtsov Square there was a Polish school for girls, run by the Polish Educational Society. A similar school for boys was in Rylski Street. The headmistress was a famous Polish language teacher, Cecylia Niewiadomska. She was a lovely old lady, who radiated kindness, tact and wisdom. She was held in high esteem by the female students and the entire teaching staff. The teachers were all sorts of people who had ended up in Russia during the war and had to make a living somehow, so they were not choosy about their jobs. For example, the famous painter Konrad Krzyżanowski was the art teacher, while German was taught by Antoni Ryniewicz, who later become the superintendent of the scientific centres in Vilnius and Toruń. Mr Bator taught Latin and our tutor was Mrs Majkowska.

To get to school I took the tram to Dumskaya Square, and from there I walked uphill to Solovtsov Square. Quite often, in order not to make a detour, I would shorten my tram ride by jumping off on the street leading to the school, as one usually stood on the tram steps. The school building was unsuitable for its purpose, as previously it was used as a tenement house. The school had several floors and the classrooms were small. Opposite the school, on the square, was the Solovtsov Theatre, and nearby, in Meryngovska Street, was the Polish Theatre. The pupils came from different parts of Poland, almost all of them refugees. There was another school in Kiev attended by Polish girls from Podolia and, of course, some refugees from Poland. They wore colourful chequered uniforms. It was the school of Mrs Peretiatkowiczowa.

Our life in Kiev was pleasant and peaceful until 1917. I went to school and did my homework. The theatre in Meryngovska Street gave us Poles a lot of entertainment. The Polish Theatre in Kiev was very prominent during the war[8]. Very famous actors like Wysocka, Osterwa, Jaracz, Lubicz-Sarnowska, Fertner etc. performed there. Classical plays as well as comedies were performed. The theatre building was large and had boxes. We attended all the plays that were performed there. It was also an opportunity to meet friends. We never imagined that in the not too distant future this building would become a place of execution for officers of the tsar's army, and that blood would flow there in rivers.

My father had a company car, an open-top Ford, which he used to go to work. I used to love going there with my father. Polytechnic professors worked in the laboratories, which protected them from being drafted into the army and sent to the front. That was because they worked for the army. There were also Poles everywhere. The factory produced soap, caustic soda, solid denatured alcohol and other products needed by the army. The lumps of soap were the size of a small room; they were then cut with a thin wire. However, the factory had to stop the production of denatured alcohol, originally intended for warming hands in the trenches, because the soldiers had started to spread the paste on bread and were getting drunk all the time. In the laboratories, soap samples were taken and refined with certain fragrances. I always came back with one of the samples.

In Kiev there was a Polish club called 'Ognisko' (Bonfire). It housed a restaurant, a café and a newspaper reading room. I remember that we used to eat there before we settled down, when we were still living in the hotel. I saw Kornel Makuszyński with his wife there. In Kiev I shared a room with Wanda Bałtutis, who went to another school – a trade school – and was a year older than me. I had become very good friends with her since my days in Kiev and stayed in close contact with her from graduation until the occupation. We were both in Paris at the same time between 1924 and 1925, then in Vilnius. Together we took part in a hunt

---

[8] Much has been written about this theatre, for example an excellent memoir by Jarosław Iwaszkiewicz.

with the 23rd Uhlan regiment, as she too had ridden horses since childhood. We made friends with foreigners. She was a dear friend of mine. She died tragically during the occupation. Here I would like to quote a mention of her from Announcement No. 13 of the Polish Association of Women with Higher Education:

> *Wanda Joanna Bałtutis – the President of the Silesian Branch*
> *'Poland had to be*
> *called by name again*
> *One's life laid down for life*
> *And eternal sleep – to sleep'*

Wanda Joanna Bałtutis was born in 1900 in the village of Shamraivka, Bila Tserkva Region, Ukraine. She graduated with honours from secondary school in Kiev. On her return to Poland in 1920, Wanda Bałtutis thought about furthering her education. After working in the country for a year, she went to Grenoble to study French, before moving to Paris, where she graduated in 1927 from the Ecole des Sciences Politiques with a degree in economics. After validating her diploma, she taught for a while at vocational schools in Vilnius and then in Kraków. Her in-depth knowledge and pedagogical skills attracted attention and in 1935 she was appointed inspector of vocational schools in Silesia, where she remained until the war. In addition to her professional work, Wanda Bałtutis took an active part in the activities of a number of social organisations, in all of which she held leading positions. Wanda Baltutis had a particularly close relationship with our association.

She was one of the most active members of the Silesian Branch and had been its president for several years. As a member of the Kraków Organising Committee, she took an active part in the organisation of the International Federation Congress in Kraków in 1936 and represented the Polish Association on several occasions at the International Federation Congresses in Paris, London and Stockholm. Then came the war and the occupation. Despite her difficult material situation, Wanda Bałtutis did not give up her work in vocational education and took an active part in the work of underground organisations. Arrested by the Gestapo in March 1944, she was imprisoned in Pawiak prison. Tortured inhumanely during investigation, she refused to give up anyone. She heroically endured all the sufferings, even though she sometimes had to be carried back to her cell unconscious on a stretcher. On 29 March of that year, she was called out of her cell. Knowing exactly what awaited her there, she said goodbye to her companions with serenity and courage. She was executed with a group of women from Pawiak – the place of execution is unknown.

Wanda Bałtutis was a typical soldier of the Polish Underground – heroic, without big words or loud declamations, with unheard-of readiness, she stood up to defend freedom and independence, knowing that she was facing death, perhaps a cruel death. That is what happened. Pro Patria semper.

During the war we stayed in Podolia and spent all our holidays in Kozhanka, near Bila Tserkva, where Mr and Mrs Bałtutis lived. The Branicki family owned large estates and four sugar factories. The area was well known to my parents – it was here that they met, fell in love and married. Years later, in exile, we rented a room from the steward of the farming estate in Kozhanka, but spent the whole day with Mr and Mrs Bałtutis in their hospitable house and orchard. There I learnt how to make candied fruit. Tennis, horse riding – I have very fond memories of that time. Wanda's sister Zosia, later married to Jan Pająk, a professor at the Warsaw University of Life Sciences, lives in Warsaw. We have remained friends, and I am still in touch with her.

I only found out about Wanda's fate in 1945, when I moved to Poland from Vilnius. It was a great personal loss for me, and I always carry her memory deep in my heart. She was a true, devoted, sincere, wise and good friend.

In 1917, during a lesson given by Professor Ryniewicz, we heard shots. We were already aware of the outbreak of the revolution in St. Petersburg and were prepared for possible unrest and danger in Kiev. Professor Ryniewicz said: 'Poland will be an independent country again.' We ran to the windows to see what was happening in the square. There was some movement, some commotion, and we could hear shots all the time. During another lesson I remember how, after a loud outburst, the maths teacher Professor Gabszewicz lifted the collar of his jacket as if to protect himself. There was a story about Professor Gabszewicz, who was known for his absent-mindedness, that once, when he was in Warsaw, he was walking down the street and mathematical equations and formulae were going through his head. Suddenly he saw a carriage by the pavement. A great blackboard for solving mathematical problems! He stopped, took some chalk from his pocket and wrote mathematical problems and formulae on it. Suddenly the blackboard began to move, and the professor ran after it, continuing to write.

The revolution became more intense. Bloody days began, officers were shot in the Merchants' and Tsar's Gardens by the Dnieper. 'Class enemies' were executed in the theatre in Meryngowska Street. At the same time, looting began. Individuals and groups tried to break into flats in nice tenement houses. So the glass door to our house was boarded up, and at night armed tenants took turns standing guard in the lift. My father also stood guard with a double-barrelled shotgun. The lift was in the middle of the staircase and was completely glazed.

My father's factory continued to work. The workers' and soldiers' councils 'eliminated' directors as 'enemies of the people'. But they had a different attitude towards the Poles. When my father was ill with gout, delegates from the council even came to see us about various matters concerning the factory. My father, as I have already mentioned, used to send me to the sugar factory in Strzyżów with instructions. He did the same while he was ill in Kiev. Once I went outside the house where my father's company car, an open-top Ford, was waiting and ordered the chauffeur to take me to Kurenivka. But the chauffeur refused. 'Why?' I asked. 'Because I am not allowed to drive women,' he replied. 'Who says?' 'Soldiers' and workers' councils,' he said. 'Where are they?' I inquired. 'The headquarters are in Kreshchatyk Street.' 'Take me there, please.'

We drove to Kiev's main street, Kreshchatyk. I walked into a room full of soldiers and civilians. They were all armed and had ammunition belts across their chests. It was obvious that they were drunk with power. They sat stretched out, with their caps pushed to the side in a devilish manner. There was a lot of commotion inside. They asked me what or who I was looking for. I asked who was in charge. They pointed at a group of people. I explained the reason for my arrival and that it was important to carry my father's instructions. They laughed at me because I was sixteen and dressed in a white skirt and blouse. They sat stretched out and I stood in front of them. Finally they whispered to each other and said: 'Nu tam my wam dajom etot awtomobil na tri dnia do waszewo rasparażeńja' (We're giving you the car for your disposal for three days). I left proud of my victory and told the driver that everything was settled and to go to Kurenivka.

At one point the city was overrun by Ukrainians who wanted to take advantage of the revolution to gain independence. Their prime minister at the time, as far as I can remember, was Gruszczyński, who lived in the neighbouring Pankovska Street, which descended very steeply into Mariinskoblogovieshtianska Street. Our friends, Mr and Mrs Parniewski, also lived in Pankovska Street. If you looked out of the bay window of our room, you could see both sides of the street. There were situations where there were Ukrainians on one street corner and Bolsheviks on the other, and they were shooting at each other. This prolonged fighting in the city caused a lot of casualties.

When the shooting stopped, I would go out with Mum. Care had to be taken not to step on human brains spurting from the shattered heads. Once, while in our flat, we saw an armoured train on the tracks visible from our windows. It opened fire. Bullets from the train flew over our house in the direction of the Ukrainian prime minister's house in Pankovska Street. My parents thought it would be safer to go out the house. But the cannon shots were accurate. Gruszczyński's house was on fire. We ran in that direction when the armoured train, having done its job, drove off. The huge tenement building was in flames. The tenants threw various things out of the burning house, including furniture, which broke apart hitting the ground. When there was relative calm, we saw an unarmed man crossing the street. A shot was fired and the man fell. My mother was very brave. She said she had to go and see him because he might have been injured and needed help. And she went, even though my father thought it was madness. But the man was dead. The fighting in the streets had calmed down. The Ukrainians had been defeated.

SWEDEN

Bornholm (Denmark)

Baltic Sea

GERMANY

Stolp
Gdynia
Danzig
Köslin
Königsberg
Kolberg
FREE CITY OF DANZIG
Elbing
East Prussia (GERMANY)
Stettin
Neustettin
Allenstein
Pyritz
Landsberg
Bydgoszcz
Torun
Frankfurt
Poznan
Plock
Ciechanow
Ostroleka
Grünberg
Leszno
Konin
WARSAW
Siedlce
Glogau
Lodz
Bautzen
REPUBLIC OF POLAND
Görlitz
Breslau
Radom
Lublin
Kovel
Jablonec
Glatz
Oppeln
Czestochowa
Kielce
Zamosc
Lutsk
Rivne
PRAGUE
Beuthen
Katowice
Rzeszow
Jaroslaw
Lviv
Ternopil
Opava
Krakow
Nowy Sacz
Przemysl
Jihlava
Olomouc
Cieszyn
Sanok
Drohobych
Borytslav
Brno
Ruzomberok
Presov
Stanislawow
Kamianets-Podilskyi
Trencin
Kosice
Chernivtsi
VIENA
Banská Bystrica
Bratislava
AUSTRIA
HUNGARY
Györ
BUDAPEST
Debrecen
Satu Mare
ROMANIA
Suceava

Memel
LITHUANIA
Panevežys
Utena
Taurage
Daugavpils
KOVNO
Svenčioneliai
Tilsit
Vilnius
Marijampole
Suwalki
Lida
Minsk
Grodno
Novogrudok
Slutsk
Białystok
Baranavichy
Brest
Pinsk
Shepetivka

R U S S I A

POLISH LANDS IN THE YEAR 1918

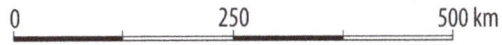

0   250   500 km

Map creation: Marcin J. Sobiech, www.exgeo.pl

——— State boundaries   ○ Cities

- - - - Voivodship boundaries   WARSAW Name of state capitals

Kielce Name of voivodship capitals

School went on and in the spring of 1918 I was promoted to the seventh grade. I was always a good student with good grades. My parents began to think about returning to Poland, to Strzyżów, where the factory had been burnt down, but my father hoped it would be rebuilt. Trains were organised to take the repatriates 'to the bosom of the Motherland'. And so, in the summer of 1918, we set off for Strzyżów in a sanitary train with bunk beds and freight wagons, together with the livestock that had been stored at the Bałtutis' in Kozhanka. There was a cow, two horses and a carriage in the freight wagon with us. For us youngsters, this trip was also a great adventure.

By chance, Tadeusz Rutkowski, a future Warsaw lawyer, was travelling with us. We made friends with him during the long journey, as the train moved slowly and stopped at stations for long periods. We would go to the engine driver and ask why we were not moving, and he would reply that it was not up to him. I remember sitting on a sack of hay in the freight wagon, close to the cow, writing farewell letters. The cow's mouth was over our shoulders. We used the cow's wet nose to wet stamps and stick them on envelopes and postcards. I was friends with Tadeusz Rutkowski for several decades. When he married Janina Brudzińska, the daughter of the first rector of Warsaw University, I was friends with both of them and stayed with them when I came to Warsaw from Vilnius for hearings. They have now passed away.

It took us a whole week to get back to Poland. We left Kiev on 12 August and arrived in Kovel on 19 August 1918. We travelled through Fastiv, Kozhanka, Kozyatyn, Berdychiv, Shepetivka, Zdolbuniv, Rivne, Kivertsi, Holoby and Kovel. I kept a note from that time, written by Tadeusz on the last day of our journey, 19 August 1918. There was no picture on the post-card, just a poem by Kazimierz Tetmajer:

> *Such sanctity around you one can see*
> *And such a halo of your pure virginity*
> *That when one sees you at close range*
> *The heart forgets about your viridity*
> *And one is just looking at your rendition*
> *Like a miracle of some sort or apparition*
> *That there is miracle – and that it is so close …*

And below, a note from Tadeusz: *As a token of the adventures we shared during the week of our return to the 'bosom of the Motherland', please accept this poem, which in my mind reminds me of you.*

A WEEK LONG JOURNEY OF THE AUTHOR AND HER FAMILY IN 1918

0   250   500 km

Map creation: Marcin J. Sobiech, www.exgeo.pl

State boundaries

Cities, towns

Railways

Autor and her family route

Main stops on the route

We returned to Poland and my father looked for a place for me in Lublin, where I was to attend the seventh year of Mrs Arciszowa's humanities secondary school. We found the palace in Strzyżów completely looted and empty. We lived in an outhouse, without furniture, in primitive conditions. My father began to collect materials to rebuild the factory. However, he was not destined to rebuild it; during Ukrainian riots in the Chełm region building materials were stolen, then the war with the Bolsheviks broke out, and finally when we moved to Galicia, then to Warsaw and eventually to Vilnius, all ties with Strzyżów were broken completely. My father decided to stay in Vilnius, his hometown.

I lived in Lublin with Mr and Mrs Orłowski, whose real family name was Sulima-Świechowski, but after 1863 they had to change it due to political reasons. My father mentioned in a conversation with Mrs Świechowska that he was asking for board, lodging and laundry for me, but that he was not asking for guardianship, because I knew how to live my life. It was a sign of great trust in me, which I never abused. Mrs Świechowska never asked me where I was going or when I would be back home, but I always told her, believing that this was what domestic coexistence and good manners required.

The author as a secondary school student in Lublin

Mr and Mrs Świechowski's daughter Jadzia and I shared a room and we became close friends. This friendship has lasted for sixty years[9]. I visit her in Olsztyn. Our friendship went through different stages: we attended the Vilnius University together, where I studied law and she studied Polish literature. Later, when she and I got married, we lived in the same house. It was only the occupation that separated us. In Lublin, Jadzia went to the Ursuline Secondary School, and I went to Mrs Arciszowa's, but the house kept us together. The school years were rather monotonous: school, homework and home. I was a good student and loved maths, so I tutored the girls in the lower grades and also helped them with French, which I knew from my childhood. I did not play sports and had no social life.

The class was small. I was friends with Halszka Leskiewicz, Wanda Puzinowska (who later became the wife of a cavalry officer, Kiedrzyński, spent a few years in the Ravensbrück concentration camp and wrote a book about it; she is a fellow at the Institute of History of the Polish Academy of Sciences in Warsaw, very socially active among women who survived that camp), Wanda Obuchowska, Lubekówna, Chajnówna, and finally Wanda Arlitewiczówna, who showed a talent for painting. She married a painter and poet, a famous Polish futurist, Młodożeniec. I lost contact with almost all my friends, because right after my graduation I joined the army as a volunteer and then I studied at the Vilnius University. Our paths diverged.

And our entertainment? Our school, like the Ursuline School, used to put vocal and poetic performances for parents, relatives and teachers. I remember successfully reciting *Listy z Sybiru* (Letters from Siberia) by Or-Ot. There were also tea dances, to which we invited boys from the humanist Arlitewicz's secondary school. At the Ursuline School there were also parties, but the girls danced with each other and the boys stood against the wall, because schoolgirls were not supposed to dance with boys. That was the prioress' opinion! Apart from the lessons, Professor Biesiekierski, a Polish language teacher, organised a philosophy club, where he gave lectures on the philosophical views of Spinoza, Descartes, Plato and so on. These were interesting lectures, but they were given only in the last grade before matriculation, so they did not last long.

From time to time my brother Kaj, who was an officer, would visit me.

---

[9] Jadzia Sulima-Świechowska married Alexander Kozłowski, an agricultural engineer. After the war, they settled in Olsztyn. They have two children and numerous grandchildren.

In those days it was something really special! He would take me to Rutkowski's pastry shop on Krakowskie Przedmieście, pay for me, buy me sweets and show me a lot of heart and interest.

We took our matriculation exam together with the boy's school where Mr Arlitewicz, Wanda's father, was the headmaster. I remember that during the exams I quietly helped the boys with their maths assignments. One of the boys was Suchodolski, who died in 1920. He was very cheerful and witty and, together with other boys, we used to walk around the park in Lublin singing *Zdechł kanarek* (Dead canary) in between the exams ...

After the exams I never went back to Lublin.

Helena in Balinpol estate

CHAPTER III

1920

⌒∾⌒

After passing my matriculation exams in Lublin in the spring of 1920, I went to Strzyżów. This time I was not able to spend a full holiday there. As I had always been very ill with my throat, had already undergone several laryngological operations and my throat was still not healthy, my parents sent me to Warsaw for another medical procedure, this time to clear the ducts.

So in July 1920 I was in Warsaw, purely by chance. I was operated on by Dr Kmita. I went alone, but to boost my courage, my Aunt Falewiczowa, the wife of General Falewicz, accompanied me there. The operation was quite difficult. I was on the operating table for about an hour and then had to sit in a chair for four days because of the constant bleeding.

I stayed with my Aunt Zofia Bormanowa in Sadowa Street. Her house was known in the family as the 'Good Heart Hotel', because there was always room for everyone who came to Warsaw.

Meanwhile, the Bolshevik offensive had begun. Fighting raged in the Lublin area, making communication with the family impossible. They left for Galicia and communication between us was lost. I did not know where they were or what their address was. The Bolsheviks were advancing on the capital. The situation was difficult. I started training as a nurse at the hospital in Solec, and at the same time I started volunteering there, so I was away from home almost all day, working and studying at the hospital, which kept me very busy. Surgery was taught by Dr Lowenstein, internal medicine by Dr Adeldt, and nursing by an American of Polish origin. These are the people I remember best because later, after this short three-week training, I had to work with them.

The work absorbed me completely. From time to time I would visit my uncle, General Wojciech Falewicz, at the Bristol Hotel. We had nice conversations, and he liked it when I hummed various songs for him. The only thing that annoyed me was that when we left the hotel, he would exit first and I would follow. I felt that as a woman, I should go first, but apparently my uncle thought I was still just a kid.

There were a lot of wounded in the hospital. Of course, there were not enough beds in the wards, so they put the wounded in the corridors, which were very wide, by the way, and the patients were not on beds but on stretchers. Our hospital was a field hospital, admitting only wounded soldiers who had received their first dressing earlier. It was hot and the wounded who were brought to us were dusty and dirty. As apprentices, I and Zosia Genelli – the daughter of a liquor manufacturer in Warsaw – were given the task of cleaning these wounded soldiers. One by one, we would take the stretcher and carry the wounded soldier to the dressing room, where we would strip him naked, lay him on the dressing table, and then wash him from head to toe, avoiding his wounds. We would dress them in clean shirts and hand them over to the nurses to dress their wounds. Sometimes a doctor had to be called.

After a while, they began to use my help in the operating theatres. For example, when performing a skull trepanation, in order to open the surgical field, the skin had to be cut and held with instruments resembling small rakes. I often performed this function. I also assisted in a leg amputation, holding the severed limb. Dr Lowenstein, not knowing my name, would sometimes call out: 'Send me the one with strong nerves.' I did what I was told without showing any fear – calmly. I remember Lt. Hłuszanin's leg was cut off. He reported that his toes on the amputated leg still hurt after the operation. He was so thin and light that, after changing his bandages, I picked him up myself and carried him from the wheelchair to the bed. As long as the patient was alive and was being treated, I did whatever was necessary. But I had a kind of unfounded fear, or perhaps even repulsion, of the dead. I could not touch them. Later, when I was working in a field hospital in Brest-on-the-Bug, where the working conditions were very harsh and the mortality rate was high – I got reprimanded because of this, and it tore at my nerves.

I remember one boy from the hospital in Solec, his name was Kostrowicki, who was wounded in the groin. Cheerful, popular, polite – he was the darling of the whole hospital. When he got better, he fled to the front without permission or discharge. Later he returned badly injured in the abdomen and died surrounded by tenderness and care. We knew his condition was serious. Everyone cried when he died. He must not have been older than seventeen!

When my nursing training was over, I got a certificate with an <u>*excellent*</u> grade, and I started thinking about going to the front. We were given fifteen written questions on the examination, each with two or three sub-questions. Later, when I was at the front, I remembered these American instructions. What a far cry from reality!

In the meantime, however, I worked in the hospital in Solec and did as I was told. The mother superior was 'Granny Idzikowska', and in addition to a certificate of completion of Red Cross training signed by the Board of Directors (Helena Bisping, Dr Józef Zaradzki, the head of training Dr Adelt and the delegate of the Sanitary Department of the Ministry of Military Affairs), she gave me a certificate stating that I had worked in the hospital, on the fourth surgical ward, specifically in the dressing room, and that I was of 'serious character, kind, tactful, and intelligent, and possessed surgical and nursing skills'.

I also received a certificate from the American Red Cross: *Helena Falewicz has attended lectures and practical instruction in nursing given under the auspices of the Department of Nursing of the American Red Cross Commission to Poland and passed a satisfactory examination.*

Sister Idzikowska promised to send me to Silesia with dressing materials, so I waited and continued to work at the hospital. I looked after a patient with tetanus, and that was the only time in my life I saw it; what a terrible disease!

I was ordered to look after Lieutenant Jagodziński, who was in isolation. His pelvis had been shattered in the Battle of Berezina. He served in an Uhlan regiment. He was lying on a water mattress and his wounds were festering, so he had to have the pelvic area drained (rubber drains with holes through which pus collected in another tube, which was cleaned by flushing with a syringe). He was a difficult patient, which was not surprising given his hopeless condition. During visits from his friends and fiancée, when I would leave the isolation room to give them privacy, he would ring the alarm bell and, on my return, he would say: 'Sister left me alone,' and I would see terror in his eyes. He would send me to the kitchen to find out what was prepared for dinner. I would come back and tell him that there would be this kind of soup, this kind of meat, vegetables, compote ... 'What kind of compote?' I would run back to the kitchen to find out what the compote was made of. When it turned out to be sweet cherries, he would grimace and say in disgust: 'There will be seeds!'

But the most important ritual was to take him to the dressing room. Two paramedics would arrive at the isolation room with a wheelchair on which the patient would be placed and taken to the dressing room, which was down another corridor. Lieutenant Jagodziński told us to lift him on the count of three. Since, in addition to his broken pelvis, he also had scabies and would grab me by the neck, I put up the high collar of my apron to protect myself from catching the disease. One paramedic put his hands under the patient's hips, the other under his legs. But several quarters of an hour passed before it could be done. He would count: 'One, two ... give me a cigarette,' and we would wait for him to finish, then 'One, two ... give me a drink; one, two ... I need some rest,' etc. Eventually, he would get around to saying out loud: 'Three.' By now we were all ready to lift him and I had my hands under his arms and the paramedics under his pelvis and legs. On 'three' slowly and carefully lifted him into the wheelchair while he screamed his head off: 'Excellent job, I wasn't in pain at all ...'

In the dressing room drains had to be cleared. The ends of a syringe were inserted into the openings of the tube drains and water was used to flush the pus on the other side of the drain. I remember that once the pus poured out onto the face of Sister Bronikowska, who was leaning over the patient. She did not flinch and only looked after herself when the dressing was finished. She washed her eyes and face with disinfectant.

When I left the hospital for the front, I left Jagodziński sick and in a serious condition. We all had very little hope that Jagodziński would survive this terrible injury. But after the war, when I was at Vilnius University, at a ball in the Vilnius Town Hall, attended by Marshal Piłsudski, who was greeted with a fanfare, I saw Lieutenant Jagodziński standing next to him. I noticed that he was wearing an orthopaedic boot. I approached him and asked if he recognised me. He stared at me for a long time, trying to remember: 'When was that?' he asked. '1920.' Then he frowned, recalling a year of suffering, looked carefully at me again and said: 'Ah, yes, you're the one who treated me so harshly.' We had a friendly chat about his illness and recovery. He had one leg shorter than the other, but he was alive and even attended balls. Not bad at all!

I was supposed to go to Silesia, but Sister Idzikowska refused to send me to the Uprising, thinking I was too young, but I was determined to go, and the opportunity finally came. Four nurses from our hospital were sent to field hospital 604 of the 11th Infantry Division, commanded by Colonel Jasiński, which was part of General Skierski's 4th Army. Among these nurses were Pffeifrówna, Salakówna – I don't remember the name of the third one – but the fourth returned to the hospital in Warsaw, claiming that she suffered from gastric neurosis and could not work in the harsh conditions of a field hospital. The four nurses sent to the front were beautifully outfitted; the uniforms and side caps were sewn by the Jabłkowski Brothers. They had red crosses on their sleeves and long trench coats with four pockets. The nurse who returned was very tall, and I was given her uniform. 'Granny' Idzikowska, as everyone called her, decided to send me to the front instead of the one who had 'chickened out'. My skirt and sleeves were shortened. I had my rucksack and bag and I was ready to go, assuming that what awaited me there would be a great adventure. And indeed it was a school of hard knocks that gave me a lot of experience, opportunities to judge people and the satisfaction of fulfilling my patriotic duty. The front was moving, the counter-offensive had begun, and the Bolsheviks were retreating rapidly after the Miracle on the Vistula. I found notes describing my journey to the front in search of Hospital 604. I quote:

'On 29 August, at 4.30 p.m., I leave for the railway station in a Red Cross ambulance, I am taken to the station by a cadet who has been ordered by 'Granny' Idzikowska to take care of me. I have a rucksack and a Petersburg-type checked bag. Granny hugs me goodbye. In the window, Lieutenant Kalinowski pretends to cry, while Zosia Genelli and Hala Solnicka wave handkerchiefs at me. At the station, the cadet makes everything easy for me, carries my things and buys my ticket, and finally I get on the train. I say goodbye to my attendant and start to read the newspaper. An officer enters the compartment, a familiar face, I try to remember where I know him from – but cannot. I can see that my companion is also concentrating on something, occasionally takes his eyes off the newspaper and looks in my direction. I talk to the lieutenant who I met at Hala Leskiewicz's – his name is Chłopecki. There are only soldiers in the compartment, all looking for their troops or headquarters. In Nowy Dwór, Lieutenant Chłopecki gets off the train, as it turns out that his division is located near Łapy. Towards evening, the passengers slowly vacate the train as we are approaching the front line, which at the time was near Mława. All who are left are the funny, energetic and cheerful cadet Szeliga-Szeligowski, two Americans returning home, and me. At my insistence the cadet lies down on the bench, and stretches his legs out towards me, I sit down and begin to think. We stopped at a station. The compartment is dark.

Only then I start to think on my sudden departure. I left without even notifying my parents or my immediate family. And where to? I do not know exactly! The hospital commander assigned me to Nasielsk, but he also took into account the possibility that the Nasielsk hospital might have already been moved. So I am heading into the unknown. For several years now, my parents have given me complete independence, so I am not afraid of what awaits me. On the contrary, I am possessed by a strange lust for adventure and the very thought that I am going to the front – me, a woman – fills me with pride. It seems that my companions look at me with a certain respect and admiration. Tired from the trip and a sleepless night, I start to snooze, but I am uncomfortable, as the sleeping cadet stretches out his legs and I have no room to lie down at all.

I feel strangely lonely, and it seems to me that I am entering a new, unknown world, a world that was perfect in my eyes. I would arrive with letters of recommendation from 'Granny', I would be well received, I would start working tirelessly for the soldiers and the Motherland! I imagine dressing the wounded, perhaps I will be the one chosen to carry the wounded from the battlefield ... Then again, doubts come over me ... To a certain extent I have absorbed my family's conviction that I was very weak and fragile and that I would not be able to handle the harsh conditions of the frontline. What would happen, then? I must add that, before my departure, I was examined by Dr Adelt, who said to me: 'I will let you go there, but you must promise me that you will try to eat as much fat as possible.' Apart from that, I am terrified by a lack of confidence in my medical skills. I worked in surgery for only six weeks. Dr Lewenstein liked me, and singled me out among the other medics, but I did not have many opportunities to apply serious dressings by myself, I was only knowledgeable about what Dr Adelt had taught us during his lectures. Anyway, I did not imagine that I would have to deal with typhoid or dysentery.

I arrive in Nasielsk at night, at 3 a.m. I go to the station and I learn there that 'Field 604' left three hours earlier for Warsaw. What do I do now? The same train returns to Warsaw, so I get back into the compartment again, lie down on the bench, cover myself with the trench coat, and wait for departure. My companion, the cadet, continued on with another transport. At 6 o'clock, I hear a train approaching, I get dressed quickly, grab my things and jump out of the carriage and see an approaching train with troops. It seems like the train is not going to stop but drives through the station very slowly, and, wanting to get to Warsaw as fast as possible, I throw my baggage into the nearest carriage and reach out to some solider, who then pulls me up inside. It turns out I am on a train carrying the 28th Kaniowski Rifle Regiment. There are eight horses and a few soldiers in the carriage. I cause a stir, the soldiers are getting up, and the train stops. They water the horses and wash themselves, and I lend them my soap. I hand my cigarettes around, as I brought a lot of them from Warsaw. Friendly banter begins. The soldiers bring me breakfast; one of them spreads butter on a bun and hands it to me. I think to myself: 'Our boys are so lovely, it's a pleasure to work for them.' The weather changes, it is starting to rain, which then changes into a true rainstorm when we arrive in Praga [nowadays a district of Warsaw] at 1 o'clock.

I go to the station with the train commander, some young second lieutenant, to find some information. It turns out that 'Field Hospital 604' left Praga heading for Dęblin at 6 o'clock. After consulting the lieutenant, who assures me that they are going to Dęblin, I decide to continue to ride with them. I do not even want to think about having to get off the train with all my luggage (and mud up to my ankles), as it is a long way from Praga to Warsaw, and I do not know the area – so I stay with the train. Soldiers bring me lunch. I eat it eagerly with a dirty spoon, wiped on a horse blanket, as the soldiers used the spoon before me. All the time the train makes stops. Passenger trains do not run at all, only military transports. We have passed the capital, I start looking around the area and I can see that this is not the way to Dęblin. (Having lived near Hrubieszów as a child and having attended secondary school in Lublin, I knew this route well).' The notes end here.

What was next? I ask around, and it turns out we are heading towards Siedlce-Łuków. Night falls. We stop at Mrozy and wait there for a long time. The carriage door is open, the horses are facing the inside of the carriage, while the place opposite the door is lined with straw, and we sleep there. This long stopover resulted in soldiers getting vodka from somewhere and some of the boys got wasted. The second lieutenant comforts me by saying that I will get to Lublin with them, and there it will be possible to find my hospital. While I was still in Praga, they assured me that the hospital would undoubtedly relocate to Brest.

We are standing at the station in Mrozy, and there is no indication that the train is going to leave. The second lieutenant, seeing me in a carriage with drunken soldiers, begins to look into our carriage from time to time to check on my safety. But the boys are not doing me any harm. Their drunkenness is amusing: they affectionately stroke the heads of their horses, speak warmly to them and call them cute names. I sat there silent, I did not speak to anyone, I only heard the cursing of the second lieutenant, who had quite a 'rich' tongue; he was a very young man, with a brown tan. You could see that he was cursing to keep up his image and to maintain order.

As the drunken soldiers arranged themselves on the straw, the second lieutenant was concerned that I was among them. At first, he walked in front of the carriage and looked in, but finally he decided to enter the carriage and lie down next to me. I covered myself with a coat, as the nights were already chilly. I pretended to be asleep. I breathed evenly and deeply, and kept still. The second lieutenant lay next to me. At one point, I felt him touch my hand. I pretend to be asleep. He began to stroke my hand gently, tenderly. My heart was beating like a drum. I pretended to wake up and roll over to the other side. The carriage was quiet, peaceful, the soldiers asleep. The second lieutenant carefully got up and left the carriage.

Again, we are waiting for the train to leave, and only at night do we arrive in Lublin, but not at the station. We stop at some distance from the station. They say that when they bring the train to the ramp, it will be unloaded. I will not find out anything at night anyway – I think to myself – so I will wait on the train until morning. In the meantime, the train leaves, we pass the station without stopping and, as it turns out, move towards the front, to Rozwadów, but not in the direction of my hospital. What do I do? I decide to get off at the first stop. It is night. With my rucksack and bag, I stand ready. The train stops, but not at the station, far from it, underneath the railway signal. I jump to the side of the track; I can hardly see anything. After a while, I spot the illuminated station in the distance, and go in that direction. Dawn is breaking. At the station, I ask whether there will be any connection to Lublin. A freight car is parked at the station. I look in. A wounded officer lies on the hay, there is a batman and a horse. I ask what their plans are. The officer tells me that this carriage is to be taken away by an engine. They promise to take me with them. But when? I go to the train driver to ask when he will be setting off. He says: 'Soon.'

After some time, when I had already packed my belongings into the carriage with the wounded officer, the engine driver calls out to me. He tells me that he would not be taking the carriage with the wounded officer, and that the engine is expected to go to Lublin. He also promises to take me. I agree, of course, and I am transferring to the engine. This is my first time in such a vehicle, but I find everything interesting. So I am riding the engine to Lublin. There are rows of tracks and trains between myself and the station, where the engine stops some distance away. I start to cross the tracks and freight trains' buffers.

Once I am in the carriage standing right next to the station platform, as I am walking down the steps, my skirt catches on the step, tears immediately and I fall onto the platform, breaking my fall with my hands. I had one finger on my left hand bandaged as a result of an injury in the hospital in Warsaw. I could not bend this finger inside my hand like the others, so it got broken. It hurt, but I am so preoccupied with my long journey, so tired and thinking so intensely about when I will finally find my hospital, that I ignore my finger and walk down the platform. A railwayman who saw me fall comes up to me and asks me what is wrong with my finger, what happened to me, pointing out that my finger is bent is a funny direction. Indeed, it is only now that I can see what has happened, and I ask the railwayman whether there is some dressing point. He points me to a sanitary carriage standing by the station. I head in that direction and climb the steps to the carriage. They take a look at my finger and conclude that I need a type of procedure that cannot be performed here. They take me to the hospital by ambulance. There, in the dressing room, they put me on the table, and the surgeon sets the finger properly, as it has come out of the joint. They put on a splint up to my elbow, bandage it, and give me a sling, and they also let me know that Field Hospital 604 has moved to Siedlce.

I am looking for a railway connection. My hand hurts. I find a connection in the evening and get to Siedlce. I go to the traffic supervisor. The hospital, as I was informed back in Warsaw, passed Siedlce and went to Brest. There is no train timetable. There are no passengers at the station. I ask the traffic supervisor how I am supposed to get to Brest. The traffic supervisor, or station master, tells me that an empty train that leaves in the morning for Brest is standing about one kilometre from the station on track number 18. He advises me to go there, get in and wait for the departure. It is night again. The train is due to leave in the morning.

I must go and look for that train. I walk, moving away from the station, it is almost dark. I count the tracks, which are plenty, and, on the eighteenth track, I can see an empty train. I walk up to the nearest carriage and open the slide door with difficulty. I feel the floor of the carriage – there is straw left after the horses. I throw my rucksack and bag into the carriage, but ... How am I going to get inside by myself? It is very high up and I have one hand immobilised. I struggle for quite a long time before I manage to get in. I slide the door shut and try to feel the floor with my hands to find a dry spot, so I can sit down. I sit in the corner of the carriage and wait. I sit there for a very long time, already beginning to doubt whether I have got on the right train. In complete silence I can hear no movement near the train. Finally, I hear some footsteps. Someone stops in front of the carriage, slides the door open, throws something into the carriage, then gets in himself and shuts the door. It is pitch black. He cannot see me, and my heart is in my throat. Finally, he lights a match and, seeing me in the corner of the carriage, says: 'Nurse, I will find you a drier, better place in the carriage, please take my coat and lie down on the straw and try to get some sleep.' This encounter and the soldier's generosity touched my heart. He was carrying dressing materials to the front. I later met him at our hospital in Slutsk and we greeted each other warmly, shaking each other's hands.

On this train, which finally left in the morning, I arrived in Biała Podlaska. The train went no further. I jumped out of the carriage to find information on the hospital, and found out that it had moved to Brest. At the station, the armoured train Śmigły stood on the side track. I approached the officers who were in the carriage and asked whether they were going to Brest. They were, and they agreed to take me. When I entered the carriage of the armoured train, the officers took great care of me. I was given water to wash myself with one hand, I combed my hair, I was given food, and we finally set off, but we only got as far as the Bug

River, where our journey was stopped due to damaged railway bridge. Having got off the armoured train, I looked for an opportunity to get to Brest, which was on the opposite side of the river. I was picked up by some military truck, which carried me across a pontoon bridge to the other side of the river and finally reached Brest, where I inquired about the hospital. At last, after a week's pursuit, I was able to report to the commander of Hospital 604, Captain Rybicki, a doctor from Kraków.

However, my dreams of working in surgery came to nothing. This was ruled out because of my immobilised hand. They made me a hospital keeper. I was in charge of provisions, that is inventory withdrawal[10], substituting food supplies[11] and the kitchen. We, the nurses, had an orderly, Tomasz, while the cook was Cwenar from Lviv. There were six of us nurses: four from the Warsaw hospital, and two from the Russian army: a younger one called Murcia, and an older, toothless, primitive, dirty woman whose surname was Kojałowicz, who kissed my hand when she said goodbye.

The hospital was in some grim barracks. The wounded lay on straw on the floor. The light was very faint. The patients were wounded Polish and Bolshevik soldiers. Of course, we treated them equally, but the conditions were terrible for all of them. Acting as a hospital keeper, I was also on night duty[12]. I walked the rooms with a lantern, giving medication or drinks to feverish patients. But the most dreadful thing for me was giving orders to the corpsmen to take dead to the morgue.

One of the rooms was occupied by patients who had been shot in the head. The conditions in which operations were carried out were atrocious. There was no disinfection equipment because it had not yet reached Brest. The operating theatre was draped with wet sheets and towels, boiled in kitchen pots. The doctors wanted to send patients with skull shots to more suitable hospitals for trepanation, but there was no transport available to take them to Warsaw. The operations carried out in Brest were not successful. This was a hopeless room, a room for the future dead. It was heartbreaking that they could not be helped, but transport was beyond our control.

---

[10] Releasing from the storage.

[11] Modifying nutrition plans.

[12] This job gave me great satisfaction. I felt a medic and not administrative staff of the hospital.

Besides the hospital commander, Doctor Rybicki from Kraków, there were two other doctors: Doctor Feliks Murdzieński, also from Kraków (who after the war worked in the Academic Nursing Home in Zakopane), and Doctor Józef Kucharski, who, having had dysentery, returned to the hospital when I was already in Brest. Dr Kucharski was the surgeon, assisted by Doctors Murdzieński and Rybicki. Dr Kucharski was very weak after his illness and could not stand for long.

Speaking of operations, I remember one that took place as the hospital was moving eastwards towards Sieniawka and Slutsk after leaving Brest. The operation was carried out in a hut. The soldier needed a ligature for a massive calf wound with considerable loss of flesh. They brought him straight from the battlefield. As we moved eastwards along the road – with the whole caravan – you could see flashes of cannon shells and corpses lying by the side of the road. Soldiers held two electric torches and a carbide lamp to illuminate the operating theatre. The operations were carried out without anaesthesia, of course. Dr Kucharski used what he called 'Hungarian anaesthesia' (I do not know why). The general idea was to terrorise the patient, to frighten him so that he would stay still during the operation. The doctor would punch the patient in the face and threaten to beat him if he moved, otherwise the operation could not be carried out. Such methods were effective. I saw the patient kissing the doctor's hand after the successful procedure. He properly acknowledged the doctor's efforts to save him, even though the doctor used a method that frightened me. No real anaesthesia could be administered because there was no one to watch over the patient after the operation, and if left unattended, the patient could suffocate on his own tongue. The hospital moved on, leaving the operated patient for transport.

The conditions in which we worked at that time were very different from what we were taught in the American nursing training. In my archives I have a paper from the nursing exam where you had to answer questions like the following: *What are the moral requirements of a girl entering nursing training? What are the nurse's responsibilities to the hospital? To the superior? How often should convalescents clean their teeth and mouth? List the items for a patient taking a bath. What temperature should the bath water be? What are the methods of reducing fever? In what position should the patient lie for an enema? What should a nurse be aware of when giving opium to a patient? What to do with the secretions of a patient with an infectious disease?* And the question *How many towels and sheets are needed to wash a patient's head?* bordered on the absurd.

After leaving Brest, the sanitary company moved forward on foot, followed by a line of horse-drawn carriages. There was no automobile. The doctors and a chaplain sat in the carriage. As I could not travel on carriages without shock absorbers, I chose to go on foot with the company. Other nurses rode in carriages. We covered thirty kilometres a day. When the doctors saw me marching with the company, they suggested that I ride with them in the carriage. I took advantage of their kindness from time to time.

The accommodation varied. Sometimes on straw in an anteroom or guard's room, where at night you had to run in the cold behind the hut to 'do your business'. I remember one night outdoors. A bonfire had been lit, and there were wooden planks propped up on one side. The heat from the bonfire was searing, while your back was very cold. Autumn was chilly, especially at night. As we followed the army in this way, seasons changed and winter came. We did not catch up with the front line during the counter-offensive. From afar we could hear thunder of the cannons and see the flashes I have already described. I cannot remember how many times we had to spend a night in such harsh conditions. After a while we wised up and stopped running behind the hut at night, because we found out that shrapnel shells could be used as a 'vessel with a handle'.

We finally reached Slutsk, where we were housed in a partially damaged monastery. There were no windows in the corridors, no cookers and it was freezing outside. This was the furthest we got on our journey. The hospital had changed. There were few injured, while the majority of the patients had typhoid and dysentery. We called the latter 'dwarfs' because they squatted over the bedpans and looked very small. Disinfection equipment did not reach us. The provisions could not keep up with us, which made fighting lice difficult. Typhoid was spreading. Dr Adler from another hospital came to visit our doctors and contracted typhoid in our hospital. We put him outside the hospital. Two nurses also got typhoid. No wonder! Every evening in the room where all six of us stayed there was a lice hunt. We took off our underwear and searched every little skin fold to destroy them. There was no one to look after Dr Adler. I was told to watch him at night, and I was also on my feet during the day: I was busy with taking stock and food supply. Once I was on my feet for thirty-six hours straight. I could never sleep during the day.

HELENA'S TRAVELS ON THE FRONTLINE

0   250   500 km

Map creation: Marcin J. Sobiech, www.exgeo.pl

State boundaries

○ Cities, towns

WARSAW Name of state capitals

Railways

Travels on the frontline

◉ Main stops on the route

46

The work in Slutsk was very difficult and exhausting. The huge corridor of the monastery was lit by fires in destroyed furnaces, with no door, only large openings, through which the light from the fire came, because the damage to the furnaces was enormous. There was a mortuary next to our room. If you went down the kitchen stairs to the ground floor, there were coffins and coffin lids leaning against the walls all along the stairs.

It was traumatising, but I had to get over myself and approach the subject of death calmly. I was ashamed that those around me might notice my lack of composure. We often sang all sorts of happy songs in the evenings, and there were cynical remarks that the stiffs behind the wall were listening to us. The chaplain was very kind. He heard confessions and sent the dead to the other world. The doctors did what they could to save lives. I remember assisting in an operation where the doctors were debating whether to cut off the patient's hand to save his life, as gangrene was life-threatening. There was no penicillin in those days, so any case of suppuration was dangerous. And this soldier was in a terrible condition. Dr Kucharski was determined to save this young boy's arm. So he cut the skin from the patient's shoulder to the palm of his hand, at 5-6 cm intervals, and put compresses on the hand – after some time there was improvement and the hand was saved. It was a great success for Dr Kucharski!

As for me, in view of the promise I had made to Dr Adelt in Warsaw to eat fat, my diet consisted mostly of bread and bone marrow. Patients were not allowed bone marrow, so cook Cwenar would beat the marrow out on a wooden board, cut the bread into slices and kindly make me a sandwich, wiping the knife on his wrapper first! The marrow made me chubby. Dr Kucharski laughed at me when I gasped – I was getting so fat I could no longer fit into my uniform and my legs were spilling out of my shoes. When I returned home, my parents were surprised to see how much I had improved.

I managed to get in touch with my parents, who had moved to the capital from Galicia. Since I was at the front, I received several letters from my mother, as my father had quickly put on the uniform and was also fighting. My mother sent me news of my father, my brothers and the whole family. She stayed with my younger brother in Warsaw. On 24 October 1920 she wrote to me:

I am really glad that you have improved so much and are feeling well, but I would very much like you to come back now, because we all miss you very much. I have enquired about the university, but nothing definite yet; it is to open in mid-November or early December at the latest. The Polytechnic opens on 15 November. Kaj has not written, but we have a message from a doctor (from Kaj's battery), who has now come to Warsaw, that Kaj is safe and sound in Zwiahel, and that his battery has taken part in several battles. Papa is also very eager to fight now; he returned from the front a few days ago, where he had been fighting for three weeks. He was mostly in Pińsk with General Sawicki, but he also went to Hrubieszów, Nowosiółki and Strzyżów. Everything there is badly damaged. Our house has no windows or doors and only three cows, two calves and two pigs survived. The cows and calves are in Nowosiółki, and as we are unlikely to return to Strzyżów, we will have to arrange for them to be transported to Balinpol in the future. Papa is now trying to get permission to go to Vilnius and will go there in a week's time. Meanwhile, I am staying here, because we are having trouble with Stach again; he was only in Modlin for one week and came back completely ill; he had a fever of forty degrees for four days and is now coughing badly with wheezing in his lungs. We called the doctor; he diagnosed severe bronchitis again and told us to keep him in bed. The fever is gone, but of course the cadet corps is out of the question. All in all, Modlin is not very good for him and I doubt he will go back there. So we have a terrible problem with what to do with him when he recovers …

Today I learnt that all the professors at Vilnius University have already left for Vilnius. There is no news from Grandma and Aunt Janina. Aunt Niusia visited today[13]. Antek is in the army somewhere in the Poznań region. Marychna is in the Legion, sharing a room with two of your friends: Puzinowska (later the historian Wanda Kiedrzyńska) and Arlitewiczówna (a painter, later the wife of the poet Młodożeniec). Wanda Wierusz-Kowalska works in the Ministry of Treasury, and Janek Wierusz-Kowalski has been sent to a dormitory in Pruszków, where he is in the first grade. Your money (400 marks) has arrived and I will run errands for you tomorrow. Many kisses, my dear child – mother.

---

[13] Joanna Wierusz-Kowalska, my mother's sister. The letter refers to her children.

I have kept another letter with more news.

Warsaw, 13 November 1920.

   Dear Hala! I received your letter and 100 marks through Corporal Fuks. Through him I am sending you some chocolate, fur to line your coat, a collar and a muff.

   It would be best if you came back now – Christmas is not far away. I have heard that the University in Vilnius will open on 15 December. Aunt Janina (Niewodniczańska, née Falewicz) urges you to go there, she writes that there is a great shortage of nurses in the White and Red Cross in Vilnius, so you can work there if you like. Grandma is well, except that she is very tired; she is staying with Aunt Mary in Balinpol, although they say the estate was looted. Aunt Janina, Maja and uncle Wincenty remain in Vilnius; Uncle Wincenty is already eating by himself. In all his letters he tries to persuade us to come to Vilnius. Papa went there yesterday to assess the situation and tell us if we can live there; if so, Stach and I will go immediately. For the time being, Papa is not breaking off relations with Strzyżów; he has spoken to Kulikowski and still hopes to work in Strzyżów, i.e. he is receiving a salary and has a factory room in Warsaw, where Stach and I live, and in the spring we will see what happens. If Papa does not arrange some a better place to live, we will return to Strzyżów and there, with Piechowski's help[14], he will build a factory. Mr Piechowski is in the army; he visited us for tea the day before yesterday; nothing has changed, always friendly. The Strzyżów project depends on his discharge from the army. Problems with Stach. The cadet corps is not good for him. There is terrible disorder, they feed him badly and it is hard to put up with. We know this from Zawisza[15]. I think we will take him from there to Vilnius. He is now on sick leave until 8 January.

---

[14] Deputy director of Strzyżów. After the war he went to Manchuria where he helped construct sugar factories.

[15] One of the many sisters of my Aunt Helena née Falewicz, General Wojciech Falewicz's wife, Maria married a deputy of the State Duma, the owner of Jotainiai in Samogitia, Kazimierz Zawisza, and had five children with him: Jurgis, Aleksander, Marja, Andrzej, Krystyna and Jan. Aleksander was killed at the front in 1919.

Tomorrow there is a big military ceremony in Warsaw to present the marshal's baton to the Head of State; many officers have come, including Captain Gronowski, the commander of Kaj's battery. He brought a letter from Kaj and fresh news. I learnt that Kaj had again taken part in big battles during the offensive and had been hit by shrapnel. Luckily, the shrapnel hit him with its flat side, preventing any serious injuries. Lucky boy! He was awarded the War Order of Virtuti Militari for his bravery. He has sent 15,000 marks for safekeeping, as there is no use for money at the front. They are now stationed near Rivne in the Korzec area. Uncle Wojciech is in Warsaw; he seems to be doing nothing. Auntie is with Andrzej in Kalisz. I am finishing up now because I have to take the package to Corporal Fuks in Smolna Street. Come and see us as soon as possible, my dear baby; Many kisses. Mother.

While at the front I also received a letter from my friend Tadeusz Rutkowski.

Warsaw, 20 September 1920.

While passing through Warsaw from the northern front to the south, I received a front letter from you. I express my sympathy for your finger and congratulate you on your post. If we ever meet (let us hope that I will not need your nursing care), we will share our adventures, and those, praise God, are not lacking in this gypsy way of life. You will also meet many people of all kinds and temperaments. I have not given you my field mail address, and I will not, because the nature of my work and the conditions lead to constant transfers and changes of address. I have barely dried off after marching in the merciless mud of Białystok with the 2nd Brigade of the Volunteer Division (11th, 201st and 202nd Infantry Regiments) and now we are on our way to Volhynia to the 8th Division. Let us hope that the weather will remain good for as long as possible. I send my regards. Tadeusz Rutkowski.

Our hospital remained in Slutsk until the armistice was signed between Poland and the Soviets. I remember the despair of the people who told us that these would no longer be Polish territories. People were crying their eyes out.

We withdrew to Sieniawka, where the hospital was now just an infirmary. Sieniawka is a small town. We finished our work in the field hospital and prepared to go home. The war had been won, and it was a joy to think about it. The winter was hard. In the house in Sieniawka, where the hospital staff were housed, we sat together in the evenings and sang various soldiers' songs: *Bury me in the cellar* ... I realised then that Dr Kucharski was not indifferent to me. He teased me and hid his feelings. After the war he came to Vilnius and asked for my hand in marriage, but I refused. Later he married Irma Hansen, a landowner. He lived in Łódź. When I met Nuisance, it turned out that he had been my husband's classmate at the secondary school in Piotrków Trybunalski. His classmates called him 'the onion'. He was blond and had a round face.

After all the patients had been transferred to other hospitals, we finished our work and went home, which was not easy. It was a frosty, snowy day when I travelled several dozen kilometres by sleigh with Cadet Szmidt from Sieniawka to Baranavichy. When we arrived at the station, the train was just leaving and we could only see the red lights at the back. We had to wait for the next opportunity and stay overnight. But where? We stayed in a cottage near Baranavichy. We, travellers, were welcomed; straw was spread in the middle of the room and we were given a blanket to cover ourselves with. Hens ran around the room roosters crowed in the morning. Cadet Szmidt and I slept well and then went to the station. There was a flock of partridges outside the door, sheltered from the frost and the blizzard.

Speaking of roosters: I had a tame one. When I was walking with the company, a rooster was sitting on a carriage, not running away, although it was not tied. Wherever the rooster was placed, it sat there obediently. When I returned to Warsaw, I did not know where my home would be, whether in Strzyżów, Warsaw or Vilnius, but I took the rooster with me, and it sat in the breadbox I carried on my shoulder. On the way to Warsaw I changed transport three times. I travelled with the rooster in a sanitary train, where I remember a medic walking around with a bucket of pea soup, offering a ladle to people suffering from typhoid: 'You don't want soup, so I'm throwing it away,' he threatened. Then we rode with the Poznań troops in a merry company of singing soldiers, who kept threatening me that they would slaughter the rooster for the soup. The rooster walked among them in the carriage. The last means of transport was a stagecoach, as it was impossible to squeeze into any other. I, with my rucksack, bag and rooster, rode standing up in a crowd. The rooster was upside down in the breadbox, and I thought it would suffocate. But no, he ended up at Aunt Bomannowa's house in Skorupki Street and was put in the bathroom. Then, on a special train to Vilnius, carrying the government delegation led by Władysław Raczkiewicz, who had agreed to take me, the rooster rode on the top of the carriage and even behaved improperly towards Governor Piwocki, who was sitting underneath. I had to intervene, but Mr Piwocki did not even notice what had happened.

Thereafter, the rooster lived until it died a natural death in Balinpol and led the local hens.

CHAPTER IV
Studies in Vilnius

ᴏᴧᴖᴏ

I met Tadzio Rutkowski when I returned from Ukraine with other Poles in 1918. When he was at the front, I was his 'godmother'; when I was at the front, he was my 'godfather'. It was on his advice that I decided the studies to pursue. After graduating secondary school, I thought about science because I had an aptitude for mathematics. But I had no passion for pedagogy and did not want to become a teacher.

Studies in Vilnius, 1921

Tadzio said that law was very interesting, that it was derived from history, psychology, medicine, sociology and that it offered the broadest education in the humanities. I listened to him and finally decided to study law. Since my parents had chosen not to return to Strzyżów but to settle in their hometown of Vilnius, I followed them there. I made it in time for

Christmas, which we all spent in Balinpol. We had lost most of our live-stock, but we still had a roof over our heads.

In Vilnius I enrolled at the Faculty of Law and Social Sciences at Stefan Batory University. I had no other clothes apart from my uniform, so I enrolled in uniform and that was how I dressed later when I attended lectures.

I lived in Vilnius at the home of my Aunt Janina Niewodniczańska-Falewicz, an interesting, talented, musical person who was a social activist in the Vilnius area and kept in touch with a great community worker, Jadwiga, the wife of General Zamoyski of Kórnik. She was also president of the White Cross. She was a very worldly person, spoke Western languages, travelled a lot, gave concerts for charity, and organised balls. I could devote an entire chapter to her. Perhaps I will still manage to do so[16].

It was then that I brought my friend Jadzia Świechowska from Lublin, with whom I had lived during my secondary school years in Lublin, and we lived together again, in my aunt's house.

I began a new chapter in my life – studying. I had a lot of work, studies, lectures, classes, seminars and tutorials. I had interesting professors[17] and took my studies seriously. To this day I have kept some of my seminar papers, such as a dissertation on John Stuart Mill's economic system, prepared for an economics seminar, and a paper on the institution of 'Trial by Jury' – prepared for a course on the history of the Western European political system. At the university I was known as 'Millowa' because of my interest in Mill's economic system.

In addition to my university studies, I worked to support myself. At home I prepared insurance documents for an insurance company. This was a very well-paid job, so my studies in Vilnius were not really a finan-cial burden on my parents, who were in a difficult situation, having to cope with the total devastation of Balinpol during the war and the losses we suffered from the looting of Strzyżów. For the umpteenth time (such is the fate of Poles), they had to 'work their way up' again.

I did well working on the registers. I could count quickly, which was an essential skill for compiling the registers.

---

[16] I used to call her 'African Auntie' (among Auntie Nina's many voyages, one was to exotic Africa. From then on we called her 'African Auntie').

[17] I have a photograph of them all and of our entire class. Perhaps I should add this photo in the appendix.

There was not much time for a social life, but as I was young and considered pretty, I was popular, and during my studies at the university I received many marriage proposals. I also had admirers among the professors. One of them was Professor Wacław Komarnicki[18] (brother of the famous Tytus), the dean of our faculty. I benefited from this admiration in two ways. The first was the honour of receiving diploma number 'one' from the Faculty of Law. The rules were stretched, because in the same year as me there was a student graduating from the Faculty of Law whose surname began with C, while mine began with F, and it was she who should have received a diploma with that number. Komarnicki, who was fawning over me, made a 'mistake' and so I became the holder of a valuable diploma.

Another matter in which Professor Komarnicki played a role was my study trip to Paris. Komarnicki saw a future for me in diplomacy and had urged me to study at the Paris School of Political Science. It was, of course, my own decision, since my best friend was in Paris, but the opinion of an eminent scholar was important.

When I began my studies, I met two adjutants of our neighbour, General Konarzewski, who was staying in Vilnius. One of them, Kazio Rudzki, whom I persuaded to study law (which he did in parallel with his military service), soon became the 'life and soul of the party' and my inseparable partner at student parties and balls. Later we became lifelong friends; he was the best man at my wedding. We kept in touch after the war, and after his death I became friends with his wife, who ran a kiosk in the Polish Hearth Club in London[19].

The other adjutant was Lieutenant Józef Sztukowski, to whom I became engaged when I was in my second year of law school. We were married on 21 August, 1925, after three years of engagement. But first I had to finish my studies in Vilnius and a year at l'Ecole des Sciences Politiques in Paris.

---

[18] A member of the Polish government-in-exile in London.

[19] Ludwika Rudzka, née Kotowska, the famous 'Kika' Rudzka (from the Polish Hearth Club in London), sponsor of valuable Polish artefacts in the Gen. Władysław Sikorski Museum in London. A very nice memoir devoted to her can be found in the fourth volume of *The Kiev Diary* (London 1980, Orbis Books) p. 14. In the Kika's kiosk in London I sold many necklaces I made from chestnuts, corn and acorns during my handicraft work.

Young Helena, June 1923

Helena at her family home, Vilnius 1923

UNIWERSYTET
STEFANA BATOREGO W WILNIE
WYDZIAŁ PRAWA I NAUK SPOŁECZNYCH

Falewiczówna Helena

urodzona w Werkach ziemi Wileńskiej dnia 1 kwietnia 1901 r.
przyjęta na Wydział Prawa i Nauk Społecznych w d. 10 stycznia
1921 roku na mocy świadectwa dojrzałości, wydanego przez
8-Klasowe gimnazjum filologiczne żeńskie Wacławy Arciszowej
w Lublinie dnia 29 maja 1920 roku. Nr. 3, odbyła czterolet-
nie studja prawne zgodnie z rozporządzeniem Ministra Wyznań
Religijnych i Oświecenia Publicznego z dnia 10 października
1920 r. Nr. 8416-IV-20 (Dziennik Urzędowy Minist. W. R. i O. P.
Nr. 22 z 15 grudnia 1920 r. poz. 140) i zdała przepisane przez
wymienione rozporządzenie egzaminy z wynikiem
następującym:

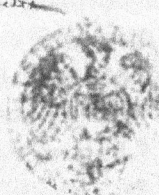

po roku I-ym   z Prawa Rzymskiego, Teorji Prawa, Historji Prawa Polskiego
(Historji Ustroju i Historji Prawa Sądowego), Historji Prawa
na Zachodzie Europy z wynikiem ogólnym dostatecznym.

po roku II-im   z Prawa Kościelnego wraz z Prawem Małżeńskim, Ekono-
mji Politycznej, Prawa Politycznego wraz z Nauką o Państ-
wie i Prawa Narodów — z wynikiem ogólnym dostatecznym.

po roku III-im   ze Skarbowości i Prawa Skarbowego, Nauki Administracji
i Prawa Administracyjnego, Statystyki, Prawa Karnego
i Postępowania Karnego i Filozofji Prawa z wynikiem
ogólnym dostatecznym

po roku IV-ym   z Prawa Cywilnego, Postępowanie Sądowo-Cywilnego,
Prawa Handlowego i Wekslowego i Prawa Międzynarodo-
wego Prywatnego z wynikiem ogólnym dobrym.

Na zasadzie powyższego, stosownie do par. 5 wymienionego
rozporządzenia

FALEWICZÓWNA HELENA

uzyskała

DYPLOM I TYTUŁ MAGISTRA PRAW

stanowiący dowód ukończenia uniwersyteckich studjów prawniczych
i uprawniający do ubiegania się o stopień doktorski.

L. t.

Wilno, dnia 26 czerwca 1924 roku

KREKTOR   DZIEKAN WYDZIAŁU

STEFAN BATORY UNIVERSITY IN VILNIUS
FACULTY OF LAW AND SOCIAL SCIENCES

Helena Falewiczówna

born in Verkiai near Vilnius on 1 April 1901, accepted to the Faculty of Law and Social Sciences on 10 January 1921 based on her secondary school leaving certificate issued by Wacława Arciszowa's girls' 8-grade philological secondary school in Lublin on 29 May 1920, No. 3, completed four-year legal studies in accordance with the Regulation of the Minister of Religious Faith and Public Education of 16 October 1920 No. 8416-IV/20 (Official Journal of the Ministry of Religious Faith and Public Education No. 22 of 15 December 1920, item 140) and passed the following examinations as per said Regulation with the following results:

after 1st year: Roman Law, Legal Theory, History of Polish Law (History of Political System and History of Judicial Law), History of Western European Law – general satisfactory result

after 2nd year: Church Law together with Marital Law, Political Economy, Political Law with State Science and Nations' Law – general satisfactory result

after 3rd year: Treasury and Fiscal Law, Administration and Administrative Law, Statistics, Criminal Law and Criminal Procedure, and Philosophy of Law – general satisfactory result

after 4th year: Civil Law, Judicial and Civil Procedure, Trade Law and Law on Bills of Exchange, and International Private Law – general satisfactory result

In consideration of the above, pursuant to Article 5 of the aforementioned Regulation,

HELENA FALEWICZÓWNA

has received

THE DIPLOMA AND TITLE OF THE MASTER OF LAW

that certifies the completion of university legal studies and gives the right to apply for graduate doctoral studies.

Vilnius, 26 June 1924

Rector

Dean of the Faculty

Before the bar examination

After the examination

CHAPTER V

Paris

❦

In the spring of 1924 I finished my studies at Stefan Batory University in Vilnius, and my dream was to go west and continue my education. It seemed to me that if I graduated from the School of Political Science in Paris, I would be able to work in the Ministry of Foreign Affairs, go on foreign missions and travel the world. My role model at the time was Mrs Kołłątaj, who had been a Soviet ambassador to one of the Baltic countries.

A friend of mine from my school days in Kiev was in Paris at the time, studying at the School of Political Science. But you had to have the financial means to study abroad. My parents, who ran Balinpol, an estate inherited from my grandparents, of which my father received the main part with a house, outbuildings, gardens, ponds, etc., were in financial difficulties. This estate – after my father's siblings had taken over the forests and the village of Gałganiszki – was relatively small, with the area of only 102 hectares (the entire Balinpol estate was over 1,000 hectares). It was also completely devastated during the war and, with the help of bank loans, my parents struggled to get the estate back on its feet; but the debts had to be paid. So I had to figure out on my own how to eke out at least a modest existence in Paris. First I agreed with the editors of the Vilnius newspaper *Słowo* (Word) and the Warsaw weekly *Bluszcz* (Ivy) that they would accept my contributions from Paris. Then I rented out my two-room flat to my future brother-in-law, who had moved to Vilnius and was looking for something suitable. He married my cousin, Marychna Wierusz-Kowalska. He was a colonel, a fortification engineer, and his name was Ożyński. He took up a post in the Vilnius strong camp. He paid me for six months in advance, and so I had the money for the journey. I did not worry about what would happen next and left. I have preserved my notes from that time. I quote:

'After a long and eventful journey, I arrive in Paris in the morning. I am a little worried whether Wanda will meet me at the station. I am dirty, tired and unkempt – I call out loudly to the porter, he takes my things and we go – I can see Wanda from afar. We get in a car and drive to Wanda's room. It is pouring with rain, we go into the city, I want to see this wonder, this heart of Europe. The most beautiful city in the world that everyone has been telling me about for years! The streets are dirty, my patent leather shoes are covered in mud, the cars rush by, I look around with a certain disappointment ...

Vienna impressed me as a great European city, clean and with grand architecture – the Danube Canal looked just beautiful, so much light and movement – I was stunned. And here is Paris – so dark, dirty, with gas lighting. The first impression was a bad one. After leaving my things at Mrs Simon's, where Wanda was staying, we go down to the underground. Another city under the surface! It is stuffy, I am hot, tired and sleepy. We ride through the tunnels. At some stops, people spill out of the carriages; at others, the train takes them in. At Place de l'Opera there are eight rows of cars, making it impossible to cross the street. The shop windows are extraordinary. The illuminated advertisements are magnificent. It is so bright you can find a pin in the street. Wearing a fur coat is out of the question, because even in a trench coat it is too hot. It all seems so strange. It was very cold the day before in Tyrol, and when I stepped onto the platform in Zurich, Switzerland, I was shivering with cold, despite my fur coat.

The first few days are busy with paperwork, enrolling at the school and at the Foyer International des Etudiantes. Wanda takes me to Julien's for lunch. So cheap. I have to drink a whole bottle of beer or a carafe of wine; I am completely green when it comes to dishes, I do not know what to order, such strange names. Faces of different colours surround me – black, mulatto, some people in between. Japanese, Chinese, you can hear different languages. I see people from Russia, England, a lot of French, Dutch and Swedes. Most of them are students. Here and there you can see a different face: a worker who has come for breakfast. Well, lunch costs three and a half francs (one zloty) and the main thing is that you can eat as much bread as you wish. Actually not bread, but rolls; they do not eat bread here, at least I have not seen it.

On Sunday we go to the Louvre. It all makes me dizzy – so many beautiful, wonderful paintings and sculptures. I have never heard of many of the famous painters whose works I see here, or even if I have heard of them, I know nothing about them. I feel that I lack a basic knowledge of art. I know nothing about architecture. It is so annoying! I had a one-track education, the law! And I do not even know that well, even though I have a master's in law. As far as social graces and cultural intelligence are concerned, the 'sine qua non' qualities necessary for a person who wants to be considered intelligent – some knowledge of literature, familiarity with known creations of human thought and mind – can give the appearance of intelligence, education. It is pleasant, but not enough …

I have already been to Notre-Dame, to Madelaine, to Saint-Germain-des-Prés (at a wedding where the gentlemen stand strangely in pairs on the right). Otherwise, I wait for letters and when I am alone, I am desperately sad. Alone among people …'

I wrote this a few days after my arrival in Paris. Our landlady, Mrs Simon, was an old woman who had eighteen children: twelve living and six dead. She could tell you their names from the oldest to the youngest, but she found it much harder to name them in reverse and had to concentrate. She told us that we were not allowed to invite any male guests, and when Iwo Jaworski (later the dean of the Faculty of Law at the Wrocław University), with whom we were supposed to go for a walk, turned up, she was appalled at our behaviour. Debrousse Street, where we were staying, was in a very elegant district of Paris, near Place de L'Alma with the Adam Mickiewicz monument. Beautiful, tree-lined boulevards and old houses with luxury apartments spread out from this square. I enrolled at the Diplomatic Faculty at l'Ecole des Sciences Politiques and attended lectures.

The law of nations was taught by Professor Charles Dupuis, international law by Professor Gidel, the study of modern Europe by Professor Rene Pinon and economic geography by Professor Ziegfried. His lectures attracted large crowds. He spoke beautifully and clearly, with excellent form and diction. A course at the school lasted two years. I knew I would only be there for one year. I took notes and prepared for exams, but I realised that formally these studies would be of no use to me because I would not get a diploma. Wanda Bałtutis studied at the Faculty of Economics for two years, but only Tadzio Bierowski managed to graduate in one year. In the first days of my stay I attended a lecture by Professor Girard. The students were so enthusiastic that they made a lot of noise during the lecture, applauding, laughing, interrupting. This surprised me; in Poland it was unthinkable to behave in such a way.

Shortly after arriving in Paris I met, by chance, Mr Kowerski, a prosecutor from Vilnius, and Mr Protopowicz on the Boulevard des Italiens. Mr Kowerski had connections at the Polish Embassy in Paris and, at my request, he recommended me to Ambassador Count Alfred Chłapowski as an unpaid intern. I was accepted and assigned to the legal department, where I met a very interesting man who became my boss – Mr Nawroczyński. He was a famous painter in Paris. He was fluent in French, especially the diplomatic language required for his position. The secretary of the embassy was Mr Schimiczek, the counsellors were Count Poniński and Count Skrzyński (brother of the then minister of foreign affairs, I think). They signed the notes and requisitions for the Quai d'Orsay. But all the documents were prepared by Nawroczyński. He did not even have a proper desk, just a table to work at. Modest, unassuming, composed – he was the pillar of the legal department. My job was to deal with requisition matters.

At the races in Paris, 1925

Polish courts would ask the embassy, through the French Ministry of Foreign Affairs, to ask the Ministry of Justice to take certain legal measures necessary for the Polish courts. These were usually requests to hear witnesses or experts for cases pending in Poland. French courts would hear witnesses or experts and forward the relevant information to the Ministry of Justice, which in turn would send the information to the Ministry of Foreign Affairs, from where it would be sent to our embassy to be transferred to Poland. These were consular cases par excellence, and in later years, were referred to the Polish Consulate in Paris. I wrote these requisitions and Mr Nawroczyński corrected them.

Our relations with counsellors and secretaries were rather formal. Mr Schimiczek has published his memoirs in the Polish People's Republic (PRL). Count Poniński would often come to work with a new cane, of which he had a collection: some with ivory handles, others carved – this was Poniński's greatest hobby. The most accessible man was Ambassador Chłapowski himself, who had a beautiful estate in Poznań. Once I was invited to a reception at the embassy. On another occasion, the ambassador and his wife came to a tavern in the Latin Quartier, where the students at the School of Political Science gathered, and we had dinner together. I sat next to Tadzio Bierowski, with whom I was friends. He was a very well-mannered and nice, intelligent young man from Lviv. His father was a very wealthy man – he owned large oil fields near Boryslav. But Tadzio was modest and used the money his parents sent him wisely. He called me his 'little sister'. After the Second World War he lived with his real sister in Gdynia. He had a house in Świętojańska Street. He never married. He used to visit me in Toruń and I used to visit him in Gdynia. He was a lawyer, a member of the Bar Council. He specialised in international law and dealt with maritime cases. He died suddenly, still young, at a meeting of the council.

Among other people from the school, I remember Mr Nekanda-Trepka, who claimed that his lineage could be traced back much further than that of the Tarnowscy. I must admit that the student community at the school was rather snobbish. The son of the later president, Michał Mościcki, graduated from this school. I was often accompanied by Sosnowski, a very nice fellow who had lost a leg in 1920 and had a creaking prosthesis. He loved to dance and took every opportunity to do so, but the ladies avoided him because dancing with an artificial leg that knocked you on your knees was not the most pleasant experience. Nevertheless, we made sacrifices for him, feeling sorry for this nice man with a disability. One of the best-known people in international circles, the president of the International Federation of Students, was Janek Baliński, the son of the long-serving president of the Warsaw City Council. Janek's father was known as a great talker, he gave endless speeches as a representative of the city. As president, Janek Baliński travelled the world attending conventions and congresses and had friends everywhere. He was a graduate of the School of Political Science. Since one of the members of the Falewicz family, my uncle Jan Michał Falewicz, had married Maria Balińska from Jašiūnai[20], Janek declares us cousins. His deputy and vice-president was a Hungarian, Franciszek Deak, whom I met through Baliński.

Once, Deak was leading a tour of Hungarian craftsmen to London. He suggested that Tadzio Bierowski and I go with them. It did not cost much, so I agreed to go to England. There happened to be a big exhibition of the British Empire in Wembley. When I announced at the embassy that I was going to London, they asked me to take some diplomatic mail with me. So for the first (and last) time in my life, I was a diplomatic courier. We travelled across the English Channel from Calais to Dover on a small ship. At first, all the passengers were on deck, but when the ship started to rock, they all fled to the cabins below, and almost everyone got sick. It was raining. I stayed on deck, sitting on my treasure, a suitcase with diplomatic mail. Someone had told me that you do not get seasick if you sing, so I started humming, and it actually worked. And when Tadzio Bierowski came to take me below deck, I was humming the tune from *The Merry Widow* (because I had already sung all the tunes I knew). I said: 'Go away, I have to sing so as not to get sick.' The soot fell on my white leather cap as I crouched under the chimney, alone on deck.

---

[20] Their daughter, sister Zofia Falewiczówna of the Ursulines, today lives in in Lodz.

Chantilly, 19 April 1925, Kociński, Carlota, me and Wanda Bałtutis

In London we were put in dormitories, where we were also given board. All day long we were urged to visit museums, palaces and parks. The heat was terrible, it being June. We were terribly tired and the Wembley exhibition also took up a lot of our time and energy. I remember taking Tadzio on a ride in a fairground. It took our breath away, flying high in the air, watching others go wild. But after dinner in the dormitory, when Tadzio suggested we go to Piccadilly to see the London nightlife, I had had enough.

The Canadian and Australian pavilions were the biggest at the exhibition. In the Canadian pavilion there was a field of wheat and a working reaper. It turned out that the stalks with the ears were hung on a string, giving the impression that it was a field of wheat. There was also an Indian camp (in white) behind glass windows. I asked what it was made of and was told it was butter frozen between the panes. The Ceylon pavilion was very interesting. In the first section you could see stones, whole blocks, with various gems on them. The second section was a cutting room for these rubies, diamonds and emeralds. There were about forty cutters sitting there. The third section of the pavilion was occupied by a jeweller's shop where these wonders were sold. They were very expensive. I still keep the pictures from London and Wembley in a beautiful green album.

The Foyer International des Etudantes accepted Wanda, and I tried to move to the Latin Quarter to be closer to her and in a more youthful environment. I met Zofia Kotowska, with whom I stayed at the Grand Hotel de l'Europe, which we called the Petit hotel d'Asie. It was a small hotel in Toulier Street, primitive and old, but this street was a branch of Souflot Street, with the Pantheon at one end and the Bel St. Michel and the Luxembourg Garden at the other. As I lived there, I was very close to Wanda and the Foyer. We went to the Louvre almost every Sunday. In the Foyer you could always get discounts on tickets for various events and free tickets that hung on a nail in the covered veranda. There was press in many languages. One could choose among freebies and as members of the Foyer, we were happy to take advantage of them. So we went everywhere we could.

Family bridge game

Father by the fireplace

Apart from the lectures and the internship at the embassy, my whole day was filled with social gatherings and interesting events. We were mostly in the company of Iwo Jaworski, Jacek Bzowski – a landowner from Kraków, their friend Bodzio Krzyżanowski, also from Kraków, Tadzio Bierowski and other people. It was there that I met Carlota Thorkildsen. She was the daughter of a teacher from Oslo, a Norwegian who had come to Paris to improve her French and was studying sociology. When I was also accepted into the Foyer, we became friends and, almost every day, Carlota would come to my and Wanda's room to chat. Sometimes she would jump under our blanket to talk and tell stories until late at night. She was a very talented and determined person. I must devote more space to her in my diary.

After the war, I began to look for Carlota through the Red Cross, I had her address and that of her parents written down. I soon received a reply that Carlota was in Oslo, that she was happy that I had found her and that she would write to me. I invited her to come to Toruń. She came and I drove her to Warsaw, which we visited with my nephew Jan Falewicz. We went to Żelazowa Wola. She was very moved by a concert and the beautiful manor house. The following year she invited me. I spent a month in Oslo and on trips she organised. In the first letter wrote to me after I found her in 1964 she described her life during the long period when we were out of touch.

She returned to her parents in Oslo, where she had worked for the League of Nations, Office for Intellectual Cooperation. Before the war, she had met a German socialist, Willy Brandt, who had been forced to leave Germany as an opponent to the Nazis and who was conducting anti-Hitler propaganda from Norway. Carlota married him and they had a daughter, Ninja, whom I met in Oslo. Willy Brandt had to go into hiding after the Germans invaded Norway. He was first in a Stalag with Norwegian soldiers and then in hiding in a suburb of Oslo, where Carlota visited him. He has described all his adventures in a book published in the United States entitled *My Road to Berlin*. He was wanted by the Germans and fled to Sweden. In Stockholm he established the International Centre for Social Democrats and continued to be involved in politics. In his book he mentions that the Polish representative was Maurycy Karniol, a lawyer from Warsaw. I knew him well and after the war, when he returned to Poland, I saw him every time I visited Warsaw, until he passed away.

Carlota stayed in Norway because Ninja was tiny and crossing the border to Sweden (although both neighbouring countries aided people in doing this) was still cumbersome. After a while, however, she also made her way to Sweden and worked as a press secretary at the Norwegian embassy. She told me that she experienced a lot of unpleasantness in Sweden because she was married to a German. The anti-German sentiment was so strong there! Brandt wanted to return to Germany after Hitler's defeat. He did, and later became mayor of West Berlin. He wanted to take her with him, but she was reluctant to leave her country. She was and is a great patriot. Berlin was in ruins and Ninja was just a baby. In Norway, everything was close to her. She told me that she obviously did not love him enough to make such a sacrifice. I suppose she regretted it later.

Brandt found a second wife, who was also Norwegian, Ruth, and this came about because in Stockholm Carlota and her husband and Ruth and her husband lived together in the same apartment. Because Carlota and

Willy worked, Ruth ran the household and raised Ninja. Ruth's husband was ill, and it later turned out that he had contagious tuberculosis and infected Ninja and another little boy who came to play with her. It took a year for the children to be cured. By this time antibiotics had been discovered – an effective treatment for this once incurable disease. Ruth's husband died soon after the war. Carlota speaks of Ruth with great respect for her character, her heart, and her tact. After her husband's death, Ruth decided to move to Berlin and married Brandt. She has three sons with him, but Ninja, who is very attached to her, used to spend holidays in Germany, visiting her father and her second mother – who was Ruth to her. During my time in Norway, I went with Carlota on one of her trips to Hammer, north-east of Oslo. Ruth bought a house there and visits to spend some time in her homeland. At the time, pictures appeared in the press showing Brandt with his wife and Ninja on the ferry from Sassnitz to Trelleborg.

I would like to return to the subject of Paris and describe the relations we had in the Foyer, that veritable Tower of Babel, to which I moved from the Grand Hotel d'Europe. The founder of this institution was an English-woman, Mrs Hoff, whose aim was to bring together young women of different nationalities. She fully achieved her goal by enabling many friendships that lasted for years. Carlota is a perfect example.

After I left, Wanda made friends with Ada Kerlsbergen, who was Dutch and whom she used to take to my parents in Balinpol. I used to take her on sleigh rides through the forest, when the horse made its first hoofprints on the snow-covered road and the spruces bent under the weight of the snow. Ada loved our cold winters and claimed it was the first time she had ever ridden in a sledge. She was a teacher of Greek and Latin in Dutch schools. At first she lived in Haarlem, where her father was a doctor and her mother the head of some religious sect. They had large gardens and an estate. After her parents passed away, Ada moved to The Hague, keeping only a summer house on her parents' estate. I think it was 1967 when she spent time in Poland at her friends', Mr and Mrs Skrzywan in Warsaw[21], visiting Wanda, with whom she was friends. On her way from the sea to Warsaw, they all stayed at my place for a night. A few years ago she came to Warsaw again and we met. This brave and no longer young woman travelled by car

---

[21] Rector of the SGH Warsaw School of Economics.

from The Hague to Poznań in just one day. I correspond with her. She is retired, lives with her sister whom she brought over from the United States, and organises performances of Greek classics in schools.

The director of the Foyer International des Etudiens was an American, Ms Watson, a charming person who spoke terrible French. Once, much to the delight of the Foyer's residents, when one of the girls approached Mrs Watson to ask her for another mattress because she was having trouble sleeping, the director, who had an English accent, called out to a boy, a cook's helper: 'Louis, Louis, montez deux matelos, elle ne peux pas dormir avec un' (Louis, put two mattresses together, she can't sleep on one). Mrs Watson had confidence in us: 'You can go wherever you want, but I need to know where you are because a parent will come and ask "Where is my daughter?" and I will not know.' So if we were going out later in the evening, we would sign the hall pass. This was also needed for the duty officer. The 'in' and 'out' board told the duty officer who was in and who was out during the day. Returning in the evening, you crossed out your name on the pass, because the duty officer kept an eye on the returns and only opened the gate until 1 a.m. If one of the students did not manage to get back by then, the gate would be closed and there would be no one to push the button to open it. Sometimes, however, the duty officer would wait patiently when he noticed that someone had still not returned on time, as those returning from the far reaches of the city were often unintentionally late.

No more than two students of the same nationality could live in the Foyer. However, there were four Russian emigrants who lived there and also worked in the Foyer, earning money by doing various maintenance jobs. The atmosphere in the Foyer was welcoming and full of culture. I remember Christmas 1924. This is how I described the evening of Christmas Eve in my notes:

'At 6 o'clock, three honks of the car horn told us that the gentlemen were waiting downstairs. We went to Cambon Street, to a small restaurant where Jacek Bzowski had ordered Christmas dinner. Great moods, festive outfits. Jacek in a tailcoat, Iwo Jaworski in a tuxedo, Wanda in light dress and I in yellow. We shared Christmas wafer and some of us were unhappy that there was no straw under the tablecloth. We had an old-fashioned potato soup, then fish, and then – horror of horrors! – I was outraged when 'mijotés' was brought to the table. It was a double offence, both breaking the fast and cannibalism. Later came the cake. We drank two bottles of wine and a glass of liqueur to go with the black coffee, and we sang Christmas carols. Then we got in the car and drove to the Foyer to admire the Christmas tree. At half past nine, there were quite a few students, all dressed up, and Miss Watson did the honours of the house. The Gospel was read in four languages: German, English, Russian and French. Then we listened to the English choir, later to the Czech choir and finally the four of us decided to sing as well: Hanka Kotowska, Janka Gessner (sculptor), Wanda and myself. We got a round of applause. We got presents under the Christmas tree. The Russian girls sang some of their folk songs, then we took over with ours. A very pleasant time is spent over tea, chatting with different people. The lounges were busy, new friendships were made.'

I met a Chinese girl, Miss Mong-Peng-Wou, daughter of the president of the Chamber of Deputies in Beijing. We met all sorts of people there, including a Javanese dancer who, in the pavilion where only girls were allowed (men were forbidden), lifted her dress to show us her muscles – thighs as hard as iron. She walked on tiptoe. She was extremely shapely and fit.

There was a lounge on the ground floor for receiving guests, where Miss Watson would often personally serve delicious tea and sandwiches in the afternoon. It cost peanuts. Guests were also received in lounges on each floor – with dimmed lights, cosy and suitable for cordial conversations. But it was absolutely forbidden to receive male friends or even male relatives in the bedrooms. This was not a prudish ban. The idea was to respect the peace and independence of our roommates, who might not know the guest and would perhaps prefer to study, sew or rest rather than make new acquaintances. Things are different now in modern dormitories, where female students bring their 'boys' into a shared room and sometimes force their roommates to leave.

Life in Paris, which made such a bad impression on me at first, was very varied. There was always something interesting to do. For example, we were told that there would be a rally of Hungarians under the auspices of the League for the Defence of Human Rights, to be led by a Pole, Dr Motz, a well-known social activist in Paris (I had once been to his magnificent apartments). The rally was organised by the opponents of the regent, Miklós Horthy, and naturally a large group of us attended. We listened to speeches that made it clear that Horthy was oppressive, but when fighting broke out we ran away. On another occasion, we learnt from the press that medical films on venereal diseases were to be shown at the Trocadéro. We were sure to see these fascinating films.

We often went to theatres and concerts. Carlota took us to see Ibsen's *Peer Gynt* with music by Grieg. I saw *Manon*, four one-act plays at Grand Guignol. In April 1925, I attended the great Franco-Slav concert at the Grand Amphiteatre de la Sorbonne, *Corbeaux* at the Comedie Francaise, a concert by a Russian choir, and Pirandello's *Cbaquin sa verite*. Not even a few days would go by without some kind of event. We would also go sight-seeing. Monuments, churches, the Louvre, Notre-Dame, La Madeleine, the Luxembourg Museum, the Cluny Museum, the Sainte-Chapelle, the Palais de Justice, the Grévin Museum, the Petit Palais, the Conciergerie, Les Invalides, the Musée d'Ethnographie du Trocadéro, the Guimet Museum, and the Winter, Spring and Summer Painting Salons. I went to the international aviation exhibition. We went to the Folies Bergère, saw Mozart's *The Magic Flute* at the Opera, *Galerie des Glaces* at the Théâtre du Gymnase, a Russian ballet, and Pirandello's *Volupte de l'Honneur*. We went to a recitation event by Kazimiera Rychterówna, who recited Norwid's *Chopin's Grand Piano*, Słowacki's excerpt from *King-Ghost*, Mickiewicz's *The Great Improvisation*, the circus scene from *Quo Vadis*, Staff's *Autumn Rain*, Makuszyński's *The Marquise*, Leśmian's *Świdryga i Midryga*, and Tuwim's *Two Winds*. We strolled around Montmartre day and night, climbed the Eiffel Tower, went out of town to Fontainebleau, Versailles and so on. With Wanda and Mrs Kotowska, we went to Normandy in Mr Bourget's (a friend of Wanda's) car to visit Rouen and Amiens. This was in March 1925. On 19 April we visited the castle and museum in Chantilly.

The social life was rich, the desire to explore France – enormous. I met many famous and nice people there. The Foyer was sometimes visited by a Pole, Mrs Korwin-Piotrowska, a friend of Franciszek Black, a well-known sculptor in Paris, whose work I had seen in the Luxembourg Museum. Black was a friend of Paderewski and previously lived in Switzerland. He came to Paris for a week, but was so taken with the city that he stayed for life. I went to his studio several times[22]:

---

[22] While in Nieborów in the winter of 1983, I learned that Black's heirs had donated many of his sculptures to Polish collections.

'Far out in the suburbs, near the fortifications, in the garden was Black's studio. Full of sculptures, large and small; in one corner – paintings, a Turkish sofa; upstairs, under a very high ceiling, a large paraffin lamp; below, a frosted electric lamp. International company. Some Latvian woman plays the piano. I meet Rychterówna and Nostitz-Jackowski. The latter is involved in a fierce discussion with the host (looking at his sculptures) about whether art should be decorative; I walk around, watching, listening.'

This is what I wrote in my Paris notes. When I was back at Black's, invited for delicious paupiettes with buckwheat porridge, I learnt that they were prepared by the master of the house.

I also went to Mr Pouchet's sculpture studio, where the atmosphere was pleasant, and there was tasty tea and figs. However, no discussions about art were held; only of dogs and hunting.

Once we invited male friends from l'Ecole to the Foyer for an evening of dancing. There were quite a few of them and they took the place by storm. They danced beautifully and talked cleverly, but the main thing that won the foreign ladies over was their attitude towards them – kissing their hands after the dance, elegant politeness. The ladies from Western Europe, especially from France, were not used to such 'noble' treatment. At this soirée, Hanka Kotowska was entertaining Janek Baliński, speaking French, because she thought Janek was French. I noticed this immediately and asked the other Polish women not to interrupt this conversation. When the cat was finally out of the bag, there was a lot of laughter. In the Foyer, we had a Hungarian excursion and at another time members of the Christian Youth Congress. In February, during the carnival, our whole group went to a Yugoslavian ball, but we did not like it there, so we took torches and went across the Place Saint Sulpice to another ball, a colonial one. There, we drank twenty bottles of champagne and almost the whole company got really drunk. Wanda was jumping, trying to catch a balloon that was overhead. I never drank too much, although I could hold my liquor, and on the way out I had to search the cloakroom for other people's coats and umbrellas and drive some home.

I have always been interested in penitentiary matters, so I visited the nightmarish Saint-Lazare women's prison and went to Fresnes, where there was a prison for petty criminals. A prison with its own system. The girls there were busy making artificial flowers for the Grandes Magasins.

Susveillate, the director, who had previously worked fourteen years in the Cadillac penal colony, told me at the time: 'They are not the ones who should be here, their parents are.' I found out how profoundly true that was later, when I was a prison superintendent for five years. I also listened to a very interesting lecture delivered by Ms Kappenburg in the Foyer, who spoke about the model prison in England. She talked about the Borstal Institutions (institutions for juvenile offenders), of which there are five prisons for boys and one for girls. The latter is in Aylesbury.

It so happened in my life that in 1941, when I was serving time in Vilnius in Lukiškės Prison, I found in the prison library a book describing these penal institutions in England.

As a member of the International Federation of Women with Higher Education, I contacted the French branch in Paris. I was invited by Mrs Monod, the president of the French branch. Mrs Monod was a historian by profession, and had written a thesis entitled *The History of the City of Lyon*. Her husband, also a historian, was a professor at the Sorbonne. In Paris there was also the American Club for Women with Higher Education, where I once attended a tea and, another time, a concert. In the Foyer, we used to receive law professors. I remember a lecture by Dr Straus on venereal diseases.

In addition to various events of this kind, I also went to the Longchamp Racecourse on 5 April, where thirty horses were running. The people who came to the races were all about placing bets. Everyone is betting, people are excited, the women are not watching the races, just plucking milkweed from the lawns for the salad that the French are so fond of ... There were a number of interesting concerts in April, such as a religious concert or a concert of Debussy's music at the Sorbonne. I also attended a concert at Balzac's little house. When we heard that Professor Marian Zdziechowski from Vilnius had come to Paris and was delivering two lectures, we rushed to hear him.

I made friends with Nostitz-Jackowski, a stained-glass painter from Poznań. He was a tall, stocky man with a gentle gaze and a pleasant manner. He accompanied me on a tour of the Sacré-Cœur Basilica. I went with him to an exhibition of Modern Decorative Art, and finally we went to the Petit Palais to see an exhibition of French landscapes *From Poussin to Corota*.

I wrote letters home about my trips out of Paris, about sights I saw, about parties, the social life and so on. I received a letter from my father dated 30 March 1925, which read as follows:

Dear Hala!

I gather from your letters that you are very distracted in your life abroad. I would have nothing against it (my writing is bad because my hand hurts, I am having another attack of arthritis) if there were enough time, means and health for it. Think carefully about what the main aim of your time in Paris is, and normalise your life so that, with the means at your disposal and without sacrificing your health (because that is the most important thing), you can achieve it. I therefore believe that 1) all trifles and vain pleasures should be put aside;

2) Poorly paid reporting commissions are not worth the effort and work.

The main aim is to get to know and understand Western culture, but not at the expense of your health. In addition – to meet people you may need in life (be careful with Mr Kleczkowski, he left the country with a tarnished reputation). It is very useful to meet a lot of people in life, but it is only a ticket to get into a certain position, while it is dishonourable to stay in that position based only on that ticket, unless you do the work and show the ability and integrity. You have these three qualities, so not every scoundrel is worth knowing, but only people of the right worth. Consider all this and see if you're doing the right thing (time and health permitting). You have not told me what they teach there, and what you like, and what your aim is for your future – that is what I care about the most. As far as we are concerned – same old, same old. I will not write about trivialities – your mom will surely give you many more details. In Warsaw I saw Jadzia Sawicka with beautiful Jadziunia[23]. Kaj is studying piano, Stach is studying furiously – what will happen with his matriculation exams remains to be seen. On the 14th, Marychna will tie the knot. Wanda says she wants to do the same on the same day; she says she is no worse. Big hugs, Dad. My warmest greetings to Wanda.

---

[23] The current wife of Professor Leszczyński, a member of the Polish Academy of Sciences.

So wrote my dear father, who concluded from my letters that I was living too lavishly, and he was right. At the embassy I learnt that in order to work in diplomacy you must have money and at least a seven-pearl crown in your coat of arms. It was said that Chłapowski squandered his fortune as an ambassador. My fate was different and I never regretted becoming a lawyer.

I wrote articles for the *Słowo* (Word) and the *Bluszcz* (Ivy) newspapers, entitled: *France in the fight against alcoholism* (in *Bluszcz*), *Reading room for children in Paris* (in *Bluszcz*); *Polish workers' emigrant community in France* (in *Bluszcz*); *Report on Rychterówna's concert* (in *Bluszcz*); *International Exhibition of Decorative Art* (in *Bluszcz*); *Aftermath of the Umińska trial* (in *Bluszcz*); *Exhibition of Decorative Art* (in *Słowo*); *Academic life in Paris* (in *Słowo*); *Foyer International des Etudiantes* (in *Wiadomości Akademickie*).

Of course, I was paid very little and my parents sent me money from time to time. But there were times when things were tight and my dinner was a cup of broth with a bread roll. Wanda and I lived very cheaply, because in the Foyer, we paid 300 francs for a room with breakfast, which in our money was 60 zloty per person. And we had medical care there, as well as discounts or even free tickets for various cultural events. But you wanted to get a real taste of Parisian life. I was invited by Mr Kowerski, Protopowicz, and other compatriots from Vilnius to the famous Olympia cabaret. But not only were we not enchanted by the artistic or cultural level, but I personally felt disgusted by the promiscuity of these women who imposed themselves on the men. My companions were to blame for my being there.

The Crescent and Star was the sign of the House of All Nations brothel at 6 rue Chabanais. It was said to be the most elegant and exclusive establishment. One day, when I was still staying at the Grand Hotel de l'Europe, Bodzio Krzyżanowski told me that he was going to visit this house. I asked him to take me with him. He agreed. We agreed that we would introduce ourselves as a married couple of journalists, buy entry tickets and go early to be there when there were no or very few customers. Of course, I said nothing about this to Hanka Kotowska, my roommate, because she would have been outraged, and at the agreed time I slipped out of my hotel room. Mr Krzyżanowski was waiting for me in the porter's lodge. We drove in silence in a taxi, somewhat anxious and embarrassed, but we did not tell the driver the address of Chabenais 6. We asked him to take us to the exchange, which was a stone's throw away.

A tall building of several floors. We rang the bell and the door opened. A noble and elegant lady dressed in dark colours came out and asked us what we wanted. We said we were journalists, foreigners, and would like a tour of the house. The 'lady' offered us various forms of entertainment, saying that they often served couples who were 'having fun' on their own. We dutifully thanked her and paid a sum of money for a tour. We were ushered into a large salon where women in ball gowns sat on upholstered sofas against the walls. They were of various nationalities and skin colours. Blondes, brunettes, Europeans, mulattoes, Japanese, Indians, blacks. Not all of them were young, some were middle-aged. They sat there and said nothing. Some were fixing their hair, others were adjusting their clothes. There were thirty–forty people inside. I wanted to talk to one of them, because I was interested in how long they had been 'working' there, what made them choose this profession, if they had families, and where they came from. But the 'lady' said that I could only do that if I first bought a bottle of champagne for 100 francs. This was very expensive (the normal price in a store was 18 francs at the most), so I had to give up my social and psychological ambitions. However, the 'lady' began to show us around the floors of the house. Discretion was assured, so none of the customers could be seen. A phone call meant that someone was going to a particular floor. The staff were vigilant, but for a brief moment I caught a glimpse of a naked woman in long black stockings walking up the stairs. It was some kind of oversight. The lady led us to the bedrooms. Inside there were many mirrors, panels in different colours, gilding and dimmed or very bright lights. In the bathroom I saw a bath in the shape of a swan. I asked the lady where the water tap was. She replied: 'This is the bathtub for bathing in champagne.' She led us into the last room. The walls were made of bricks, like in a tower. In the middle there was a pillar on which were various instruments, like in a torture tower. 'On sefouette,' she said. *This is for sadists.* She took us to Edward VII's room. It turned out that the king of England was a guest in this house. They prepared all sorts of devices for him, and the chair looked like a gynaecological chair. After the tour and a farewell to the *patronne*, we left through a different door from the one we had used to enter the building, passing through a cavern artifi- cially decorated with stalactites and stalagmites, across a narrow wooden bridge with birch railings, about a metre above the ground, until we found ourselves on the street.

Looking back on my stay in Paris from the perspective of more than fifty years, I admit that the lectures at l'Ecole des Sciences Politiques and the writing of requisitions at the embassy were not particularly useful to my career as a lawyer. But the city made me passionate about art, painting, sculpture, architecture, everything that pleases the eye and without which the world would be grey, dull and physical. Perhaps it was then that my desire to collect beautiful things was born. With the money I earned I bought only the things I could afford, but they were beautiful, and this continued throughout my professional career. I loved to look at the patterns of handmade carpets. I bought old Meissen porcelain, jewellery, engravings and paintings. I did not want a villa of my own, I did not have a car before the war, but when I saw something in an antique shop that fascinated me, I wanted it.

Of course, it was far from the rich collections of the wealthy, but to the best of my ability and financial means I arranged a seven-room apartment in Vilnius, where I enjoyed living. Whether I visited Paris again in 1963 or London in 1963 and 1968, I was always drawn to museums and antique shops.

So perhaps the time I spent in Paris in my youth was not wasted.

CHAPTER VI

Nuisance

❧⌘☙

That was the nickname I gave my husband at the beginning of our marriage. Why such a sinister nickname for such a cheerful, good, gentle and well-behaved man? There was nothing sinister about him. He was tall (nearly 6'4), strong, dark blond with wavy hair, which I envied, as I always had to go to the hairdresser for a perm. His eyes were grey-blue, his face long, his nose aquiline with a high bridge. Powerful as he seemed, he was gentle and composed. He never let anger get the better of him and had a smile for anyone who did him a favour, whether it was a porter or a

Helena and Józef, Krynica, 1933

housekeeper. He was very observant of people's behaviour, and when I gestured in conversation, he would grab my hands, as he considered this behaviour terrible.

During our engagement, which lasted three years, I initially addressed him in my letters as 'Maciupeńki' (Little One) and only later as 'Zmora' (Nuisance), and this nickname soon became widespread. How did it come about? When I was in Paris during the academic year from September 1924 to June 1925, attending the School of Political Science, after having received my master's degree from the Faculty of Law and Social Sciences at Stefan Batory University in Vilnius, I met many of my schoolmates there, as well as students who lived in the Foyer International des Etiudiantes. Of course, in addition to studying and visiting Paris, we kept in touch with our male friends, who occasionally spent evenings with us in the lounge of the Foyer, or we went to the various cafés. I remember the Rotonda in Montparnasse, where painters exhibited their work, where you could dance and admire the artistic world of Paris, or the Russian restaurant Zolotoy Petushok, where the food was very similar to Polish food (buckwheat, beef roulade, blinis, etc.). Sometimes we went to another Russian restaurant, K-Nam, in the Latin Quarter, where the lights were dimmed and music encouraged dancing. My fiancé was working at the Polish embassy in Moscow at the time. Separated by thousands of miles, we longed for each other immensely. That is why, in the midst of the hustle and bustle, the dancing and merriment, I would sit at the table, sullen and thoughtful. My colleagues saw my misery and tried to cheer me up, complaining about this 'nuisance' over there in Moscow, the cause of my sadness. That is how I came up with this nickname, which did not exactly fit the figure and character of my fiancé, but others around me found it creative and funny. After ten years of marriage and the birth of our son, my husband's nephew Konrad Malewski wrote the poem *Nuisance*.

'Nuisance' –
a word that, whispered in the evening
by the pale lips of the nanny,
freezes a scream of terror
in the throat
of a child, for whom a wicked thought
in a dream creates a monster
'Nuisance'
A word that in the evening
over the child's head whispered,
awakens dreams colourful
and dear
about how it will be wonderful,
when the morning comes
to reach out little hands
and wait until the dreamed
and longed for comes –
'Nuisance'.

My husband was a cavalry officer. His parents lived in the Raków estate near Piotrków Trybunalski, and Józek commuted to school in Piotrków. He failed his final exams in Russian because he knew the language so well that when he did not come to school and was asked for the reason, he replied: *ja myślel czto wczero było świato.* (I thought yesterday was a holiday). He passed his matriculation exams later, in Russia, where as a foreigner he was treated with more lenience. After being admitted to the cavalry school in Elizavetgrad, he joined the Russian army and served there until the revolution. He told me that while the fate of officers during the revolution was generally tragic, Poles were treated differently. Not a hair on his head was touched, and the workers' and soldiers' councils allowed him to remain in the regiment until the end. At that time the Polish 3rd Corps was being formed, which he joined, and under the command of General Żeligowski he returned from Odessa to Poland, to Lviv, where the 14th Jazlowiec Uhlan Regiment was stationed.

He described how they had to cross the railway bridge on foot to return to Poland; they had to lead the horses over this bridge. It was an openwork bridge, designed for railway traffic, not for vehicles or pedestrians. It was constructed of raw planks and nervous and frightened English thorough-breds were led along this very narrow passage, but showing great intelligence and caution under the circumstances. Soldiers led the horses one by one, holding the bridle. The horses saw the danger of putting their hooves through the holes, which could break a limb, so they walked slowly, snorting, pricking their ears, placing their hooves carefully on the planks, and nothing bad happened to any of them.

Józef, Helena and her mother Wanda, Balinpol, 1937

My husband served for some time in the 14th Uhlan Regiment in Lviv and then became adjutant to General Daniel Konarzewski, our neighbour. The general's estate, Punżanki, was only five kilometres from Balinpol. Location of Punżanki was beautiful: a large brick house stood on a hill, overlooking a lake surrounded by more hills, on which the general had planted 5,000 fruit trees – Antonovka apple trees. Of course, the general rarely came to his estate, as he held various high positions in the army. For a while he was also the minister of military affairs. I once attended a dinner at the general's house in Mostowski Palace, where Mr and Mrs Konarzewski lived. I remember that the youngest child in the house at the time, six-year-old Grześ, got under the table and started biting the ladies' legs. The general pulled him out and picked him up. Grześ started hitting his father's bald head with his fists screaming: 'Let me go, or I will call you "evil". As a favourite child, he was quite spoilt.

Once the general came to Balinpol, to my parents' estate, with his adjutant Lieutenant Józef Sztukowski. He was related to the general because the general's brother was married to Nuisance's sister, Janka Sztukowska. Did he make an impression on me then? I think not! He was interesting to talk to and looked very handsome in his uniform, but he paid no attention to me.

The general's second aide-de-camp was Lieutenant Kazimierz Rudzki, whom I persuaded to study law and who graduated the same year as me. He, in turn, became my 'adjutant'. He led dances at public balls, danced a lot, at which he excelled, and then turned up whenever his presence was required, for any game or mischief. He was a great companion and it was he who 're-introduced' me to his army colleague, Lieutenant Sztukowski.

This visit proved decisive. The handsome officer fascinated me with his manner and conversational skills. He was a man who had learnt many things on his own. I was told by his colleagues that, during the war, when the squadron was stationed in a village, everyone would go to buy eggs or chickens and feed themselves. Józek would sit down in a ditch with an English grammar book in his hand, and study. He was well read, had broad horizons, a literary mind, an easy way with words and rhymes, and he spoke foreign languages. A few years after we were married, when we were on holiday in the south of France near Toulon, an elderly French lady accompanied us on one of our walks, and whenever in a conversation I struggled to find the right word, Nuisance would always come to my aid. He himself spoke French shyly and was ashamed of his mistakes.

The next day, after his first visit with Kazik Rudzki, a messenger brought me a basket of chrysanthemums with a visiting card that read:

> *The echoes of a broken song fall silent,*
> *a golden meteor far away in frozen oblivion,*
> *the windows in the ballroom are closed*
> *... or someone's life has just turned over a new leaf...*

Despite the flowers and the poem, he was formal and cool towards me, which started to bother me and as a result I began to pursue him myself. The usual roles were reversed. For the flowers, I gave him chocolates. In a conversation I found out that he needed white collars sewn under the collar of a military trench coat. I sewed them for him and took them personally to where he lived, in the villa housing the military offices of General Konarzewski, at the foot of the Castle Hill (Rennenkampf Villa).

He usually visited me with Kazik, who probably saw what was going on and that was the reason for his sadness and sorrow. Józek wrote poems and sent or handed them to me personally.

> *Life did not spin me golden mirages,*
> *spring did not weave me youthful delusion,*
> *the moon did not shine silver on stained glass of my dreams,*
> *fable did not wrap my temples in rainbows.*
> *I was like a barge tossed on the rough sea,*
> *among uncharted waters with no borders nor end,*
> *sometimes visioning the northern lights*
> *or the sun blazing bloody fire.*
> *I fought long, valiantly without respite,*
> *I walked like a priest, then again a blasphemer*
> *– a plaything of destiny*
> *but never a farce of a woman's heart.*

His poems were sad in tone. Long before we started to think about marriage, he wrote:

> *I cannot offer you happiness, girl*
> *Your pain, your suffering I wish to have.*
> *Your tears – my love's tribute,*
> *My embrace – a spider's web.*
> *Through hard and cruel struggles*
> *You shall cross life's bloody fields.*
> *I shall look into your sad eyes*
> *And I shall bless your pain.*

But he vividly remembered a moment when his heart skipped a beat. It was at the races, at Pośpieszka in Vilnius. My brother and I arrived in a carriage harnessed to two sturdy, beautiful chestnuts with plucked tails and trimmed manes: Sparrow and Camel. I sat in the front seat with my brother, who drove, and a soldier sat in the back. We pulled up in style. I was a student at the time. I saw him from a distance, he was in the company of military men. He just came to say hello and left. Much later he told me that he liked me very, very much back then. And during the races, I kept looking for his silhouette in the crowd ... He fascinated me with his reserve.

He visited often. He never complimented me, but rather criticised me ironically, saying that my 'hips had developed at the expense of my brain', or that I had a 'broomstick figure' because I was wide at the hips and had a small head.

When we declared our love for each other, on 23 May 1922 he wrote:

> *Sacred moments of sincere confession*
> *clear as the blue of the morning hue,*
> *a fable quietly rises to the heights*
> *of a lonely soul thirsting for love.*
> *But there are also moments*
> *when the spirit of desire*
> *shakes like the leaf of a slender aspen*
> *the scarlet of blood in the veins and fiery avalanche*
> *turns long hours of separation into ashes.*

He later confided to me that his coolness was due to his composure. He did not expect me to accept him as a husband, but finally we revealed our feelings and decided to get married, as we were in love. We kept it a secret, but my family was aware of my feelings and I could see that they were reluctant to see the humble lieutenant as a suitor for the hand of their only daughter. My brothers both made sharp remarks, saying that it would happen 'over their dead bodies'.

A stranger, a stiff lieutenant, who did not even try to win them over! What followed was an exchange of letters between my father and my fiancé, as my father realised that I was not yet earning my living and that a lieutenant's pay was not much. My fiancé started his reply very politely:

'Dear Honourable Marshal!' (my father was the vice marshal of the Vilnius Sejm, which decided to incorporate the Vilnius region into Poland), but the content of the letter was more or less as follows: 'I am alive, Hala is alive, and we intend to be alive together ...'

Later, when we were married, my parents were very kind to my husband. They always spoilt him when he came to Balinpol, and my mother often said that Józek was warmer to her than her own sons.

After graduating from the Faculty of Law and Social Sciences, I decided to continue my studies. My dream was to go to Paris, where my dear friend Wanda Bałtutis was studying at the School of Political Science. I knew the language and I wanted to work in the Ministry of Foreign Affairs or in foreign missions. It seemed to me that if Mrs Kołłątaj could become a Soviet ambassador, I could become a clerk at the Polish embassy.

My Nuisance left the army and went to work for Jan Malewski, his brother-in-law, who had a textile factory in Łódź. This was short-lived, however, as the job did not suit him and he returned to the army. Unfortunately, he forfeited his seniority and later, when his peers were promoted to colonels, he was still a lieutenant. When in the army, he left the country after some time to be employed by the Polish embassy in Moscow, where he served as press secretary. From there, he sent me a poem:

> *I'd like to look into your eyes today*
> *Serene in pensive reverie.*
> *Lay your head on my shoulder*
> *Can you feel my heart beating?*
> *My spirit wandered amidst nothingness*
> *On life's wasted soil.*
> *I've loved nothing but You*
> *Your love I only ever craved ...*

This calm, composed man was a romantic and a good writer, the evidence being his later newspaper articles and occasional satirical works on the law and courts. Once we were sitting in Sztrall's patisserie in Vilnius and Józek read that the state lottery had announced a competition for the slogan for the Millionaire's Lottery. He took a paper napkin from the table and wrote on it:

Million – stars in the sky,
Million – zloty in need,
Million – the girl in love,
Million – the main win.

He put the poem in an envelope and sent it to Warsaw as his entry in the competition. After some time, a postal order for one hundred zloty arrived. It was a considerable amount (twenty dollars), and he was very pleased. He immediately went to the largest and most famous pharmacy of Mr Pružan, where he liked to spend money on various perfumes, scented waters and soaps, and bought me a pigskin case with a cover and a monogram (with a crown). We parted ways in September: I went to Paris to continue my studies, and my fiancé was sent to Warsaw for a while, and later to Moscow.

It was in Paris, as I said, that the nickname Nuisance was coined. We were so far apart, in love and pained. He sent me a new poem:

If you knew of my heart bleeding,
How it throbs in my breast with futile longing,
To look into your eyes just once more –
You would be here with me.
You would be next to me, you would approach quietly
Radiating with secret love
And placing your hands on my poor heart –
You would stay with me.
If you knew that my weary thought
Wanders like a ghost in the dark night
To catch you in its thirsty arms –
You would be here with me.
You would be next to me.
You would be next to me and on my forehead
Scorched by pain and daily misery
Place your nourishing lips
Why aren't you next to me?

He was in Moscow, I was in Paris, and I returned in June. Finally, on 12 August 1925, he joined me. I met him at the train station in Vilnius and we went straight to St. Anne's Church, where we were joined in holy matrimony by Rev. Prof. Świrski, later bishop of Łomża. Kazik Rudzki and director Władysław Milkiewicz acted as witnesses. The family was not there. I did not want to upset them, so I did not present them with a fait accompli. My father accompanied me to the station that day. I was meeting my fiancé, and my father, who had been engaged in community work, was leaving to open an agricultural exhibition near Vilnius. He offered to stay with me, but I urged him to go. He was to return the same day – straight to Balinpol.

Helena in Balinpol estate

The wedding was a bit unusual because the church was closed at the front to avoid onlookers and we entered through the sacristy. I wore a dress from Paris, white with a hand-painted stripe at the bottom, a black bolero jacket and a small hat. After the wedding, we took a walk to the Nobleman's Club, located in a wooden villa by Castle Hill, and had lunch there with our witnesses. Later we packed up our belongings, and took the train to see my parents.

A carriage was waiting for us at the station in Santoka. The horses' harness was decorated with roses, and Stasiek Szujski on the coachbox looked very serious. This made a very pleasant impression on us. We drove four kilometres through the forest and by this time we felt reassured: there would be no grumpy faces at home. And indeed!!! All the furs that had been in Balinpol were lying on the porch, forming a soft carpet on the steps and on the porch floor. According to the superstition in the borderlands, the path for newlyweds must be soft, to ensure a soft life for the newlyweds. (Furs were still available in those days, for it was not until much later, during the war, that the Soviet partisans came and took them away.)

My father and mother greeted us on the porch with bread, salt and hugs. From then on, throughout our life together, they never showed any resentment towards their son-in-law. On the contrary, they spoilt him and treated him to whatever he liked. We settled in Vilnius, but after a short time Nuisance had to return to Moscow, as his leave had ended, and we went together.

When we returned to Vilnius from Moscow, I began my training as a judge (which took two years), and then as a barrister in the office of Walenty Parczewski. Nuisance was initially in the 2nd department, but he did not like this work, and he returned to the army, to the 23rd Uhlan Regiment, stationed in Biały Dwór near Podbrodzie. During this time we led separate lives, travelling long distances to see each other.

Biały Dwór was about seven kilometres from Podbrodzie railway station, about sixty kilometres from Vilnius. When I used to go from Podbrodzie to Biały Dwór to see my husband, there was no other means of transport than a horse. Sometimes it was sleeting, the weather was terrible, and the saddle and knees got wet when I rode through the forest to the headquarters of the 1st Squadron, which was commanded by Nuisance, who had been promoted to rittmaster. Biały Dwór was an estate left by a Russian and occupied by the army. The place, very close to the Lithuanian border, was surrounded by forests, and was ideal for hunting and skijoring. The Pohulanka training ground, where drills and manoeuvres were held, was about twenty kilometres away.

In Biały Dwór Nuisance had a small black-and-white cocker spaniel, a very intelligent animal. Once, when Nuisance was taking part in drills in Pohulanka and lived in a tent, or a wooden shelter built and used only during drills, he came to his pallet to find the dog, Dodo, lying on it. The dog, upon discovering his owner's departure, had followed its instincts and found him nearly twenty kilometres away from home. The dog was tired, so he got some sleep and then went to the field kitchen and sat down, waiting for a meal. After his visit, Dodo wandered between the tents and returned the twenty kilometres back home.

There was another dog in Biały Dwór that Nuisance wanted to tame, as its previous owner, the lawyer Romankiewicz[24], had been happy to give it to Nuisance when the dog tore off his tuxedo sleeve. But that dog caused trouble in the squadron too. Once it attacked a soldier, knocking him to the ground, and every time he tried to get up, the dog lunged at his throat. The batman mounted his horse and hurried over to Podbrodzie, where Nuisance was in command of the regiment, so that the cavalry captain would return and free the soldier. The big fawn-coloured boxer died tragically when it attacked Lieutenant Konopka in Podbrodzie, as Lieutenant Konopka pulled out a revolver and shot the dog. Despite having a bullet lodged in its head, the dog made it to Biały Dwór before dying.

The prodigy of the area was a real wolf, tamed and raised from a puppy. The wolf grew into a huge animal and got on very well with Dodo. Sometimes the wolf would want to play with the dog and would jump at him, but if Dodo did not want to play and growled at the wolf, the wolf would immediately walk away, even though he was incomparably bigger and stronger. It was a true friendship! When we rode the horses along paths and forest tracks, Dodo and the wolf would run behind us. It was interesting to see how the wolf behaved when a vehicle, carriage or sleigh came from the opposite direction. The wolf did not want to meet strangers and would go into the woods and bushes so that no one could see him and then, as soon as they had passed, the wolf would reappear beside us. At the post office, the ladies working there were terrified when the wolf climbed up and put its paws on the counter.

Once, when I came to Biały Dwór, I was told that the wolf had escaped. In the evening we decided to look for him in the woods. Nuisance used to summon him with a whistle. So we went into the depths of the forest, where it was very dark, armed only with an electric torch. Nuisance whistled and whistled, and to me this expedition seemed hopeless, but

---

[24] Romankiewicz was Russian, a member of White Guard who served under Denikin and somehow managed to get to Poland after his troops were defeated. He studied law in Kyiv and was a lawyer in Vilnius. We became very friendly. After the war, I visited him in Cambridge.

after a while the wolf jumped out of the thicket, threw itself at Nuisance's neck and licked his face. What happened to him later? Nuisance took a flight in a touring plane, invited to Latvia and Estonia. The wolf was left in Biały Dwór under the care of an orderly and a housekeeper who served three other officers residing there. Apparently they did not want the trouble of feeding the wolf and let him go. There was no one to 'whistle' it home and the wolf was never seen again.

Nuisance loved all animals and was sensitive to their suffering, or man's cruelty towards animals. The story was told in his family that when he was a young boy, he would go into the countryside and let all the dogs off their chains. Some dogs were very aggressive, but none ever bit him.

I remember another incident, in our house in Vilnius. Our house-keeper Karolina noticed mice in the kitchen and decided to set up a trap. The trap was a bucket of water into which the mice would fall when they walked along a stick. I do not remember that complex structure very well. One morning Karolina came into the dining room with a happy face, said that she had had a good 'catch' and invited us to see how many mice she had caught. When Nuisance saw a few mice floating in the bucket, he immediately rolled up his coat sleeve, grabbed any that were still alive with his big hand, and rushed outside to release them.

I would also like to recall an amusing incident that happened on the first day after the 1st Squadron moved to Biały Dwór. Nothing had been furnished yet, the soldiers were quartered on the ground floor and Nuisance was given a cot on the first floor in a completely empty room. In fact, the whole floor was unoccupied. As Nuisance lay down to sleep, he felt something walk over him. He was so tired from the road that he did not pay much attention. But something was lurching towards his face and finally reached his neck. So he flicked his hand and the thing fell to the floor. After a while he felt something moving under the sheet, in a gap between the mattresses. This was too much! He stood up, slipped his hand between the mattresses and felt something soft and warm. Sleepily, in the dark, he carried the creature into the next room, went back to bed and fell asleep. When he got up in the morning, remembering the trouble he had had that night, he opened the door to the next room and saw a white rat curled up in the corner. Where did the rat come from, a rat that is drawn to people and not afraid of them?

It turned out that one of the sergeants had a tame white rat that had lost its owner during the move. The rat had always slept on the neck of its keeper, so when it happened to find itself in an empty and cold room, it tried to warm itself and crawled into Nuisance's cot. It walked all over the bed, determined to get to his neck, lie down quietly and make itself comfortable.

I loved animals and I always had dogs around me. In my childhood and later I always had dogs, once I had three adult cocker spaniels and six puppies, nine in total! As a child I had a tame squirrel, a deer in the garden and so on. So the love of animals was another thing that Nuisance and I had in common.

During several years of living apart, when I was working in Vilnius and he was stationed in Biały Dwór, we used to travel to each other's homes, and we both looked forward to these visits. When we visited military families or civilian acquaintances and they were not home, Nuisance would leave my visiting card with the note 'with my husband'. As to my fellow barristers, I would revisit them personally, as I considered them friends. As a modern woman fighting for equal rights, I felt compelled to express my views on this subject. Officers, Nuisance's colleagues, would sometimes wonder how he could be married to a woman-lawyer: 'She will always want to get her way. You have nothing to say at home, she will always have the last word.' Nuisance would reply, holding his hand half a metre off the floor: 'You couldn't be more wrong, it is quite the opposite. My wife talks so much in court and uses up so much energy there that when she comes home she is this small. She agrees to everything, does not argue, and there is no disagreement between us whatsoever.'

Making use of his rhyming skills, I used to ask him to write barristers' Nativity plays, which were performed first in the famous Zacisze restaurant and then in the bar council's building, where various events were held, most notably a gala dinner on Christmas Eve. I dressed up as Santa Claus, put on a robe, a biretta and a false beard, and carried mischievous symbolic presents in my basket. We read these rhymes, the guests laughed, and I handed out the gifts. Of course, Nuisance did not know all of my fellow barristers, so I briefly outlined their personalities, which he summarised in four lines. Here are a couple of such limericks:

A tiny house by the Blum's alley
proclaims vendetta against the mighty,
with the commoners, however, she does not mingle,
as 'La Passionaria' is etiquette jingle.

This one was about my friend Halina Sukiennicka, a lawyer. She lived in an alley and had clear socialist inclinations. At the time, the prime minister in France was socialist Leon Blum. Later, when she had a car and a nice villa, Halina's opinions softened and she no longer had such leftist views as when studying at the Stefan Batory University or later when acting as defence attorney for the communists tried in Vilnius.

About lawyer Gorzuchowski, known for his rather messy conduct:

Every proper gentleman
to find a good chair
must iron his trousers
at least once a year.

About barrister Łuczywek, who lived in the bar council building above the restaurant:

If you want to cheaply
Seduce some lady deeply,
Eat a sausage, drink a beer:
Let our Łuczywek appear

About barrister Andrejew, who was a great speaker, a defender in criminal trials:

Your speech as smooth as Ganges flow
Your words like honey-flowing dough
And though the client is a common thug
Golden-voiced advocates do never bug.

About barrister Rodziewicz, a well-known civil lawyer who liked to drink:

> *He no longer drinks vodka,*
> *He makes somehow slack,*
> *Takes care of his health,*
> *Treats himself with cognac.*

Another limerick, about Halina Sukiennicka:

> *She found out the work delight –*
> *the words that bring the light,*
> *But to discover a woman's strength*
> *She needed to cheat on her man ...*

There were many of these four-line poems, as they were written for the barristers' Christmas Eve parties organised every year. Each time Nuisance was hired to write the limericks.

Nuisance always took care of his health. As a cavalry officer, he had many opportunities to drink, but no one could force him to drink, not even a shot, if he did not feel like it. His colleagues would often try to provoke him by proposing various toasts at regimental celebrations or other occasions, like 'to the Marshal!' – Nuisance did not move; 'to the president!' – Nuisance would sit still and not touch his glass ...

He would not let me drink either, claiming that every glass that went through the kidneys left a permanent mark there. But there were rare occasions when he drank, and what was even worse – alone. He did this at balls. He almost always went in civilian clothes. He would dress in a tailcoat and, before going to the ball, he would drink a beer glass full of cognac on an empty stomach. Why on an empty stomach? I asked. 'Because if I had eaten anything, I would have had to drink three glasses to feel the slightest effect of alcohol, and I do not want to strain my kidneys.' He claimed that when he drank, the orchestra played better, the ladies were prettier, the floor was smoother, and conversation seemed more interesting ...

Having a very low heart rate of forty beats per minute (like the long-distance runner Nurmi), he could run two kilometres and only then reach the heart rate typical for other people.

He played tennis, swam and hunted; in 1936 and 1937 he was a member of the Vilnius Aero Club, so active in sports aviation that he was elected chairman. When he completed his ground training and flight training, flying RWD-8 and RWD-13 touring planes became his greatest passion, and I became infected as well.

Nuisance was a humble cavalry officer, but he believed that the force he served in should be abolished or relegated to a museum, and that in wars of the future aviation would play a decisive role. He wrote a series of articles on the subject. Only two have survived in my archives: one dated 23 March 1936 and the other 28 May 1936. I will try to present them in excerpts, as the articles printed in *Słowo* are very long. The excerpt from March 1936:

The Role of Aviation in the Future War

The Great War did not create an aviation doctrine. The worldwide turmoil found aviation in its infancy, but nevertheless, from the very first days of the war, the role of this new weapon became particularly important. The tasks for aviation are becoming increasingly diverse. The possibilities, both strategic and tactical, are enormous. It all depends on the technical conditions of the equipment. Human effort and ingenuity, fuelled by the war climate and driven by unlimited resources, give a powerful boost to aviation as we see it today. It is entering a period of maturity before its time. Neither the mental strength of the pilot nor the properties of the equipment meet the growing demands. A man fails, a machine breaks down. An aircraft offers no guarantee of safe flight. We all remember the 'flying coffins' and the pilots who used substances to boost their confidence.

All that is now a thing of the past. The current aviation equipment, having undergone a series of complex tests, guarantees flight safety in every respect, and the high expectations for pilots will make for a strong and healthy aviation crew. As far as current aircraft character-istics and properties are concerned, we have significantly increased the capabilities in all directions in comparison with the war standards. The speed of a bomber aircraft, reaching up to 400 kilometres per hour, is already an ominous warning at the very moment of the declaration of war that their loading capacity of many thousands of tonnes may, at any moment, threaten to destroy the capitals of the belligerent states. Air force will cast a sharp eye from the sky, tearing out the secrets of our strategic plans and regroupings. Army cooperation aircraft, capable of landing on any prepared terrain, will become the ideal and indispensable means of communication and personal contact between commanders. The threat of an airborne assault, protected by adequate armour against arms fire, will become a nightmare for larger military groupings, especially for cavalry, for whom an airborne assault, even with minimal material losses, will disrupt the execution of their task. We are aware that aviation has become an inextricable part of warfare and that every commander, whether planning at a higher operational level or operating at the level of the lowest tactical unit, must always consider the activity of aviation when making decisions in wartime, whether working with it or defending against it. We arrive at these suppositions and this reasoning by studying aviation operations during the war and by drawing on years of post-war experience. (…)

Are we reasoning correctly? A general in the Great War remarked wittily that we were always preparing for the war of the past. Will aviation play the same role in the wars of the future that we see today? Various opinions are already forming, and various alarms are being raised, testifying to the reversal of ideas and the collapse of some age-old laws and beliefs.

England, for example, whose 'splendid isolation' has hitherto been guaranteed by their powerful navy, wakes up one morning to find that it is no longer an island. They raise the alarm and rapidly expand the air fleet. During the conflict with Italy, the naval hegemony did not put its prestige to the test and decided against engaging in an unpreced-ented duel with the air fleet that the Italians, in anticipation of the Abyssinian war, have expanded immeasurably. Strong aviation, in any case, is the motto of Italian armaments. Italian aeronautical doctrine states that no country can win a war unless it has first gained an advantage in the air. (…)

The rapid expansion of bomber aircrafts in all countries gives an idea of the direction in which the air doctrine is developing.

Thus, the centre of gravity of the future war will lie not only in the interaction on the battlefield nor in the destruction of living forces or strategic objects. Air action will involve paralysing the country's nerve centres, destroying industrial hubs, causing chaos in the steady rhythm of work, engaging the reserves that constitute the real force in modern war. After all, we know very well that not all the states will be able to prepare the reserves necessary for conducting a war. (…) Therefore, aviation's task at the very moment of the declaration of war will be to prevent the enemy state from reorganising peacetime existence for the purposes of war. (…) In the future war aviation will become, first and foremost, the starting weapon. (…) The air force must always be supplied with the latest equipment and aircrafts should be mobilised in a matter of minutes. This is what our neighbours are doing (…). We are concerned looking at an aircraft with a 450-horsepower engine that, despite its powerful roar, does not reach the speed of a modern 130-horsepower touring plane (…).

As modern aviation equipment with ever greater capabilities becomes available, the potential usability of aviation changes as well (…). Whereas in the past fog or low clouds prevented enemy aircrafts from operation, now, with the use of blind flight mode and radio-goniometric instruments, aircraft can appear unexpectedly over major cities, hurling thousands of lightning bolts from an overcast sky (…). Taking all this into account, we are gaining an increasingly clearer view of tomorrow's aviation doctrine (…). It is an offensive weapon, where attack will always prevail over defence (…). We know from experience that the accuracy of anti-aircraft artillery decreases as aircraft reaches higher altitudes, while the accuracy of the aircraft is still adequate (…). In the future war, aviation will emerge, above all, as an independent weapon, the superiority of which, if not decisive, will in any case make a difference to the outcome of the war. In turn, when used as an auxiliary weapon, it becomes an integral part of any action, determining its success to a large extent.

The current political situation has been a kind of alarm bell that war is always possible. Starting a war without a strong air force is tantamount to defeat (…). Finding the means to raise the air force to modern level, guaranteeing national independence, should be the most pressing issue of our state.

Józef Sztukowski

The other article was entitled *Let's have the courage*. This is what my husband wrote in May 1936:

Great wars create doctrines upon which future generations are trained – to learn the art of victory under the guidance of experienced leaders. These doctrines must be flexible, constantly updated, based on both experience and prediction, and closely linked to the development of modern technology, the advances of which are constantly introducing revolutionary disruptions into even the most stabilised notions of warfare. And yet people (...) who, through hardship and sacrifice, have acquired the experience of war, consider themselves the bearers of the secret knowledge that has been revealed to them in the face of life and death, and try at all costs to transmit the experience of the last war in an unalterable state to the next generations. These people are preparing for wars that have already been fought, and which, by analogy, have found their tragedy in history, whether in the defeats of the Prussian and Austrian marshals in the Napoleonic campaign or of the Muscovite marshals in the Russo-Japanese war. What these people do not realise is that they are putting the noble interests of defending the state against the massive interests of individual forces (...).

Italy provides us with an instructive example of how to understand the demands of modern warfare: 4,000 kilometres from its supply base, in extremely difficult terrain and climatic conditions, with the hostile murmur of the world's most powerful navy and economic sanctions imposed by some forty nations, it is gaining the upper hand in terms of the main weapons and was victorious in the Abyssinian campaign thanks to the extensive use of motorisation and, above all, aviation.

Without going into a moral assessment of the war itself, far-reaching conclusions must be drawn from this campaign, especially with the regard to the sensational actions of the air force (...). Mussolini was a pilot; his two sons and his son-in-law fought in the ranks of the 'La Disperata' squadron as line officers trained and brought up on General Douchet's theory, that no country can win a war unless it has first gained an advantage in the air (...). Aviation wins a war ...

In our country, aviation has yet to take its rightful place. On the one hand, it must gain mass acceptance; on the other, it must overcome inexplicable resistance. While the general public is very sensitive and responds readily to any appeal made by aviation, the authorities are strangely reticent and indecisive.

The recent aeronautical information campaign that has stirred up the public, which is increasingly united in its demand for serious measures in the field of aviation (...). These great traditions, which resurrected our army, gave us victory and revived our independence, conceal a painful gap. Let us have the courage to admit it. We have no tradition of a legionary air force. On 6 August 1914, no Polish aircraft crossed the historical border and created a legend that would inspire the victorious power of the Polish bayonet and sabre. We have to fight for these traditions ourselves. The Air Force is waiting for its Messiah to unfold its wings, eager to fly. Let the example of the Italians teach us that casteism in the armed forces is disastrous and that progress brings aviation to the fore. We must let it happen.

Let us not develop our aviation in an atmosphere of defensive tactics. Let us remember that air defence is determined by attack. Let us not wait for enemy aircraft to hover over our cities with their threat of destruction, but let us destroy them at their own bases before they take off. Let us understand modern aviation doctrine, let us demand a unified leadership that believes in the great mission of our country's air force.

Józef Sztukowski

A humble officer of low rank, a cavalryman, wrote what proved to be so painfully true three years later. But neither General Rayski nor General Zając, who headed our air force, did everything they should have done to develop this type of weapon, and when Germany attacked Poland in 1939, they had 7,000 aircraft, while we had only 700.

In addition to articles of a political nature on aviation or reportage, Nuisance once answered in verse a puzzle published in *Wiadomości Literackie* (Literary News) under the title *Podróż Pana Grypsa naokoło świata* (Mr Gryps' journey around the world), in which one had to guess from the pictures (on the basis of an architectural fragment), where Mr Gryps was staying. And here is the introduction to the answer:

Whether you're in Pale, Ozone or Ipsa,
whether you earn your bread with your brain or otherwise,
listen to my song about Gryps,
who was generally quite an unlucky boy.
His father did not serve in the Legions,
his mother survived marriage without divorce,
in the dust clouds on the shiny tyres,
in his own glory he did not seek a profession.
He simply could not boast an aunt
(a crime among dear relatives)
who, though respectable, if rumours are true,
did not have the merit of privilege.
Unable, therefore, to dream of a career,
in constant fear of the spectre of starvation,
Mr Gryps rejoiced quite sincerely,
when he found a job as post clerk.
He stamped stamps with dignity,
showing contempt for factory invoices,
but a strange affection for
scripts, newspapers and foreign letters.
He explored the whole world from end to end,
taking in the rhythm of life from tiny emblems,
dreaming of the land of the rising sun,
absorbing the scent of exotic flowers.
He loved his golden tale more than life,
and dreamed in vain for several months,
and as his back humped over his arduous work,
a hundred thousand fell upon his quarter.
Mr Gryps, like an express train, was quick to think
and did not put off his decision for years;
he took his leave, studied the map closely
and set off on his journey around the world.

After this introduction, Nuisance described Mr Gryps' journey in verse, based on the pictures in the magazine:

And so, through the nation joined in union
offering a guarantee of peace,
through the fertile fields of Romania,
Mr Gryps headed for Constantinople.
Constantinople revives ancient history,
and welcomes messages from Lechistan.
Mr Gryps did not see the Pillars of Hercules,
but met the donkeys of the Dardanelles.
Knowing that 'the grass is always greener ...'
he visited the ancient ruins in Athens,
and finally made it to Jerusalem,
to get souvenirs for all of his aunts.
In Egypt, Mr Gryps had a hard time
when, having strayed from the city,
he almost died in the jaws of a crocodile,
but redeemed himself with chocolate sweets.
Further through the deserts of Sudan,
our traveller was led by a caravan
and from the sandy top of a mound,
enjoyed vivid flashes of a Fata Morgana.
And now look – as with a possessive swagger
'Duce' receives the parade on horseback,
thousands of tanks along the road ride
for havoc, captivity, conquest and annihilation.
In India, the fakirs perform all sorts of miracles,
interwoven in every day dread,
Mr Gryps wonders why their Buddha,
is being led down the garden path by the English.
In Madagascar, Mr Gryps was surprised
to see familiar faces from Nalewki Street
in small stalls, among piles of percale.
Finally, in the land of fiery heat,
wandering among China's scorching walls,
Mr Gryps longed for a Polish bar

when he was served a dish of bats.
On his trail lies a mighty country,
stronger in spirit than other states,
what makes them so valiant:
rice, harakiri or earthquakes?
Coming from a country of anniversaries and celebrations,
when he stopped one day in Australia
Mr Gryps did not disappoint his countrymen,
he honoured Kościuszko with a wreath of azaleas.
Following the Soviets, he established a new route,
aiming for southern America,
traversed the South Pole
and broke the record for flights to the Arctic.
To the wilds of Mexico a dictator has moved,
whose demise had long come,
Mr Gryps will tell how the bloody saviour,
from a fierce lion has turned into a mouse.
Now discretion! After the travelling toil,
Mr Gryps found himself in the boudoir of stars,
I don't know what was his plan in divine Hollywood,
I hope it wasn't counting stars.
Mr Gryps saw all sorts of wonders in Detroit,
a rather dark conclusion he brought for us,
their Ford production coincides with ours ...
with the caveat that the daily – is annual.
Mr Gryps, while exploring the streets of New York,
suddenly fell into an unusually gloomy mood,
for when he found himself in Chinatown,
Shanghai bats came to his mind.
England is a country of rigid etiquette,
of great tradition – as anyone would think,
Mr Gryps was nevertheless inclined to ask:
why does it rule the colonies without ceremony?
Standing in front of Gioconda's splendid visage,
Mr Gryps mused quietly, and thought:
it would all go to auction soon,
with empty coffers left by Blum's government.

Berlin, return, the horizon is drowning in fog,
today the Germans are regaining their voice,
why are these thousands of hands raised?
To greet – or to strike a blow?
To the Literary News is heading,
As soon as Mr Gryps arrives in Warsaw,
he intends to publish his memoirs,
as the first step of his literary glory.

I have included the whole piece, as I believe it shows some of Nuisance's characteristic views and humour.

Before he left for Moscow in 1924, knowing that our separation would be long and that we would not see each other again until the autumn, he wrote: Warsaw, 3 June 1924:

I'm leaving today – and I'm thinking of you
as if I have buried my love in a grave,
that the beautiful flowers of my dreams
will be turned by life into cemetery weeds.

After all, the lonely days will long pass,
autumn will silver the fields with cobwebs,
birds will chirp in the blue sky briefly
and poplars will hum with golden rain.

The nightingales will fall silent with the meadows
where the butterflies are coloured in rainbows,
the cold will cut the buds of the late rose,
and only dead stems will be left of flowers.

And I am so sad that in my young years,
which at their end shone with aurora,
pain and suffering will weave sharp thorns
and squeeze my heart with a thorny collar.

When the whole world awakes from captivity,
and the emerald seas burn with blossom,
I look for the withered leaves on the poplar…

We were supposed to meet in the autumn, but he arrived from Moscow on 12 August 1924 and we were married that day.

Although Nuisance's writings were always sad, he was not a gloomy person. He was cheerful, although a little strange. I remember once, when guests came, Nuisance was in his room. I came to tell him who had come, and he said: 'I will not meet them.' But after a while, when he heard us talking about oriental carpets, which he loved, he came out because he liked the subject and was familiar with oriental art. He knew the names of various carpets, the techniques of weaving, and he and Colonel Kędzior, who later became an observer of the Spanish Civil War, always had a lot to talk about. He would immediately test the red colour on the carpet with a handkerchief to see if it was plant-based dye or aniline. Of course, he was only interested in handmade carpets, not machine-made ones.

Whenever he went to Warsaw, he would look in the antique shops in Chmielna Street or Gutmajer's shop in Wierzbowa Street, and if he saw something interesting, he would spend his last penny to make the purchase, and if he did not have enough money on him, he would have it sent to Vilnius cash-on-delivery. Our entire seven-room flat in Mickiewicza Street in Vilnius was decorated with Turkish shawls and oriental carpets. On Sundays, Nuisance would walk around the flat in his pyjamas, rehanging his engravings and paintings, changing carpets, moving and rearranging them, and this was his favourite activity. He used to say that when he looked at an oriental carpet, he found more and more patterns and colours, and everything was so harmonious, elegant and beautiful. This hobby of his started in Moscow. His boss was also a collector. They both went to markets and antique shops, and by the time I got to Moscow, our whole room was filled with oriental rugs and shawls. Nuisance's passion lasted until the outbreak of war in 1939. A Vilnius antiquarian, Boltupski, would often show up on our doorstep saying that he found another beautiful oriental carpet. Of course, Nuisance would go to the antiquarian the same day and almost always bought one. The selection was not large, so every opportunity was tempting. It was different in Warsaw, where there were piles of carpets in antique shops, and just looking at them could make you dizzy. These were, of course, very expensive ...

On 3 May 1926, a few days before Piłsudski's May Coup, Nuisance wrote a poem entitled *The old legend rises from the dead.*

> *When the world is surrounded by a nightmare*
> *And the daytime hustle goes silent,*
> *The legend rises old*
> *And the Ghost-King awakens.*
> *From the age-long sleep he is roused,*
> *He grasps his sword with both hands,*
> *At the head of a fighting horde*
> *He wants to chase his enemies away.*
> *But the silence of the night is not broken*
> *By the sound of heavy weapons,*
> *Not for battle glory*
> *The old legend's moan calls for.*
> *It is the moan of the nation's conscience,*
> *The pernicious call of the ancients,*
> *It is a moan of pain and disappointment,*
> *It is the cry of Polish blood.*
> *It cries out for rights for its will,*
> *For a strong Polish rudder,*
> *To take the boat that is sailing into captivity*
> *And pull it out of obscurity.*
> *It cries out for peace for its work,*
> *So that the Polish abundant land*
> *Becomes without feuds and clowns*
> *A legend of yesterday.*
> *And new faith flows into the heart*
> *When the daytime hustle sounds.*
> *... The legend will rise from the dead – old*
> *And the Ghost-King will awaken.*

After Nuisance left for a mobilisation grouping on 28 August 1939, I found his old wallet. Inside were letters I had written when he was in Warsaw and I was in Vilnius. These letters were badly damaged, torn at the folds, yellowed. They are the best proof of how emotionally involved I was with him, how much I loved him.

I quote the letters in full:

'My sweetest Dumpling, my dearest baby. I sit at home alone and can only think of you – I do not pick up a book, I have no desire to do anything, I just long for you terribly. I walk around the apartment, I look at your face in the photograph, I find you in every corner of the place, I lie down on the sofa and closing my eyes … I see you, I dream of your caress … You came to me longing and poor, and you are gone again, and it seems as if you have not come back at all, and that you have been gone for so long.

I feel a kind of physical pain – a longing for you, I need you not only for me to feel immense happiness, but to stay alive, literally. Now I cannot imagine how it was possible that before I knew of your existence, I was in this world and felt good.

You, my little baby, you made me fall in love with you, you were the first to interest me, and you raised issues with me that I began to feel passionate about through my association with you. You've awakened in me a kind of hidden sensuality, you've shown me what a kiss is, a caress, you've taught me to love. You've made me a woman. You've shaped my whole emotional and sensual sphere, it was actually exposed when I looked at you, I captured your thoughts and words, I found this mutual understanding. Suffice it to say that now I am only yours, my beloved, exclusive and afraid not to lose what I currently have.

In my daily life I feel you as something very beautiful and very close to me, but at the same time it sometimes flashes through my mind that I love you more than you love me, but after your return from Warsaw, as soon as I saw you, when we went into my room, when I kissed those dear tears and wet eyes of mine – I felt blissful that I am something very close to you after all, that you love me, that my life is perhaps as dear to you as yours is to me. When you told me how you felt, I felt immeasurably happy that I was needed by you, that I was loved and that my previous thoughts were terribly wrong and caused by my fearful love.

H.

Another letter. Vilnius, 11 January 1929.

My dearest Nuisance!

Yesterday I was delighted to receive your letter and then the telephone call; this immediately put me in a completely different mood and I went to a ball and had a great time until 6:30 in the morning. Then I slept until two o'clock in the afternoon and now I'm up. At the ball I was always among the officers of the 4th Uhlan Regiment, while at the refreshments (because there was no dinner), I sat with Świerczyńska, Obiedzińska and Messrs Świerczyński[25], Obiedziński, Rozwadowski, Anton and so on. I danced with Przewłocki[26] who took me away from Budzyński during the cotillion and was very charming. He said that he was waiting for me, that he wanted to dance with me at the provincial ball, etc. He was very kind and cheerful. I wore my immortal gown and you can imagine what an impression I made. I received so many compliments! Even Marychna Smolska and Ożyński said that I should never take this gown off, that I would not look so good in any other, etc. I had my hair done very well, so when I left the ball and looked in the mirror, I was so pleased with myself! Don't laugh, my love – long story short, the party was perfect – the gentlemen drank the health of their cars!

I want to go to the provincial ball on the 1st of February, so please make sure you can come home on the 1st. This is a must. I'm going to have a new lilac gown and I really want to go to the ball with you. Parczewski has left for Warsaw, he's coming back tomorrow, I have little work to do. All that awaits me is a trip to Nowogródek in search of the parish records for Parczewski's big trial. I only wish it weren't so cold, as it's easy to catch a cold.

Baby, I'm looking forward to seeing the snake skin, but maybe you'd better buy a carpet for the dining room I'm dreaming of, and there will still be time to buy the snake. The carpet must be large, so that when the chairs are moved away from the table, they don't get caught on its

---

[25] A friend of writer Jarosław Iwaszkiewicz. He served as a model for the writer in the short story *Panny z Wilka* (The Wilko Girls).

[26] Brigadier General Marian Roman Przewłocki.

edge, and when the table is pulled out to its full length, the carpet must be long enough. The type of the carpet you will determine by yourself in Warsaw. I'm sending you a photograph taken by Łuczyński, the only one that was good, and I'll also send you another one, taken by Marci-nowski when we met in the street. I am sending you lots of kisses. Friends at the ball decided that my only flaw was my love for my husband. I am waiting for your account of your trip to Piotrków and Trzebnica. Hala.

Letter number three. Vilnius, 11 February 1929 (written while Nuisance was ill in Warsaw).

My dearest Nuisance!

The telephone in Warsaw is out of order, I cannot get hold of you. Are you well? You're not keeping in touch at all! Stefan neither writes nor telegraphs. I am terribly anxious and terribly sad not to be with you, honey. I want to come to Warsaw and will probably do so soon. Maybe Wednesday evening. I feel so sorry for you, baby, that you have been so abandoned. I dream of coming to you and being with you 24 hours a day. Why are you so silent? Send me a wire, I will come right away. Parczewski took a regular train to Warsaw today. At the moment Dean Zawadzki is travelling by an express. I am sending the parcel and letter through him. Parczewski promised to visit you and let me know if I should come. It is so hard for me to see them going to Warsaw while I have to stay. Parczewski is such a scoundrel. He can see how upset I am by all this. He could have sent me to Warsaw, and yet he refused, saying that surely you are not seriously ill. I am so terribly sorry that you have a wife who loves you so much, and yet you are alone. Honey, order me to come. If you are still sick, I will come. You know, keeping someone in the dark like that can lead to despair. Today, I had one case in the Justice of the Peace Court. Tomorrow, I have an honourable appear-ance in the District Court. The day after tomorrow, I have the Biszewski case in the District Court, for which I have already received one hundred zlotys in advance, and then I am free. I have nothing else to do until 20ᵗʰ February. On the 15ᵗʰ there was supposed to be a meeting of barrister's trainees at my place, but I cancelled, because I want to come to you on the 13th. You cannot leave the house so soon after the flu, so we will sit together in your room and it will be fine. I'm sending you a million kisses, my Dearest Love. I love you so much and I feel so bad without you. Your Hala.

I read these letters after Nuisance left for the front. I read them again and again, waiting for any news of him. Then came my husband's last letter from Kozielsk. I left it with Janek, whom he loved so much and whom he was never to see again.

Helena's Wedding Day 12th of August 1925

Father and son, Balinpol, 1936

Nuisance with Pumpkin, 1936

Józef and Jan

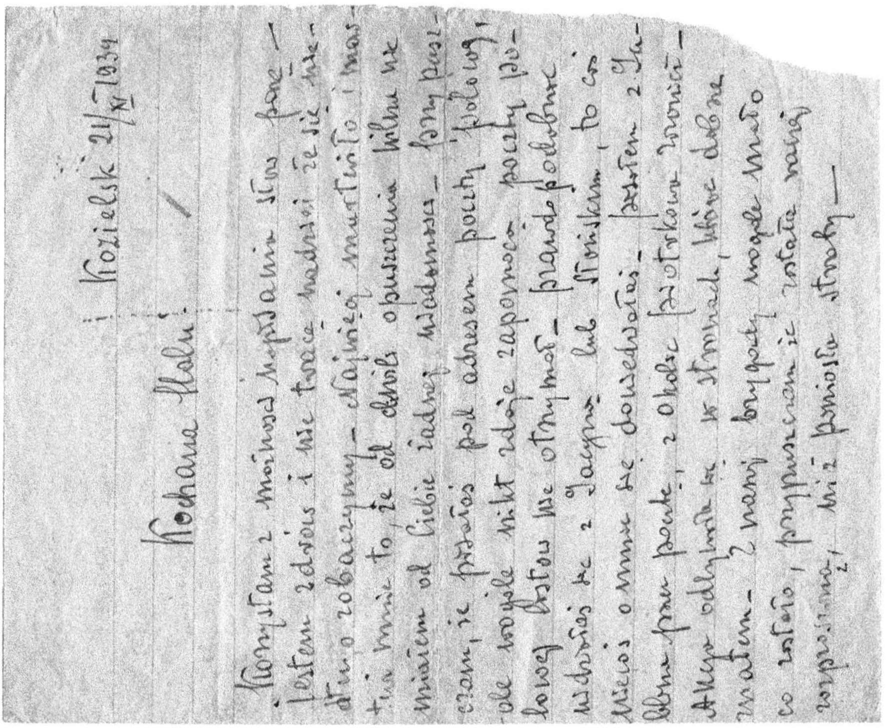

Kozielsk 21/XI 1939

Kochana Halu!

Korzystam z możności napisania słów parę — jestem zdrów i nie tracę nadziei że się niedługo zobaczymy — Najwięcej martwiło i martwi mnie to, że od chwili opuszczenia Wilna nie miałem od Ciebie żadnej wiadomości — przypuszczam, że pisałaś pod adresem poczty polowej, ale wogóle nikt żadnej za pomocą poczty polowej listów nie otrzymał — prawdopodobnie widziałaś się z Jacyną lub Stolińskim, to coś niecoś o mnie się dowiedziałaś — pisałem z Jabłonnej przez pocztę, z okolic Piotrkowa również — Akcja odbywała się w stronach, które dobrze znałem — Z naszej brygady wogóle mało co zostało, przypuszczam że została raczej rozproszona, niż poniosła straty —

Słyszałem natomiast dość smutną wiadomość, że zginął Leszek Kowalski — wiadomości tej jednak nie sprawdziłem — więc może być nieprawdziwa — W Jabłonnie mówił mi, że zginęła od bomby lotniczej matka gen. Bartkowskiego — Seferyński podobno żyje w niewoli niemieckiej — Florczak zginął, co prawdopodobnie wiesz — Widziałem Pawełkowskiego i Aleksandra Mohla — Wogóle znajomych spotykałem bardzo dużo — Ciekawy jestem co słychać z Mamą, czy została przy Was — i jak jej sprawy — Zostawiam twój adres — Odpisuj tylko pojedyńczo na mnie listy — Będę czekał z utęsknieniem wiadomości od Ciebie, gdyż wszelka troska o Was jest obecnie największym moim zmartwieniem — Ucałuj wszystkich serdecznie odemnie, Mamę, Julisię itd — Wszystkim naszym wspólnym znajomym serdeczne pozdrowienia —

Adres — С.С.С.Р. гор. Козельск Смоленской обл. Почтовый ящ. №12 — Иосифу Владиславовичу Штыковскому —

CHAPTER VII
Moscow

ଏ৵৶ଚ

On 25 September 1925 I wrote a letter to my mother from Warsaw:

My dear Mother! Tonight at twelve o'clock we will probably leave for Moscow. They should give us our passports and visas at two o'clock.

Yesterday, together with Nuisance, we were at the Zwolińskis[27], the house was full of women, apart from auntie and four daughters, Janinka Puzynianka[28] was there also. We visited the Bormanns', and today we plan to visit Aunt Zenka. I bought shoes with rubber soles and I feel like walking on cotton wool, they are so comfortable and quiet. (…) Please write to me often and in detail about everything, because although Nuisance is so tiny, it was very sad to leave home now.

Lots of kisses to you, to Auntie[29] and Stach. Hugs. Hala.

Another letter came from Moscow: 28 September 1925:

Dear parents!

Yesterday, Nuisance and I arrived in Moscow. We had a very comfortable journey, we got a sleeping car as soon as we departed from Warsaw. We left Warsaw at midnight. At the railway station Hela Skolimowska and Zula Zwolińska bade us farewell, with flowers (which touched me to the core). The next day at 11 a.m. we arrived in Stołbce, then we crossed the border, still in a Polish train. The Bolshe-

---

[27] My aunt Zofia Falewiczówna married a participant of the January Uprising of 1863, Mikołaj Zwoliński, and had four daughters: Zula, Hela, Maryjka and Wala and a son Olutek.

[28] Her elder sister Alexandra Falewiczówna married Prince Xawery Puzyna and had two daughters with him: Janinka (later member of Congregation Sororum Canonissarum) and Basia 'Barbie' Grużewska, who died in Argentina.

[29] My mother's sister, Joanna Wierusz-Kowalska.

viks entered the train and controlled our passports. In Negoreloe they searched our personal belongings and although they meticulously inspected everything, including the black silk fabric, they did not find anything to declare. In Negoreloe we saw Cziczerin, who was on his way to Poland.

At home, after a bath, getting changed, and having dinner, we put on the gramophone and, in the evening, we all went by car to the dog show: Major, Nuisance, Lieutenant Rawicz and me.

Major's Doberman pinscher Teddi made his debut at the show. Very far away, in one of the pavilions of an industrial exhibition, in pens – wonderful dogs. The barking was terrible, a noise that made your ears hurt. The major's dog Teddi lay on a Persian rug, and won three medals: two silver and one bronze. There was a puppy at the show (Teddi's brother) whose mother also got a prize and whose father was the star of the event. The owner of this dog, a friend of our acquaintances, offered the puppy to Nuisance, so we took it straight to the car and home. It is a lovely animal – imagine that it was born without a tail, which is proof of a great breed!

Last night the puppy squeaked a lot, so Nuisance took it to bed and it calmed down. The flat is fine, my room is very nicely decorated. Nuisance's Persian shawls hang on the walls. A thin lace cape on the bed, kilims, lovely trinkets, etc. But soon we will move to an even better flat. At the moment Rawicz is playing the piano, the major has gone somewhere. Nuisance is reading newspapers and I am writing. We went for a walk in the city this morning. Traffic is heavy and the streets are littered, although there are rubbish bins and big ashtrays everywhere. In the streets, a large grey crowd, badly dressed. I saw soldiers and secret police. Yesterday, on the way to and from the exhibition, our friends showed me all the government buildings, offices, secret police quarters and so on. Everyone is looking at us, they think we are foreigners, probably Americans.

Please write and tell me all the news in detail. I'm very much looking forward to the news and often think of home, which makes me tearful. Lots of kisses to you, Father and Auntie. Give Stach a hug for me. Hala.

The third letter is dated 9 October 1925.

Dear parents!

I'm looking forward to hearing news from Balinpol and I can't wait until Sunday, hoping to find a letter in the diplomatic mail. I want a long and detailed letter, like the ones mother used to write to Paris, about everything – the cows, the farm, daily life and news in the family. I feel perfectly well, even though I have nothing to do. Nevertheless, I'm busy all day long and I'm not bored at all. I sew, I mend Nuisance's things that are still here. I read the newspapers, play with the dogs, who are terribly nice, put on the gramophone, and sometimes Nuisance takes the car and we go somewhere for a nice walk. We went to Sokolniki recently and I enjoyed it very much. We paid a visit to all the dignitaries in the Legation, where we were received with great splendour and glamour. We have already been revisited.

It turned out that Counsellor Wyszyński's wife was Zosia Wyszyńska, the daughter of the director of Klemensowo, who once came to Strzyżów. We fought wasps in the flowerbed in front of the house, but she doesn't remember that. She is not very amiable. There is also the wife of one of the officials in the Legation, and my former schoolmate from Kiev, née Linde; she was the class dumbhead. The nicest person, who I think will become my great friend, is Mrs Brückner, the wife of the secretary of the Re-evacuation Delegation. Major Kobylański is ill. He had a tooth extracted and then developed an ulcer with complications. He's bandaged up, swollen, and I'm looking after him a bit, forcing food into him.

Next week we are moving into a new apartment, in a grand villa that formerly belonged to some very rich jeweller. It is being completely renovated, with a second bathroom, etc. The members of the attaché office will occupy the entire ground floor (four officers and myself), while the first floor will be occupied by some of the bigwigs from the Legation. Next to the house, in the garden, there is a new tennis court which cost 800 dollars to install. They say it is better than the one the English have here. The servants will live in very nice basement quarters. Our food will be prepared on the first floor, but we are supposed to eat downstairs! There's a lot of talk now about moving, settling in, buying furniture and so on. I'd love to move in and unpack as soon as possible. Nuisance is busy, always reading newspapers and writing reports. He is very 'small' and getting smaller. It is snowing here today, and not for the first time.

I don't feel the Bolsheviks here at all. It's peaceful and safe. They've been selling a strong 40 percent vodka here, for a while now, so there are lots of drunks, and if you drive a car through the streets in the evening, the chauffeur has to manoeuvre between passers-by who are swaying from side to side as they walk. How are things at home? Has Aunt Niusia[30] left? How is Kaj's health? Has Stach enrolled at the university? Our Nal is lovely, naughty and, although small, he's already a handful. My dear Mama, write often to your daughter, who thinks a lot about home and wants to know everything. (...) Lots of kisses to Father and Auntie. Please hug Stach for me. Hala.

So we moved into this grand villa where had a huge room, a former living room with a fireplace. We also had a separate bathroom. Nuisance had, of course, laid the oriental carpets he had bought in Moscow on the floor and hung Turkish shawls on the walls, so it was cosy, although there was not much furniture. We ate in the hall, usually the four of us: Major Kobylański, Captain Grudzień or Lieutenant Rawicz, Nuisance and I. The major had a nasty habit of interrupting as soon as anyone at the table tried to speak, as if he did not care what anyone had to say. He was a snob, but an elegant, tall man, a bachelor. His sister was the wife of Michał Mościcki, the son of the future president of Poland. Such connections must have gone to his head.

The villa was located on Arbatsky Piereułk, a small street leading to a very busy street, the Arbat. Nuisance was constantly typing, because he was a press secretary. He read all the newspapers and reported what might be of interest to the general staff. I explored the city, went out alone and walked around. I did a little shopping. In his spare time, Nuisance played tennis with the secretary of the Japanese embassy, Machida. This little man had to jump very high when serving to get the sharp ball over the net. I often talked to him. He was nice and told me he had a fiancée. He had a picture of her, but he had never seen her before in his life. I was

---

[30] Joanna Wierusz-Kowalska née Więckowska.

astonished and asked him how he could marry a person he had never met, without knowing if they were right for each other. He replied very seriously that his parents had assured him that they had made the right choice and that he would be very happy with her. However, as I found out much later, the opposite was true.

The second secretary of the Japanese embassy was Imaida. Both names sounded grotesque in Polish, as the first was pronounced 'ma, czy da?', meaning 'Does he have or does he give?', and the other was pronounced 'i ma, i da,' meaning 'He has and he will give'. We were once invited by Nuisance's sparring partner to the opera-ballet *The Corsair*. He asked us to go to him first and then we would go to the Grand Theatre together. Nuisance dressed in black, I put on a black velvet gown and a mink cape and we went to Machida. He had two rooms in the Japanese Legation. We entered a connecting room, behind which was his bedroom. In the first room he sat us down at a table with a gramophone on it. He put on a record and looked at us. We were all dressed up. He was dressed casually. So he decided to change. A servant put two glasses of tea by the gramophone for us. Machida went to his bedroom and then appeared in the room where we were sitting, with no shoes on his feet, holding his trousers in front of him, dressed in a loose shirt and with his suspenders hanging down at the back.

He went into the hall to give his shoes to the butler to clean. He was carrying the shoes in his hand. When he returned, he sat down on a rowing machine and began to exercise. We drank tea and watched him move back and forth on the seat and wave his arms. When the butler brought him his clean shoes, he sat down beside me, put on his shoes and adjusted his sock while talking to us. He then went to the bedroom and returned elegantly dressed in a dark suit. This kind of casual, unembarrassed behaviour is said to be characteristic of the Japanese.

We went to the opera. The show was magnificent, the stage was dripping with gold, the costumes were very rich. The famous dancer Gelcer was performing that night. We sat in the front row, right in front of the parapet, behind which was the orchestra. The parapet, lined with red velvet, was worn and torn. The dignitaries sat in the boxes. Many of them were bearded and wore rubashka shirts with collars buttoned at the side. During the interlude, the audience ate in the auditorium, took out sandwiches wrapped in paper, ate sausages and made a racket, talking loudly

Helena before the ball, Warsaw 1937

and shouting to their friends. I made a terrible faux pas when I saw a slant-eyed man in the ground-floor box I asked Machida if he was also Japanese. I could see Machida's indignation. How could I mistake a Chinese for a Japanese? But he forgave my racial ignorance and we remained on good terms.

We felt well in Moscow, although we were aware of the constant surveillance. Opposite our villa, on the other side of the alley, was a low house where, behind a curtain we could see a man sitting for hours at the window[31]. We knew he was on duty. Nuisance told me that there was always a motorbike parked right behind the villa, and every time a Legation car drove out of the gate, the motorbike would follow. Before I arrived, Nuisance often went to the swimming pool. There were three

---

[31] The 'participant observation' method is still used in the computer era. There is no institution more respectful of tradition than ... the police.

types of pool: women's without swimsuits, men's without swimsuits, and a general pool with swimsuits. When Nuisance undressed, the motorcyclist did the same; when he had finished swimming, his 'ghost' also got dressed. But once, on his way home, Nuisance looked over and saw that the motorcyclist was not there. He asked the chauffeur to stop and said, 'We'll wait for the motorcyclist. Apparently his bike broke down, and if he doesn't follow us, he'll suffer the consequences.'

They waited for this man to arrive. It was a sign of Nuisance's sense of humour. Jaksatyr, the counsellor of the Legation, reacted quite differently to this surveillance. Wherever he went, whether to a shop or the cinema, he was followed by an individual whose presence annoyed him so much that he asked to be transferred to headquarters, to the Ministry of Foreign Affairs in Warsaw.

A cold winter has come. Of course, nobody cleared the snow from the pavements, so people walked on trampled, uneven snow. People would fall over[32]. We had shoes with rubber, non-slippery soles and neither snow nor slippery pavements bothered us. However, such shoes had never been seen in Moscow before, and the locals immediately identified us as foreigners. A cabdriver, for example, would come up to us shouting 'Inostraniec pojedziem' (Let's go, foreigner) or a boy selling newspapers would shout 'Inostraniec kupi gazietu' (Buy a paper, foreigner).

I once had a very unpleasant experience in Moscow, involving a dog. Major Kobylański had a dog called Teddi, which I have already mentioned. He was proud of it because it won medals at dog shows. However, Kobylański showed little interest in the dog. He did not show him any affection, and as a result the dog was not attached to him. Nuisance, on the other hand, was very fond of this dog and took him for walks. When there was a dog parade organised by the Association of Doberman and German Shepherd Lovers, Nuisance took part in the parade, leading Teddi on a leash. He was a member of the association and received information by telegraph or letter: 'Rodiłoś piat szczenkow z koich tri biez chwosta' (Five puppies were born, three of them without tails). We bought one of those, without the tail for sixty dollars and named it Nal. The dog later came with us to Vilnius.

One day, I went into town with Teddi. The dog was so well trained that

---

[32] How familiar. Could it be the calling card of the system?

he walked to heel without a leash. We were already far from home when Teddi saw a dog across the street. Teddi darted across the road towards the dog and within seconds was run over by a bus. The dog was lying on the road, still alive. I ran up to him and picked him up in my arms where he died. You can imagine what was going through my mind at the time. Someone else's dog, a valuable one, that the major bragged about. How could I look him and Nuisance in the eye at home? How could I tell him that Teddi had died? I could not go home. I carried him to a carriage and when I arrived at the attaché's office in the courtyard, I called for a servant to take Teddi's corpse to the storeroom. Nobody was at home and I did not have the courage to stay in the apartment, where I might meet Nuisance, so I went into town again. I did not return for lunch or dinner. It was late in the evening when I did return, tired and upset, after wandering aimlessly around the town. The servant had already told the household about the tragedy. They were worried about me. Nuisance's eyes were red from crying. He and the major already knew everything. He said nothing, but from that moment on I felt that his attitude towards me had changed. This composed man had a justifiable grudge against me. This incident with Teddi had taken a heavy toll on me, especially because of Nuisance, who was very attached to the dog.

In Moscow I was an unemployed housewife, so I walked around the city a lot, and we often visited the Re-evacuation Commission headed by Professor Kuntze. There was also Professor Morelowski, with whose wife I kept in touch later, in Vilnius. After the war he became a professor of art history at the University of Wrocław. It was he who brought Jagiellonian tapestries from Canada.

After a year in Moscow Nuisance was called to Warsaw. We took Nal with us, which involved a lot of red tape. We needed a permit from the Ministry of Agriculture to export a purebred dog, a health certificate for the dog and proof of vaccination. At the border, the customs officials wanted me to pay customs duty. I was outraged and explained to the customs officer that Poland should be grateful for bringing such a purebred dog, a rarity in our country, that could improve the breed. Nal's father – Alaks von Kaucenhoff – was indeed magnificent! I saw him at a dog show. The dog helped discover 140 offences. Sitting next to him was a policeman, who was his handler. We were travelling in a sleeping car with a Greek diplomat. I asked him to take the dog and I would take his briefcase or suitcase and we would go to the train together. And so we did. When I stepped onto the platform without the dog, the customs officer asked me about the dog again, because if I refused to pay the duty, they would put Nal in a cage and I would have to buy him back in Warsaw. I replied that I no longer had the dog, because I had given it to the Greek ambassador. I have to admit that I deceived the customs officer, as deputies or ambassadors had a 'laisse-passer'. In the carriage, the deputy gave me back the dog and I gave him the briefcase. It turned out that the heating in the sleeper was broken and it was freezing outside, so I would have been very cold in our compartment at night had it not been for the dog, who lay against the wall at my back and kept me warm.

When I got back to Poland, I started my training as a judge, passed the exam and then started a two-year barrister training. Actually, I remember Moscow as a break in my long and busy life.

I would like to describe one more detail of my husband's journey from Warsaw to Moscow. The wives of Wieczorkiewicz and Bagiński[33] were travelling to Moscow in the same carriage. They had some problems on the way. My husband looked after them and later received a thank-you letter from the Soviet authorities.

As I have already mentioned, Nuisance was transferred to the 23rd Uhlan Regiment, taking command of the 1st Squadron in Podbrodzie and then in Biały Dwór. This meant that we were separated for five years, only visiting one another. Finally, Nuisance was transferred to the headquarters of the Cavalry Brigade under the command of General Rudolf Dreszer, where he worked until the outbreak of the war. At last journeys to Biały Dwór were over and we were together.

After ten years of marriage we had a son Jan called Pumpkin[34]. How happy Nuisance was to have this child! When Jan cried, he carried him in a sleeping bag and spent all his free time with him. Little Pumpkin would ride him like a horse or sit on his shoulders. The two of them would roll on the carpets and go for walks together. He would show him ships on the Vilija or locomotives. He loved this child immensely and was so happy with him.

---

[33] Wieczorkiewicz and Bagiński were communists who tried to blow up the Warsaw Citadel. They were initially sentenced to death, then they were to be exchanged with Polish spies in the USSR. However, both of them were shot dead by an escorting police officer Muraszka (!).

[34] Jan Maciej Paweł Sztukowski was born in Vilnius on 25 July 1935.

At the railway station, Pumpkin cried when someone took him from his father's arms. He wasn't meant to see how his beloved son grew, and the son he left behind as a four-year-old does not even remember him.

A great injustice was done to this half-orphaned child, deprived of a loving father. Nuisance died tragically, murdered in Katyń. His last letter came from Kozielsk. Wachtmeister Korbel of the 1st Squadron of the 23rd Uhlan Regiment told me later that he met Nuisance near Brześć during the September Campaign. Nuisance was hesitant about where to go, but he trusted Russians more than the Germans. And yet, all my cousins had returned from the German prisoner-of-war camps! Nuisance remained in the Katyń forest forever.

CHAPTER VIII

Sport In My Life

෴

Having parents who loved sport and following in their footsteps, I was active from an early age, doing exercise and sport. My father was an excellent rider, he knew a lot about horses, loved horse racing and used to take us to the races whenever we were in Warsaw. He never bet, but he would watch the horses in the paddock and give his opinion on their form, stamina and chances in the race. Later, when we were in Vilnius, he organised horse shows. He brought Swedish draft horses to the Horse Breeders' Association to improve the breed of our working horses. He wrote for the magazine *Jeździec i Hodowca* (Rider and Breeder). My mother also used to ride horses before she was married, using a side-saddle. She was also an excellent swimmer, she could easily swim across the Bug River, where Strzyżów, the sugar factory where my father was director, was located. In fact, most of my childhood sporting activities took place there. There was a tennis court by the house and all the members of the household (except my father) played tennis. There was also plenty of opportunity for horse riding. We, the children, had ponies, and there were also horses kept specifically for riding; we kept Hiawata, from the stables of my uncle, General Wojciech Falewicz, from Marwa near Kaunas. The other, a beautiful black docked mare, was called Łaska. There was also a useful mare which walked in a foursome – a trained bay mare, but she often stumbled due to injured legs. My mother warned me that if I rode this mare, I might fall off if the horse stumbled at high speed. My father, however, who brought me up very independently and like a boy, replied that it was not far from the ground anyway.

In Strzyżów, we children had complete freedom, and sometimes our parents did not know what we were doing or where we were. Having no swings we decided to make them ourselves. One of us climbed up a small tree and tied a rope to the top, and we made a loop at the other end. Then someone would step into the loop and jumped and ran around the tree. The rope would wrap around the trunk and then unwind. At that moment you would be lifted up, and the rope would unwind. Once, when I was really high above the ground, the rope snapped and I fell, breaking my collarbone. But nobody cared too much, I was not even bandaged, and our childish follies continued. We climbed trees a lot. In the garden behind the palace, there were big chestnut trees with widespread branches. Each of us had their own chestnut tree, where we made our base with hiding places in the hollows. Not far from the house was a pond that became a slide in winter. We used sledges to slide down the hill.

After Strzyżów our carefree life was interrupted. We left for Russia, and it was only during the holidays spent at Kożanka, the Branickis' sugar factory, that I had the opportunity to ride horses with my friend Wanda Bałtutis. After my return to Poland, I got back to Vilnius in 1920, when I came back from the front, but busy with my studies I had no time for sport.

In Balinpol, which has been looted during the war, life was very modest and at first there were no riding horses. However, my cousin Tadeusz Falewicz, a well-known horseman, had a horse called Rosenfel, which won him 45 thousand zlotys at the races. When this horse retired from racing, Tadeusz sent it to us as a sire, so I had the opportunity to ride a racehorse, which was very difficult.

Later, when I married a cavalryman, every morning the batman would bring us two saddled horses and, before going to work we would take a nice ride out of Vilnius, usually towards Karolinki. We were always accompanied by our Doberman pinscher Nal, brought from Moscow as a puppy. Nal was a purebred, excellent at jumping through a wheel hanging in the doorway or over a few rows of chairs. Nal knew that the horses would be brought to us and early in the morning, he would sit on the windowsill waiting for them. When the horses were brought over, he would jump out into the hallway, barking with joy. In the street he would jump up to their mouths but fortunately the horses were not afraid of him at all.

As I said, the only means of transport between Podbrodzie and Biały Dwór was a horse. It was not far, only seven kilometres, and I would change into my riding clothes in the casino in Podbrodzie and then, during my entire stay in Biały Dwór, I would rarely get off my horse. We were riding through woodlands and fields, even to Pohulanka – a military training site 20–30 kilometres away. Once we rode from Biały Dwór to

Orniany, at the invitation of Mr and Mrs Michał Tyszkiewicz. It was there that my mentor, Walenty Parczewski, looked after the affairs of her husband, Count Michał Tyszkiewicz, the owner of a large estate in Orniany with adjoining properties in the district of Święciany, and it was there that I met Ordonka. I used to travel to Święciany to attend court hearings on behalf of my mentor, and also appeared before courts in Vilnius. The Orniany estate was close to the Lithuanian border. About 15 kilometres from Biały Dwór was the 1st Squadron of the 23rd Grodno Uhlan Regiment, commanded by my husband. It was a large forest estate, probably 10,000 hectares. The main part (the palace) was destroyed during the war, but it was partially rebuilt afterwards; several large rooms were renovated so that the owners had somewhere to stay when they came.

Michał Tyszkiewicz also had a flat in Vilnius at 3 Maja Street, close to Kasztanowa Street (where I found shelter much later, in 1944, when the Tyszkiewicz family no longer lived there). Michał Tyszkiewicz wrote song lyrics for his wife, travelled around Poland, and rarely visited Orniany.

Once, before the war, I travelled by train from Vilnius to Warsaw in the same compartment as a group of actors returning from performances. Among them were Jarossy and Ordonka. At that time I was appalled by Ordonka's behaviour; she was very noisy and caused a lot of turmoil in the compartment, chattering away and sitting on men's laps; in a word, she behaved like a spoilt child. Much later, when we were invited to Orniany one summer, it was quite different. The only means of transport was a horse, and we had to go through the woods, along narrow paths and forest tracks, surrounded by beautiful old trees. Sometimes we would take a random shortcut and had to go single file.

The person in front would warn the others to watch out for branches hanging over the path at the height of the rider's head. At that point we would raise our hand to cushion the impact of the branch on our head or, if possible, push it away. We were never sure where a given path would take us, and hoped not to accidentally cross the Lithuanian border, as this could cause international complications! On arrival in Orniany we were warmly welcomed by our hosts. Ordonka's brother was staying with them at the time – a modest young man, a postal clerk from Warsaw, Mr Pietrusiński. He told me that he loved spending time in the country, and that he would get up in the morning and go barefoot to pick and eat strawberries in the garden, go for walks, and so on. Ordonka seemed very short to me, she wore white trainers without heels, moved like a little girl and was very cheerful.

It was suggested that before dinner we should walk or drive to a nearby lake to swim. I did not have a bathing suit, but Ordonka offered to lend me one, and I do not know how that was possible, since Ordonka was short and slim, and I was fat and 168 cm tall, but the suit fitted me well and the swim was wonderful. I admired Michał Tyszkiewicz's posture at that time; he was beautifully built and had fine legs, thin at the ankles. We then returned to the manor, where dinner was served. Here, of course, Countess Tyszkiewicz was at the fore. The butler, wearing white gloves, served the platters from the left side and addressed Ordonka as Countess ...

During the meal the mail was brought in by someone from Podbrodzie. Ordonka recognised the handwriting when a letter was handed to her, and exclaimed: 'Oh, it's from Hemar.' She opened the envelope and inside was a sheet of paper with a text written for her. She was very pleased and began to read the lyrics. Although she was reading it for the first time, she

The author in Michał Tyszkiewicz's (Ordonka's husband's) car on the way to his palace in Orniany

did so as if she was on stage. We were all surprised and delighted to hear her delivering this text. Apart from my husband and me, there were also officers from the 1st Squadron at the dinner: Lieutenants Konopka and Danielczyk, and probably Lieutenant Janowski. Hemar's text, like other texts for Ordonka, was distinctive because Ordonka put a lot of feeling into every sentimental or tragic line. Her songs were very moving. Whether she was on stage as a poor seamstress sitting at a machine, or playing an old Jewish woman, the mother of a son who comes from America and dies in a shipwreck, she could squeeze tears out of our eyes. And when she sang about love, it was heartbreaking.

In Vilnius she not only gave concerts, but also acted in plays. She always knew how to dress properly. Her gowns were long and flowing, in a rainbow of pastel colours. She looked tall on stage. She had no figure by nature, but she knew how to make up for it. She did not have a strong voice, but she knew how to use it brilliantly and her singing, which sometimes turned into parlando, captivated the audience and her immense talent was widely recognised.

During the war, for about a month, when the mass deportations to Russia were taking place, I stayed in Ordonka's flat with her dresser and two large Saint-Bernard dogs. It was winter, and during that whole month, every evening I took my son, who was eight or nine years old at the time, and would go there with some necessary things to sleep on. We would spend the night there and go home in the morning. The idea was not to be at home at night ...

The actor Łukasz Łukaszewicz, a good friend of Ordonka, lived in her flat. I admired his care for the dogs. Food was scarce. Łukasz worked as a waiter in a restaurant, where he collected various leftovers from the plates and brought them home. The dogs slept on the rug next to Łukasz's bed, looking into his eyes with tenderness and affection. They were grateful. When it was time to repatriate, Łukasz took both dogs with him. Later, in Poland, he gave one to a lady he knew in Gdańsk and paid her to keep it. He travelled to visit the dog! The other one stayed with him, then fell ill and died.

I know that when Ordonka went to the Soviets, she performed in the military theatre of the Polish Army that was being formed there at the time. She found herself in Lebanon, where she contracted tuberculosis and was ill for a long time. She was said to be very spiritual, patient and good to those around her. I was told she died like a saint. She was buried in Beirut. On a trip there, Łukasz found her grave in the cemetery and left flowers. Ordonka's husband worked for Radio Free Europe and died in Munich. I did not know that Ordonka was also a talented painter. When I was in London in 1976, I visited friends, Mr and Mrs Gołkowski, who showed me a painting by Ordonka, signed *Hanna Ordon.*

A story recently told on television by Jerzy Waldorff reminded me of something else. When Mr Borowik, Michał Tyszkiewicz's representative, came to pick her up in a carriage to take her to Orniany, Ordonka asked why the horses were so thin. Borowik complained that they had no oats, and Ordonka took 500 zloty from her purse to buy oats for the horses ...

I digress to tell this story about Ordonka, because it is also related to horses.

Later, my husband and I were invited to Orniany for a wolf hunt. I had hunted more than once, as my father and brothers were keen hunters, but I had never hunted wolves. There were not many people with rifles – the host, Michał Tyszkiewicz, several officers and my husband and I. The battue moved towards the hunters, lined up every few dozen metres, and, behind the hunters, a rope with pieces of coloured material was hung at a low height. If a wolf is pushed towards this rope and sees it, it will stop and not jump over it, and then there is a chance of catching it. Tyszkiewicz had heard from the forester that wolves were in the backwoods, but we were all curious as to which direction they would run and who would have the opportunity to shoot them. We were all excited. Any one of us could have a wolf coming at us. As the battue drew closer and the decisive moment approached, I looked left and right towards the rope where the wolf could stop, my shotgun ready. I saw the wolf at the rope as it turned its head towards me in all his glory: broad head, long neck fur. I moved slightly preparing to fire, and in this short moment the animal had turned and disappeared. Whether it was this wolf or another, one more wolf had been shot on that hunt.

The second time I hunted wolves with Mr Mieczysław Bohdanowicz, there was a lot of excitement, but the wolf got away somewhere and the hunt was unresolved.

I remember that my father presented me with a 28-calibre shotgun. It was a light gun made by Manufacture Liegeoise d'Armes a Feu. The first game I killed was a woodcock on an evening flight. It was difficult to shoot because it was almost dusk. Woodcocks fly high, making a special sound that tells the hunter that a woodcock is flying over a young forest, but you do not know from which side it is coming from. Woodcocks are very fast. When the bird fell after my shot, it was very difficult to find it, fortunately a hunting-trained pointer retrieved it immediately. My hunting companions then smeared the woodcock's blood on my face, as was customary for the first hunting kill. I hunted rock ptarmigan, sometimes wading up to my knees in mud or jumping from clump to clump, crossing water-filled ditches. Ptarmigan is also a rare bird and not every regular hunter has had the opportunity to hunt them. We used to have a hare battue On Christmas Eve in Balinpol. Hunters, relatives and friends of my brothers were invited. I, of course, took part in these hunts as well. We moved from litter to litter in sledges and at the agreed time and place, Mum would turn up and bring the freezing hunters delicious hot bigos *(Polish dish of chopped meat of various kinds stewed with sauerkraut)* with mushrooms, which we ate outside by the sledge. Mum would leave, and we would continue hunting.

I came to Podbrodzie one day because the next day, 3 November 1929, the hunting run was to be held. Of course, after the run, all the officers of the regiment gathered in the officers' casino. There was a festive dinner and so on. I did not go to Biały Dwór, but my husband and I stayed the night in the guest rooms of the casino. Wanda Bałtutis[35] was there with me as well. She was a friend of mine from my time in Ukraine in 1917–1918, and later we had studied together in Paris. In Vilnius I took my attorney apprenticeship and she worked in education. We had come from Vilnius not for sport but for socialising. We were woken up in the morning because everyone was getting ready for the run.

Lieutenant Konopka had a great mare, Noc, who jumped perfectly, but he himself did not compete, because he was the contre-master. He asked me to ride his Noc in the run. I never did hurdle jumping, and all the jumping I had done was in a field over a ditch, so I had no intention of taking part in this run. Lieutenant Konopka explained to me that the only thing to do was not to disturb the horse, that she was a great jumper and would take any obstacle. I did my best to avoid this and I had no intention of humiliating myself. On the other hand, I wanted to give it a try, because taking part in such a difficult race would have been an honour. So I gave in

[35] I have already written about Wanda Bałtutis.

to his arguments and rode this wonderful horse. Wanda also managed to find a horse and rode with me.

I will quote the report in the Vilnius newspaper *Słowo* of 8 November, placed in the sports column: *Hunter's Run on St. Hubert's Day in the 23rd Uhlan Regiment:*

On St. Hubert's Feast Day, 3rd November this year, the traditional Hunter's Run took place in the 23rd Uhlan Regiment in Podbrodzie. Ten officers and two horsewomen: Mrs Helena Sztukowska and Ms Wanda Bałtutis. The run was held under the direction of the master Major Święcicki on a varied and skilfully chosen terrain over a distance of seven kilometres. The competitors had to overcome six obstacles: a hurdle, a ditch, a fence of thin poles, a fence in the village, abatis on the road and another hurdle. The Hunter's Run was very varied and lively – a steep descent from the mountain and crossing of the Dubinka River. The run was held in difficult conditions, as the weather was not favourable and rainy, making the ground soggy and boggy. However, there were no incidents during the race. In a bravura finish, which started with a sign from the master and a shout 'hilala', Mrs Falewicz-Sztukowska was the winner, beating all other contenders. The other horsewoman, Wanda Bałtutis, completed the entire route flawlessly as well. The applause for these brave sports-women was endless.

So much for the run. But I had no idea how much excitement and anxiety there was in taking part in such an event, unprepared and on a horse I did not know. When the horse jumped into the Dubinka River, all was well, but the banks were so steep that the horse could not get out, and it took a long struggle before it climbed out of the river. The river may not have been wide or deep, but it had almost a vertical bank. I remember climbing a very steep hill overgrown with small pine trees and bushes. We had to stand in the stirrups and hold on to the mane with one hand to keep from slipping out of the saddle. Then we galloped into a clearing, fenced off with perches on one side. Horses in a bunch, and there were sixteen of them, get very excited when galloping side by side. At the jump I leaned too far forward and let go of the reins, and upon landing I may have held the horse too tightly because Noc hit me in the jaw with her head.

It hurt a lot, but I moved my jaw to see if it was cracked or broken and we were still galloping when, to our surprise, Master Święcicki jumped over a closed yard gate into a farmstead. We had to do everything he did, so we jumped over a very high fence (gate) one after the other. The last obstacle, behind the farmstead, was blocking a narrow road and was also very high. I jumped. Whether the horse was infallible or I was lucky, it went well. Finally we galloped into a large training area with a perch at the other end – this was the finish line. Now the pace was faster because it was a flat ride and then … victory!

I also had the opportunity to ski behind a horse in a training field where there was quite a lot of snow. The horse, ridden by a soldier, was wearing a harness with two long ropes with a bar at the end, that the skier held on to. The horse galloped and everything was easy when you were going straight but in curves you had to position the skis so that they could make a turn. So you had to tilt the ski inwards towards the bend and put one ski (the outer one) forward. The worst part was that when the horse galloped, it threw up lumps of snow that blinded the skier. You needed very strong legs at the ankles to do the manoeuvre. And that crazy speed was magnificent! Later, in Balinpol, I tried skiing behind a sledge with a rope tied to it, but it was not the same as skiing behind a horse. Once there was a skijoring competition in Pośpieszka and three officers took part, including Nuisance. He was the last to finish, but he came home with a beautiful crystal, which I still have, and announced: 'Admittedly, I came last and didn't get the crystal, but I bought it for myself as a prize.' We also skied behind sledges in Biały Dwór, because there were sledges but no other equipment

In 1935–1937, Nuisance became involved in sport aviation, completing a pilot training course and becoming very enthusiastic about it. He even became president of the Vilnius Aero Club. But we never flew together. Pumpkin was already one year old and Nuisance was afraid that he might lose both parents in a crash, so he suggested that I fly as a passenger with Captain Janusz Kurnatowski, who had just been appointed to the Aero Club by the Minister of Communications. And so it began! Even during my first flight, when there was a double yoke, he explained the operation of the ailerons and elevators. He gave me the yoke and told me to fly. Space is plentiful in the air, a plane is not like a car, which constantly encounters obstacles. So keeping the plane at the same altitude for longer flights is not difficult. It was worse when you had to take off or land. But I learnt to do that as well after a while. On my first flight, when I closed the throttle to land, Janusz calmly said: 'Keep the nose down, or we'll go into a spin.'

The training began. So, the take-off: the light aircraft would accelerate on the runway and at one point Janusz would say: 'Pull the control stick up.' Those were exciting moments! Landing was more of a problem. I am in the air at some distance from the airport and proceed to land, nose down. I am already low when I see cottages or potato fields below, so again the throttle and up again. I make a loop, come closer to the runway, close the throttle, descend, I am over the airport, but just when I have to touch the plane down, the runway ends and there is a potato field again. So back on the throttle, up again, I come around again and come in for a landing. I had to try several times to measure the adequate landing distance, depending on the altitude and when to close the throttle and what pitch angle to apply. Later I got better, Janusz praised me. But there were times when Janusz landed himself using his control stick. I had good knowledge of the area, and once I flew to Lake Narocz with Captain Babiński. People used to say that he had his own junker plane, which he used to fly from Warsaw to Cracow, but it would take him a week because if he saw smoke coming out of a chimney on the estates he was flying over, he would assume that dinner was being prepared, so he would land wherever he could and show up at the house, where he was invited to dinner. In addition, the engine kept breaking down, so he would land in unlikely places, such as meadows or squares, to make repairs and continue his journey. When he felt vibrations in the engine, he would land again. He held the record for the number of landings outside of an airport! It was a substantial number.

So we were flying over Narocz and close to Lake Svir, I pointed to Balinpol, located to the north-east. Coming back from Narocz, just by Lake Svir, Captain Babiński took that direction and I realised that we were flying to Balinpol. But the question was where to land there. We flew quite low over the estate, with telephone wires going in different directions, we flew over the lawn and tall spruce trees. I was horrified at what this man was doing! It was the RWD-8, a two-seater where we sat one behind the other and finally, on a patch of stubble behind the living quarters, the captain landed beautifully. The take-off was even more difficult as the

Lawyer – pilot

ground was uneven and provisional stubble runway was short. We stayed in Balinpol for about an hour. Pumpkin was afraid of planes. When Nuisance flew over Balinpol throwing sweets at him, Pumpkin would shout 'Close the windows, close the door!' and refused to leave the house. When he was a toddler just beginning to talk, when asked where his mummy and daddy were, he would point to the sky ...

I loved talking to pilots about their adventures. Once an aviator, a major, a highlander by origin, told me how he was in Grudziądz, flying a military plane over a lake. The plane started to burn and he jumped out with a parachute over the lake. Fortunately at the last minute, a gust of wind carried him ashore, where he landed safely, about half a metre from the water. 'I then got on the train and went to the Gate of Dawn to thank Our Lady for such an ending.'

Lieutenant Henryk Wirszyłło, a pilot, also told me a story about how his plane (or rather the wooden structure under the engine) caught fire over a forest. When he was about to land and was in a dive, the fire came towards the cockpit where he was sitting, so he had to land with side bearers and just happened to be over a young birchwood. 'It will be soft here,' he thought, and slid over the tops of the birch trees, touching down softly and safely. People came running and put out the fire with earth. Another pilot recounted a forced landing in the branches of a large tree. The wings fell off and he remained in the cockpit, suspended between the branches and unable to get out, until local people came running and helped him down.

Nuisance thought Janusz did not like flying. He always said that he would just fly to the woods and be back shortly, but after such an accusation, Janusz

Kobylnik, 19 June 1937, Helena as a pilot

decided that we would fly a long distance, to Grajewo, where the commander of the 9th Horse Rifle Regiment was my cousin – Tadeusz Falewicz. It was a sudden idea, and so we flew to Grajewo without any of the things we needed for the night. I was in charge of the plane the whole time, but it was Kurnatowski who landed on some square in Grajewo. My brother was not there, only my sister-in-law Zosia Falewiczowa, née Lubańska. She called another pilot from Warsaw, Captain Ojżyński, who flew in and we had a great time there, but the next day we had great difficulty with taking off. We could not take off from where we landed, so we rolled around looking for suitable space. It was marshland all around and, and there was only one place where the headland cut into the swamp. Kurnatowski decided to take off from this headland slightly above the marsh. He accelerated, got to that makeshift runway and just as the headland was ending and Janusz was taking the plane up, the plane started to descend and I was sure that we were going to fall into the swamp. But really low above the swamp the plane took off and rose into the air. Emotions ran high ...

Another time, we flew to the estate of Mr and Mrs Bohdanowicz near Stara Wilejka. We had to land on a field of clover, which is a good place to land if the clover is not too high. However, the clover there had not been cut and there were rows and rows of stone piles on it. In fear not to catching the stones with the wings, Janusz made several attempts to land, and finally chose the widest strip between the rows of stones and landed safely. Again, the take-off was worse. The clover interfered with the wheels, so I had to take the train to a place where landing was possible and Janusz took off alone. The plane was lighter with just one person in it and it worked out all right.

We flew a couple of planes from the Aero Club to Nesvizh. A festival was to be organised there, so a lot of people were going to come together and we wanted to give an air show. One of the planes was flown by a sports pilot, Kurec, who weighed 160 kilograms and for whom RWD had made a special large cockpit. He was the son of the owner of a cardboard factory, a very rich man, so he was able to adjust the plane to his individual needs. Our arrival caused a sensation among the inhabitants of Nesvizh. We were all accommodated in a Jewish hotel. There were so many guests that visitors from the provinces even slept on the floor in the hotel corridor.

We were invited to dinner by Radziwiłł, together with several officers of the 27th Uhlan Regiment stationed in Nesvizh. The young Prince Radziwiłł was a reserve officer of that regiment[36]. We all turned up, pilots and officers alike, at the magnificent residence, a castle in the shape of a horseshoe. We were served by butlers in rifleman's uniforms and white gloves. But the food was meagre and cheap, and when we got up from the table, the cavalry officers approached us and invited us to their casino, where they discreetly promised us better food. In the evening we arrived at the casino of the 27th Uhlan Regiment. Young Radziwiłł came with us. The food was indeed excellent and alcohol was flowing. People drank eagerly and the atmosphere was very cheerful. I was tired from the excitement of the flight. The next day we had to return to Vilnius. The hour was late and I wanted to go back to the hotel, but the officers would not let me

---

[36] Probably Prince Antoni Jerzy Mikołaj Radziwiłł, born in 1912 (son of prince Leon, 17th Ordinat of Nesvizh).

out. Finally I slipped out and ran along the sidewalk, as one of the officers rushed after me to take me back to the casino. But I managed to reach the hotel, made my way to my room, passing people sleeping on the floor in the corridor, and locked myself in. The officer who was following me knocked on the door, but I persuaded him to go back because I had no intention of coming back. So he left and I was getting ready to go to bed and had already put on my dressing gown when someone climbed up to the open window. It was a very hot night. It turned out it was the same officer. Being very drunk, he climbed up to my window and finally sat down on it and said that he would not leave until he had taken me from the hotel to the casino. There was a long discussion with the tipsy lieutenant (I can't remember his name), but seeing my persistence, he went back alone to party until dawn with the pilots.

I also remember a flight from Warsaw to Vilnius with my passenger Zygmunt Buyko (now a legal adviser in Katowice). We took off from Mokotów airport in clear weather, without checking any weather forecast. On the way it turned out to be terribly windy. We were buffeted terribly. Poor Zygmunt Buyko sitting behind us (the RWD L3 was a three-seater) felt terrible. We decided to stop in Grodno, where we landed to the horror of the airport crew, as the meteorological announcement cancelled all flights. I had a school friend in Grodno, Buszkiewiczowa. I called her on the phone and she invited us all to stay with her. The wind was raging, the aura was changing, so we gladly took advantage of her hospitality and spent the night there. Buszkiewiczowa was a very sociable person. She lived in a two-storey villa and welcomed us warmly with a dinner and substantial quantities of alcohol. After a hearty meal, Buyko, tired of travelling by plane, took the train to Vilnius. Janusz and I stayed the night.

I was to sleep in the other room on a large high bed, and Janusz in the study of the absent master of the house. I was tired, so I went to bed immediately after dinner, while my companion and my friend stayed downstairs in the dining room, chatting and sipping drinks. I found the bed intended for me was uncomfortable because it was higher in the middle than at the sides. So I decided to play a prank on Captain Kurnatowski and swap the beds. I put two armchairs on the big bed under the duvet. When Janusz came into the study where he was supposed to sleep, he found me. I told him I would not leave the comfortable sofa and we began to tease each other. He threatened to jump on the sofa anyway, but eventually went to the room where I was to sleep. After a while he came back saying that someone was already sleeping there. He rubbed his eyes thinking he was having a drunken hallucination, but eventually he realised there was furniture under the duvet. In the morning we flew back to Vilnius.

Later I met Buszkiewiczowa in Ciechocinek, where I was being treated and living in the villa Sienkiewiczówka, while she, as the wife of a major, lived in in the villa Pomorzanka. She persuaded me to go to Miller's dance. We had no friends in Ciechocinek, so I was reluctant to go, but she was confident and said that everything would be fine. So we went. There were taxi dancers, elegant gentlemen with refined manners. I suspected they were officers of the former Russian white army. We had a wonderful time dancing with great dancers, and as we danced, I kept thinking how you pay for such a service. During the last dance I put a banknote in my partner's pocket, he kissed my hand and the matter was settled.

One time we were all at the airport and Janusz suggested we take a flight. When we were in the air, he said we would fly to the sea via Warsaw. I was at the controls of the plane the whole time. We landed in Mokotów, Janusz invited me to his studio apartment in Polna Street, where I was to spend the night, while he went to Warsaw and came back in the morning to take me to the airport and fly on to the seaside. Before leaving, he made me a great dinner out of tinned food. He had a large stock of it. He was a real food connoisseur. (Decades later, when we met in London, he also cooked me a multi-course meal with wine to go with each course).

We flew to Gdynia. At one point the aircraft was buffeted and tossed around, black clouds surrounded us and there were flashes of lightning. We thought it would be safer to return to Warsaw, but when we saw the same weather conditions on our tail, we continued the flight north. It got completely dark. Janusz took over the stick, as it required a lot of strength to control it and keep the plane level. The situation was dangerous because the downpour drastically reduced visibility and also we were in danger of being struck by lightning. We thought we were heading in the right direction, as we had a compass and an altimeter. Light touring aircrafts had modest equipment.

The storm passed and we flew over the sea, where the shore was illuminated by settlements. Janusz had been silent during the storm, and now he told me that these illuminated settlements below us were East Prussia. A forced landing in such a situation involves a lot of red tape and is always dangerous. We did not have the necessary documents. We would be detained by the police authorities and so on. And I had a trial in two days in Pastavy[37] that I had to attend. So we were very anxious, but we descended to assess the situation and look for a suitable place to land. However, Janusz was wrong in thinking that this was Prussia, as we were over our own coast. It was getting dark. Janusz showed me the lights that marked Gdynia, Sopot, Oliwa and Gdańsk, but the airport was in Rumia.

The airport was lit up. We landed on the tarmac, which was completely flooded. The airport staff ran to us through the water, thinking the plane had nosed over, and when they saw us disembark unharmed they were extremely surprised that we had dared to fly in such a terrible storm. All flights were grounded and the airport was empty. The storm even caused some damage to the airport, breaking several constructions. We took a taxi at the airport and went to a hotel in Gdynia. When we booked the rooms, Janusz took a bottle of champagne out of a bag and said to the porter: 'Keep it cold.' Janusz Kurnatowski was an intelligent man, full of imagination and wit, and a gentleman in every respect. We had dinner, I was tired after all the danger and excitement and went to bed while he went into town. He came back very late, I think, and when I woke him up in the morning he was completely dazed, jumped out of bed, stuck his head under the tap and refreshed himself. He told me he had met a naval officer he knew and sat with him for a long time in a pub. We made our way back, this time without storm or danger, via Warsaw, where again Janusz disappeared somewhere to visit friends and his mother. When we flew to Vilnius, he told me to take over the stick and fly because he was tired and wanted to get some sleep.

In 1936 a rally of sport aircrafts from all over Poland and owners of private planes from Vilnius was held at Lake Narocz (with an area of 84 square kilometres – the largest lake in Poland before the war). A couple, both doctors, Michalak was their name, flew in from Cracow. There was also Senator Rudowski, the owner of the Półwiesk estate near Rypin, who came with his twelve-year-old daughter Magda. Senator Rudowski had three daughters studying in Warsaw and was a great enthusiast of sport aviation. In Półwiesk, a field of clover was used for

---

[37] A town, county seat in Vilnius Region, relatively close to the Daugava river (Latvian border).

take-off and landing, and name Półwiesk was written in big letters on the barn roof. There was also a windsock to indicate the direction of the wind. He used his light plane to carry provisions for his children in Warsaw. His young daughter Magda was able to use the professional terminology while recounting their flights. She often flew with her father and was also enthusiastic about the sport.

In preparation for this rally, the Aero Club asked the head of the Kobylnik district, Mr Marian Gumowski, to organise a lunch for the participants. I have preserved Gumowski's letter to the Aero Club in response to this request, which contains capital remarks worth quoting here:

Kobylnik, 22 June 1936
Marian
Gumowski
Head of the Kobylnik District

To the Vilnius Aero Club
in Vilnius
Arsenalska Street
Attn: Mr Pilsiak

With reference to the planned programme for 28th June, as I have personally discussed with you, honourable gentlemen, in Kobylnik on 11th February, awaiting the announced letter with any further changes and details of the guests' arrival and stay, I hereby kindly ask for information, as soon as possible, whether and to what extent the reception is to be prepared and whether the participants can be counted on to cover the costs of the joint dinner.

For my part, I suggest the following arrangement:
All the guests, it would seem, would have to be divided into two categories: the first, that would easily cover the expense of about four zloty for dinner and about five zloty for dinner with black coffee and liqueur. This would include cold hors d'oeuvres: cold meat, Dutch and cream cheese, stuffed fish – pike, fried whitefish served cold and pike in jelly, royal herring, quality vodka, beer and soda water. Soups: chicken broth with noodles and borscht with dumplings on a cool day

and on a hot day hot borscht would be substituted with cold beet soup. Second courses: stuffed chicken with lettuce and maybe we can move one of the fish from the cool appetisers, e.g. whitefish, to the hot second course, to be served hot. Dessert: cream, lemon and cream ice cream, wild strawberries. The price of the dinner would increase by two or three zlotys, depending on whether and how much more expensive alcoholic beverages – wine and cognac – would be consumed.

The second category of guests, who could not afford such a considerable expenditure for a single dinner, would be seated at one end of the table, and would not be offered the more expensive items – liqueur, wine and cognac, as these would be served to the first group only. This would reduce the cost of the dinner to four zlotys, as mentioned above, or these costs could be completely crossed out, if you, honourable gentlemen agree, provided that the latter category is not too numerous. Anyway, this is left to your discretion, gentlemen, and subject to further discussion. If you gentlemen consider something from the above proposition not suitable or customary for pilots, or if you find the prices not acceptable, I kindly ask for an immediate reply, so that the plans can be altered and modified in time, giving us time to purchase the goods not available on our local market. Please also kindly inform if a flag is to be hoisted on 28 June, or perhaps a cross unfurled as on 14 June this year.

Yours sincerely, M. Gumowski

P.S. The use of sailing boats as well as of motorboats is already settled.

Reading in 1977 what was written forty-one years ago, in 1936, it is hard to believe that such an exquisite celebration could be held in a remote village and for so little money.

After the sports event, my husband and I received very heartfelt letters of thanks from Mr Rudowski, to which Mrs Rudowska and her daughter Magda added their names. The senator wrote: *Once again, I would like to thank you most sincerely for your kind hospitality and to apologise for the fuss caused by our visit. We hope that we will have the opportunity to return the favour, at least in part, by hosting you in Półwiesk. Your area is beautiful and its inhabitants kind. (…) Magda is writing an account of the return journey. The mechanics at the Warsaw Aero Club decided that the rudder was bent or warped and needed to be repaired, so we stopped in Warsaw for a day to have it repaired.*

We saw Mr Wołodia in Warsaw, who is due to land in Półwiesk on his flight to the coast, so we're expecting him. We send you our kindest regards and hope to have you as our guests soon, even in July.

Wołodia, that is the fat Wołodia Kurec, who, because of his corpulence, had the cockpit of his touring plane specially converted.

In this letter, dated 3 July 1936, Magda Rudowska wrote the following about the flight:

Dear Madam!

We have very fond memories of the Vilnius region in general and of your hospitality. As we agreed, I am writing to describe our flight home. We encountered severe turbulence all the way to Grodno, then a little less when we climbed to one thousand one hundred metres. We flew for almost two hours. We arrived in Grodno at half-past two and stayed until five. We had lunch and went to the river. There, we bathed and warmed up, filled up with petrol, and hurried to Warsaw. This part of the flight was great and very pleasant. We arrived in Warsaw at half past six. The next day we were supposed to fly to Półwiesk, but something broke in the rudder and we couldn't leave until the following day, at four o'clock. On Monday morning, one of the pilots from the Aero Club died in a crash. On Wednesday evening we visited Mr and Mrs Prauss, Drzewiecki was there and he told us his impressions of Africa – extremely interesting things. We got back at eleven o'clock and got up at four in the morning; I couldn't get up at all, I wanted to sleep so badly. We had an awful lot of stuff, but the take-off went well. We had tail wind from the left and we arrived in Półwiesk at six o'clock. The flight lasted fifty-five minutes. Everyone slept until Ewcia woke them up. We flew for another fifteen minutes over Półwiesk and another estate to give my sisters time to get dressed. Then then I told them about everything in detail.

Thank you again for your hospitality and please come to Półwiesk. Many kisses and regards to your husband.

Magda Rudowska

I cannot describe all my flights in these memoirs. There were so many. However, I remember the emotions I felt when I was flying with Lieutenant Zakrzewski and we had to land on a small square. He would descend for a glide landing, tilting the plane sideways and lowering the altitude. This was something new to me. It must have been something he learnt from aerobatics.

At that time I was not yet familiar with the technique of a control swap, when the controls are changed in deep spins. It was exactly this kind of spin that led to the death of the pilot Gidwiłło, who flew to Zułów (where the marshal was born) on the marshal's birthday to wish him a happy birthday.

In 1938 the International Rally of the Polish Automobile Club was held on 25th June. The first stage led from Warsaw to Kupa village on Lake Narocz. This quiet village on the banks of Lake Narocz turned into an automobile town. Motorists from Vilnius came out to greet the visitors, who warmly welcomed the arriving competitors. All the hostels were full and even a saloon carriage was provided by the railway management for the racers to use. Technical service and catering were efficiently organised.

The Vilnius press described this rally, attended by sixty-two cars (sixty-one of them reached the finish line), in a report entitled *Sky-high salute*:

> *At about three o'clock in the afternoon, the RWD touring plane piloted by attorney Sztukowska, accompanied by the instructor Captain Krzykowski (error: should be Kurnatowski), flew over the car park. The plane made several spins over the car park and then landed on the airstrip in nearby Kobylniki. Mrs Sztukowska was on her way to visit a relative, who is vice-commander of the rally, and to pay a visit to the motorists.*

In the *Polska Zbrojna* (Armed Poland) magazine of 27 June 1938, there was a report on the first international rally, won by Mr Wessely from Vienna, who drove from Warsaw to Narocz in five hours and forty-two minutes. The report mentioned that the competitors were greeted at the finish line by the pilot Mrs Sztukowska and a troop of cavalry[38].

Foreign and Polish competitors were impressed by excellent organisa-

---

[38] In truth, I did not see any cavalry at all.

tion of the event, they loved Narocz, the beautiful route, especially the Vilnius-Narocz route. There was order and discipline on the roads and the directions were excellent. Everyone was content. When the drivers were not too far from the finish line, I flew over them at quite a low altitude and was able to observe their efforts. There I met my brother-in-law Stefan Sztukowski[39], a well-known Warsaw motorist and member of the Warsaw Aero Club.

An incident also occurred during my flights, in Budsław, when Janusz and I were returning from Mr and Mrs Oskierka. At the airport, Janusz was about to taxi for take-off when he started the engine, and at that moment the plane nose-dived so that the spinning propeller hit the ground. I immediately shut off the throttle, for which I was praised, as Janusz had not.

Finally, I would like to recount the last tragic event in the summer of 1938. Janusz and I were on our way back to Vilnius from Narocz when the horizon ahead of us turned completely black, and that meant a storm coming! We were hoping to squeeze through a gap in the clouds, but there was no crack anywhere in this blackness. It was not raining yet, but the clouds coming in indicated that it would rain any minute. In a touring plane you should be able to outrun a regular thunderstorm, as the speed of the aircraft is greater than the speed of the wind. We looked around in those clouds, trying to figure out how to sneak northwest, but it was impossible. Turbulence began. These were difficult moments. It took a lot of strength to keep the plane levelled with the control stick. There was no question of continuing the flight home and we decided to return to Narocz. There wind was raging. It was not yet raining when we turned back, no longer orienting ourselves by the windsock or the wind tee on the ground, but by the smoke coming out of the chimneys of the houses we were flying over. This was how we determined the wind direction, as you always take off and land against the wind. We landed safely and, seeing the storm approaching, began to secure the aircraft. We folded the wings and tied the aircraft down with cables to hooks driven into the ground. It was the RWD-13 with a closed cockpit. It started to rain, so I went into the cockpit to take shelter from the pouring rain while Janusz

---

[39] Lt. Col. Stefan Sztukowski, anti-aircraft artillery officer, a well-known motorist, husband of the excellent operetta actress Lucyna Messal and later of the well-known singer from the Qui Pro Quo theatre Olga Kamińska (a specialist in Russian romances). Stefan died in Warsaw in 1984.

was still doing something to secure the machine. He was wearing a light-coloured suit, so as I wanted to give him his rubber coat, which was in the boot behind the rear seat, I got up to open the zip and give him the coat.

At that moment, the plane was picked up like a feather by the wind, the cables snapped and I, sitting in the cockpit, was rolled by the hurricane, tumbling with the plane and banging against the interior of the cockpit, which had a whole array of brass instruments, edges, etc. I was fortunate that the wind did not carry me into a field or meadow, but into a young forest. And after many somersaults, the plane finally stopped on a tree. Janusz ran after the plane, fearing I was already dead. When he reached me, he started to break the cellophane windows to get me out of the plane. I had not lost consciousness and was not in pain. I told him not to break the glass but to open the door for me, which was on top because the plane was on its side. It had shattered wings and a damaged cockpit (the engine was fine). Then Janusz opened the door, reached inside and helped me out. The hurricane was raging, the smaller trees were down, the branches of the tall trees were blown around and broken, it was pouring with rain. Janusz decided to move away from the plane because the wind could change direction and we might be hit by a 300-kilogram engine. I had left my shoes on the plane as they had slipped off my feet during the somersaults, so I was barefoot, as the thin stockings had been torn right off. We walked until we were some distance away and crouched under some bushes. The hurricane was still raging. I noticed that my white dress, which was soaking wet, was beginning to turn pink, so I asked Janusz if I was hurt, as I felt no pain. He replied that I had a cut on my head from which the blood was flowing and staining my dress pink. I asked him for a handkerchief and put it on my head to stop the bleeding.

We had to seek help. So we got out from under the bushes and fought our way to a cottage, to find out where there was a town to get a doctor. We were told that Dr Dybowska lived across the fields of stubble in her manor house about two kilometres away. We had to make our way over fallen trees blocking the road. The storm was still raging, but had somewhat eased. We went out into the field in the direction we had been told and walked barefoot across the stubble towards the doctor's buildings. The stubble hurt my feet, but I was in such a state of shock that I felt no pain: water was running down hair and onto my face, creating curls of 'perm' on my face and turning my dress red. I was a living image of misery and despair. The doctor set about dressing the wound. She cut the hair around the wound, which turned out to be fifteen centimetres long, cut sharp as if with a knife, all the way to the skull. The stitching did not hurt at all, even though the scalp is thick and the crescent-shaped needle was forcibly driven into the edge of the wound.

I was put to bed. Janusz left, having arranged a car from the police station in Vilnius. I stayed with the doctor. I was so badly bruised that not only my arms, but also my toenails were blue. The next day a car was sent for me, but the doctor would not let me go, claiming that I might have a concussion and that it was not advisable to drive over one hundred kilometres in this condition. But after a few days the car returned and I set off for Vilnius. On the way I met General Rudolf Dreszer and Nuisance, who were on their way to field training exercises, and whom Janusz had already notified very briefly about the accident. Nuisance took photographs of this meeting and took a picture of General Dreszer with the crashed plane. They went to the field training exercises and I went home. On the way I saw wide stretches of the forest cut down by the wind.

At home I developed a fever and called for a medical consultation from an internist and a surgeon. The internist found nothing serious and the surgeon, after removing the bandages, found an abscess. Penicillin was not available in those days. My head was so swollen that it was as soft as a pillow. I was taken to hospital. In several places the haematoma turned into purulent plum-sized lumps. The doctors tried to drain between the wound and these suppurative areas, where they placed long pieces of gauze. When changing the dressing, they took them out and put in clean ones. But my condition did not improve, it got worse. So the doctors decided to perform an operation, they opened the purulent area, cut the skin and pushed it back to get direct access to the purulent places and clean them properly. The procedure was performed without anaesthesia. And the two months I spent in hospital testify to the seriousness of my injury. When I returned home and started attending court hearings, I was called Elizabeth Arden, as the advertising label of the cosmetics company.

In the *Wieczór Warszawski* (Warsaw Evening) newspaper, issue 192, there was an article entitled *Bodies, ruins, destroyed forests – the result of a terrible hurricane.*

Postawy, on 8 July. A special commission visited the Postawy district to assess the damage caused to the population by the hurricane that hit the area two days ago. On the territory of Miadzioł, Postawy and Kobylnica districts, the storm destroyed 85 settlements, 36 residential houses and 355 farm buildings. Many people were killed by lightning. In the village of Syrki, a fifteen-year-old shepherdess Julia Kowinko was killed by lightning. In the town of Stary Miadzioł, a collapsing thatched roof crushed sixty-five-year-old Mowsza Iskryn, who died instantly. Similarly, Aleksy Koczergo died under a collapsing barn in the village of Koczergi. As the hurricane approached, two women were in a boat on Lake Batoryn. A strong gust of wind made a huge wave which capsized the boat and the two women – Aleksandra Metko and Maria Czerniawska – drowned. Their bodies have not yet been recovered. As the lake is extremely deep, they will remain in its depths forever. In addition, a plane piloted by Jan Kurnatowski, who was seeking shelter from the storm, was badly damaged on a makeshift airstrip near Lake Narocz in Kobylniki. The total damage caused by the storm is estimated at half a million zlotys. The authorities organised emergency aid for the victims, many of whom were literally left without a roof over their heads. In three districts of the Postawa region, crops were completely destroyed. Forests were affected particularly hard. In large areas trees have been uprooted and are lying side by side. Many thatched roofs were carried away by the wind for several kilometres.

When I had fully recovered, I went to the airport to see if the accident had left me traumatised. Would I still have courage to fly? It turned out that I wasn't traumatised, but our plane, Kokoszka Wileńska (i.e. common moorhen of Vilnius – the name of the touring plane) was no longer fit to fly. Except for the engine, everything was broken and crushed. Janusz left to join the regiment in Lida. I had neither the RWD-13 nor a companion. That was the end of my beloved, exciting and unforgettable flying experience. My career as a pilot was over ...

A medical certificate I have now found in my archives shows that I appeared before a medical board, which, after examining me, decided that I was fit for the gliding course I wanted to take. The war thwarted the plans of us Poles, and after the war, I only enjoyed flying passenger jets, as it reminded me of my youth.

Some more things about Janusz Kurnatowski. In 1939 he made his way to France via Romania. He was in Lyon, from where he sent me the news. After the fall of France, he got to England, where he served in the Polish Air Forces. He often flew and fought over Germany. Once he fainted in a plane where he was an observer. His superiors withdrew him from combat flying and transferred him to instruction. He married a younger colleague of mine from Kiev, whom I was tutoring in mathematics at the time. She reminded me of this when we met in London in 1963. Her name was Ela Bisping-Podlewska, Janusz was her second husband and before she was married to Count Lubieniecki. It was only after the war, when I visited my brother in London in 1963, that we called each other by our first names. When I was staying with Barrister Sukiennicka, Janusz visited me there bringing a bunch of red roses. I said to him: 'Janusz, there were so many rumours about us before the war, so many suspicions, and we never even kissed.' And he replied: 'Maybe we should have.'

In 1968, when I was in London on my way back from Mexico and Canada, I saw Janusz again. Later they were writing to me regularly. Janusz got seriously ill, I assumed it was lung cancer, as he was a heavy smoker. He was breathless, coughing, in a lot of pain. He wrote asking me to come and see him, he sent an invitation, but I did not go. From what Ela wrote I knew he was constantly in hospitals, he looked bad and felt terrible. He was well cared for. I wanted to remember him as a wonderful companion and a handsome man. I did not want to see him in the state he was in at that time.

In a conversation with Janusz you had to 'read between the lines'. Nothing he said could be taken literally. He himself knew that others knew, but called it 'nonsense'. He was secretive, very composed, and well mannered when in social situations. He was well read. He rubbed shoulders with painters, actors and Warsaw bohemians. He was charming! He taught Professor Pruszkowski how to fly an aeroplane. Later Pruszkowski bought his own touring plane and flew it to Venice for the Biennale art exhibition. Janusz was friends with Zabetta Pruszkowska, Tadeusz Pruszkowski's wife. He had many female friends in general ...

When war broke out, his mother was in a boarding house in Balinpol. Then she lived with me in Vilnius. She had a successful cataract operation. She was a very intelligent, well-read person who spoke several languages. After a few years she fell ill and I took her to Balinpol. She died there and was buried next to my father and brother in the village cemetery. When I told Janusz about this, his eyes filled with tears. He was grateful to me. After a long and serious illness, he died in London in 1975.

I found the letters he had written before the war. I will quote some of them; 24 February 1939:

... No, there is no mud in Lida ... the wide airfield is covered in white snow, not deep, admittedly, but deep enough to cover the ugliest. I feel inside the dull glare of these days of white and sunless; that's how I am, as this white glare has laid itself on my scars and on my petty affairs ... It is bad that you are ill, that you are in pain. I have heard that you were at the Lawyers' Club on Shrovetide, but perhaps that is not true. You ask if I have a lot of work – yes, a lot, a whole lot, but that is good. I am terrifyingly active from the early morning: teaching, convincing, persuading, pointing, urging, pushing, pressing, even speaking out sharply when needed and it is good as it should be. And in the evening, at my place, I am like a speaker who, after a great oration in front of a large audience, disappears into the shadows backstage ... he wipes the sweat from his forehead with his hand, dims his 'fiery' gaze, calms his movements and nerves down, relaxes his muscles and lets his thoughts run free. Then again, numerous doubts immediately arise, but that is what life is all about ... Janusz.

P.S. Beautiful thanks for your nice letter, Mrs Hala. Write more, please. I will not come to Vilnius, because they do not invite me the way I would like, and I want a lot ... but I give up easily. J.

And another letter, undated.

Please don't write me nice letters, because they mix my reality. I have already set my sights on her, I have mocked her and accused her – but nonetheless I hurry to the post office and seize the letter like prey, I carry it to my den, and only there do I read it. Ah, Hala, you horrid thing – I want to strangle you again ... Janusz.

And another letter, dated 17 July 1938.

The hot, full summer envelops the world. The skies pour heat on the earth like hot water into a basin. Free lazy thoughts and movements parched out of all sense. And what were you doing in Warsaw, dear Hala? How was it? Or when you left for Morszyn?

Who did you actually meet there, because the action was arranged, that much is obvious! And yet I can't help thinking that I was not mistaken, not even for a moment when, as I said in jest a long time ago, I thought subconsciously: nice, urging for more lasting feelings, superficial, a bit casual ... I saw it on the balcony. J.

The fourth letter, dated 28 July 1939 (to Morszyn, where I was undergoing treatment):

Oh, oh, oh! She's lying down, she's fasting, looking terrible, pale, weak, fat ... But why are you so pale, weak, fat ... and so far away from me. J.

Janusz was very fit. When he was younger, he won a championship in the 400-metre run. I saw his strength and agility with my own eyes at the Kobylniki airfield. When he wanted to start the plane and the starter failed, he spun the propeller himself. Of course, he jumped off after each swing to avoid being hit in the head by the working propeller. The propeller ignited the engine and the unmanned aircraft began to take off. Apparently the gear was engaged. Janusz ran after the plane, caught up with it and jumped into the cockpit holding his body with one hand while turning off the throttle with the other. He was so physically and nervously exhausted after this incident that we returned to Vilnius the next day.

Janusz did not like to dance. More than once I urged him to dance, but he just replied: 'I very much enjoy holding a woman in my arms, but why should I run around the room with her?' He called me a cold lizard, while I defended myself by arguing that lizards were not amphibians, but warm-blooded creatures.

Reminiscing my flights over Narocz Lake, I would also like to mention Colonel Count Konstanty Przeździecki[40] of the 14th Uhlan Regiment. The

---

[40] The fourth commander of the 14th Jazlowiec Uhlan Regiment from 8 Feb 1922 to 16 Dec 1925.

colonel had a motorboat and a floating cottage that was pulled from shore to shore by the motorboat. The cottage had a canvas cabin for changing, a roof for sunbathing, and the cabin had sofas, tables, a radio and monthly and weekly magazines in various languages. For lunch we would go to a hostel on the lake shore and after lunch we would return by motorboat. There were canoes attached to the side of the cabin, and we would row them across the lake. Sometimes we would arrange to meet the colonel on a certain day in Kobylniki, where Przeździecki waited for us with his beautiful car and would drive us to the hostel where we would all spend the night.

After all the difficult experiences we shared with Janusz during our flights, he would tell his friends: 'I can't get rid of this lizard. One might have thought that after the last accident she'd be in a wheelchair and finally out of my hair, that she'd lose her energy and nobody would like her anymore.' Janusz made such jokes, but it was clear that he thought otherwise.

Janusz Kurnatowski's cousin, Mrs Irena Lorentowicz, included his photo in her memoirs. She also spoke warmly of him. In her dedication to me, she mentioned our mutual affection for this unusual man.

Helena in Zakopane

CHAPTER IX

My Three Prisons

❧

1st anniversary of Marshal Piłsudski's funeral, 12 May 1936, Vilnius

For three years I worked as a correctional caseworker in Vilnius prisons. It was a very interesting social work. I often pondered on the fact that until the moment of passing the sentence, the criminal was dealt with by intelligent people, i.e. the investigating judge, the prosecutor, the judges, psychiatrists and lawyers – people with higher education. Whereas once the sentence has been passed, when the time has come to punish the convicts, but also to rehabilitate them and prepare them for return to society, the only people who dealt with the prisoners were the 'tormentors', limited individuals, absolutely unqualified to civilise them. After all, who has occupied and still occupies the positions of a prison guard? When thinking of it, I came to the conclusion that this position was little different from that of the convict. The certitude that, after serving the required number of hours, the guard is allowed to return home, to his family, to freedom, does not change the fact that he spends most of his life within the grim walls of the prison and his main task is to make the punishment as harsh as possible. People who are sensitive and gentle with the prisoners are not well suited for the job, as the management of the institution requires them to adopt certain attitude that makes the incarcerated feel the discomfort of prison and fear disciplinary measures, as punishments determine their privileges or lack thereof. The prisoner who served too many punishments may be considered 'incorrigible' and ineligible for early release. To this effect, prison guards are usually ruthless, harsh and unpleasant in their dealings with prisoners. The work in prison, the negative attitudes surrounding them and their contact with often incorrigible recidivists contribute to their further demoralisation.

As a correctional caseworker, I got to know these people well and once I witnessed the dismissal of a very good and intelligent guard, simply because the female prisoners liked and respected him for his fair approach. The prison guards employed in Lukiškės Prison, which housed a thousand prisoners, were individuals who neither knew pedagogical methods nor how to apply them. After being sentenced, the prisoner would fall into the hands of simple-minded, cold-hearted people, totally unprepared for 'educational' work they were supposed to perform, without any training in this difficult but also interesting and extremely important work.

While dealing with criminal cases and visiting my clients, I heard a lot from both male and female prisoners about their circumstances. At that time the Prison Patronage was established in Vilnius, and I chose to join it. The president of the patronage was the professor of criminal law Bronisław Wróblewski, the secretary was Mrs Sumorokowa, the wife of a land registrar, while I enthusiastically took on the work of correctional caseworker. Some of the cases I described in my court diary, and once, when an inmate asked me to defend her, I accepted, considering it a community service, and defended her pro bono. I made a lot of 'friends' at that time and I consider that period of my life as very interesting.

The Appellate Public Prosecutor's Office granted me the right to enter the prison at 'any time of the day or night', but whenever I went to see my client upon written request, I always had additional authorisation from the investigating or judicial authorities.

I visited the prisoners separately and talked to them alone. They confided in me their sorrows and tragedies of their family lives, and in my observations I found the female murderers the most interesting group of criminal prisoners. They committed their crimes mostly in severe mental agitation, and their attitude towards 'professional' criminals (like thieves) was very contemptuous. They were the elite, the prison aristocracy. Having collected a lot of material, I suggested to the then director of the Vilnius station of Polish Radio, Witold Hulewicz, that I would like to talk on the radio about several patronage issues. Upon obtaining the consent I gave a series of lectures on different categories of convicts. I discussed the judicial system for juvenile offenders and the situation in Lukiškės Prison[41], mentioning, among other things, the occasional law violations. More often than not women diagnosed by psychiatrists as mentally ill or unstable were detained in regular prisons, even though by court orders they should have served their sentences in psychiatric institutions. Instead of being hospitalised, they were unlawfully imprisoned with healthy women, adding to the distress of other female detainees, tormented by cohabitation with the mentally ill. I recall that my lecture on this subject was very harsh; I spoke about the violation of the law and the inhuman acts committed by the authorities[42]. My agitation was so strong, that a report about my speech was sent to the Ministry of Justice and the Appellate Prosecutor's Office.

Immediately after my first radio broadcast, *Women Who Kill*, I was called – still at the radio station – by Witold Hulewicz, who was evidently moved by the topic and asked me to continue raising these issues on the radio. I tried to my best abilities to inform the public about these disturbing issues.

I performed the duties of a correctional caseworker for about five years and I don't think anyone filled this position later. Visiting Lukiškės Prison, I never imagined that soon, during the occupation, I would be taken to this institution twice by the Gestapo and spend many months in the same prison cells.

But yes, during the war I became a Gestapo prisoner.

The first case was defensible. I was accused of having sent a certain

---

[41] I kept copies of radio talks from Vilnius in my archive and will try to prepare them separately.

[42] Op. cit. p. 189.

amount of dollars to Warsaw, where my family was facing financial troubles. I found out that my niece Hala Falewiczówna, known as the wild child of the family, was seriously ill with tuberculosis, while her father (and my cousin) Andrzej was in a prisoner-of-war camp in Murnau. His wife, Zofia Falewicz née Lenczewska, was looking after her ailing mother-in-law, General Falewicz's wife and her teenage son Jan. I sent them a twenty-dollar gold coin through a lady who often crossed the border and was an acquaintance of my cousin Olo Bormann. Olo gave my money to this lady, whose name was Halina, and who dealt in cosmetics, but as bad luck would have it, at that particular time she was detained at the border. She confessed that she had received the dollars from my cousin Olo, who in turn ratted me out. And so we all ended up in prison, not knowing anything about each other's circumstances.

I remember that I was in Balinpol at the time, in the orchard, when a very upset Ludwik Sempoliński, who was hiding with us under the surname Kalina[43], came to me and said that I was wanted by the Gestapo. He urged me to hide in the garden, as they might or might not look for me there, as currently they are talking to my mother, who assured them that I was not in Balinpol but in Vilnius. The weather was lousy, it started to rain as I lay down on the ground and hid in raspberry bushes. Sempoliński had also remained in the garden to avoid being seen. He came to me several times, telling me not to come out because the Gestapo were still there. Finally he allowed me to come out saying that they had left, but instead of me, they arrested my mother. I hurried to Vilnius to find out what was going to happen to my mother, but I could not go to my apartment, as it was already being searched. I found refuge with my university friend Zwierka at 3 Maja Street. Having arrived in Vilnius, I found out that during the search, when the Gestapo officers were taking away various things, Zygmunt Kowalewski, a refugee from Warsaw who was staying there, asked the Gestapo men what it all meant. When he was told that it was a search, he replied that it looked more like a robbery. He then heard *Kommen Sie mit* and was arrested. Gestapo tortured him to tell them where I was hiding and as he could not stand the suffering, he gave me up.

---

[43] Ludwik Sempoliński, was wanted by the German authorities in 1939 as the Hitler-parodying performer of Hemar's popular hit *Ten wąsik, ach ten wąsik* (That Moustache) from the Qui Pro Quo theatre's programme *Orzeł czy Rzeszka*, hid in our house for an extended period of time.

Then the Gestapo came to 3 Maja Street. When I heard the doorbell, I opened the door thinking it was the master of the house coming back. *Sind Sie Sztukowska? – Ja – Kommen Sie mit.*

A Gestapo officer in black glasses escorted me to the Gestapo head-quarters located in the courthouse in Mickiewicza Street near the Lukiškės Square. The detention centre was in the basement. Through the windows under the ceiling you could see the feet of passers-by. There, in the washroom, I met my tenant, whose face was blue and bloodied, and bore the marks of the torture that had been inflicted on him. I had no grudge against him. I had already learnt that my case was minor and I saw that his suffering must have been terrible.

In my cell there were also two young Jewish women, one of whom had been arrested for escaping from the ghetto and the other for sleeping with a German. They were young and cheerful and had no idea of the danger they were in. In the mornings we were ordered to clean the corridors. They both were eager to do the task, as they could look into other cells in the process. I remember them telling me that in one of the cells there was a young man, kneeling and praying. They opened the cell and gave him something to eat. The prison staff were Lithuanians. It must be remem-bered that the Lithuanians collaborated with the Germans, and thus only the highest administrative positions were held by Germans. The ordinary guards were Lithuanians.

The young Jewish women told me about the course of their investiga-tions and that the German officer interrogating them, Martin Weiss, was a tall, dark-haired man in black glasses. I met him when I was arrested the second time.

The prisoners wrote their names on the cell walls. Among many others, I found the name of my friend Stanisław Węsławski, a lawyer who did not manage to return home from the Gestapo prison. I met him once when we passed each other on the stairs of the building. It was just a moment. He was short-sighted and did not have his glasses on; I greeted him quietly as we passed each other, but he had no time to reply. I found out later that he had been shot. After the war his wife lived in Toruń, where I also settled with actors of the Drama Theatre from Vilnius. Stanisław Węsławski's sons live in Poland, one is a cellist at the Warsaw Opera and the other, an engineer, has settled in Gdańsk.

The treatment we received from Lithuanian guards was varied. Some-times we were allowed to air our mattresses in the yard, which was a sign of kindness, as it allowed us to go outside. On other occasions I was called a 'Polish pig' by a young, handsome and elegant Lithuanian sentinel.

My stay in the Gestapo detention centre was short. I was interrogated only a few times and then sent straight to Lukiškės, where I was locked up in the prison I had come to know so well, albeit in dramatically different circumstances.

They put me in a large cell with young girls who seemed indifferent to their imprisonment. They spent their time trying to make contact with other prisoners in the neighbouring cell. I admired the skill with which they tapped on the wall in Morse code. They knew the names of all the inmates, communicated with each other and helped with matters relating to notifying the families or requesting to carry out urgent matters. All the women were extremely disciplined and had to follow orders. In the neigh-bouring cell was Miss Prokopowiczówna, who was engaged in underground activities.

If there was movement in the corridor in the early morning, it meant that someone was being taken away for a beating. Our cell had a high window, but it was dangerous to climb up to it. If the 'stork' – the guard sitting on the roof – saw a face in the window, he had the right to shoot without warning. But somehow people still managed to look out of the window. One of the girls would then cover the peephole in the door, while another, assisted by the other female prisoners, would cautiously look out to see who was being taken to the covered lorry in the yard. I remember the day when Miss Prokopowiczówna was taken to be executed.

After being there for a month, I was released together with that beaten man and my mother. I was no longer interrogated in prison. Olo Bormann was also released.

My second case was much more serious. I was arrested while hiding a sixteen-year-old Jewish girl in Balinpol. I did so at the request of my acquaintance, Mrs Abramowicz-Wolska[44], who asked me to rescue her best student, a Jewish girl. She was born in France and had finished primary school in Belgium, so her French was fluent and she could pass

---

[44] In recent years, Mrs Abramowicz-Wolska lived right next to me, next to Senatorska Street in Warsaw.

Helena with her son Jan 'Pumpkin'

herself off as French. She begged me to take her to Balinpol, where my seven-year-old son lived. Mrs Abramowicz brought this girl, who did not look Jewish at all and who, during the six months she stayed with us in Balinpol, did not speak a word of Polish. She pretended to be French and even in her conversations with the servants she used gestures to communicate, so as not to betray her origin. Her documents were false, of course, but the name on them was Teresa Zielińska (while her real surname, as far as I remember, was Szubicz, but I may have got her name wrong).

All was going well, but our Treuhandler (administrator) on behalf of the Germans, a very decent man by the way, warned my mother that it was unsafe to keep Teresa in Balinpol any longer. I managed to transfer her to a neighbouring estate, but unfortunately she was arrested by the Gestapo. I have no idea who gave her away. After some time I received news that Teresa was in the Vilnius ghetto. Shortly afterwards I received a written summons to the Gestapo office. Remembering the previous reaction of the Gestapo when I was not found in Balinpol and my mother was taken in my stance, I decided to obey the summons. Knowing what was needed in prison although not allowed, what had to be hidden somewhere deep so that the authorities would not find it, I packed and with this 'package' of essentials, dressed warmly, in ski trousers and boots, with prohibited items sewn into my fur coat (like a pencil, pocket knife, needles, thread, etc.), I set off for the well-known courthouse.

It was winter, 11 November 1942 (Independence Day). I showed the summons. I was interrogated in the building, not in the detention cellar where I had been taken before. There were seven interrogators. I pleaded not guilty, insisting that I did not know Teresa was Jewish, that I had taken her to my mother's house, where my son was living, so that he could learn French. They shouted at me: 'Das ist eine Lüge[45].' I tried to persuade them that they could go to Balinpol and question the servants, who had never heard Teresa speak Polish. When she needed anything, she communicated by gestures. I said that I trusted them to be fair and uncover the truth. I was so convincing that at the end of the interrogation they said I would be taken to Lukiškės and the case would be 'looked into'. Then an eighth Gestapo officer entered, a tall, dark-haired man with dark glasses. I asked him calmly *Sind Sie Herr Weiss?*

He asked how I knew him.

I replied that the two female prisoners with whom I had previously been in the same cell had said that he was a handsome, tall brunet, had 'Schwarze Brille' and that he was fair. He then lined up the other seven officers and asked me if I knew their names, but I did not.

The conversation ended. The Gestapo officers wanted to check what I had in my bag, but I told them that I knew what was allowed and what was not, and that everything in the bag was allowed.

I was led across Lukiškės Square to the prison I knew so well. On the way, the Gestapo officer stopped a woman and asked her: *Jude?* The woman showed her identity card, which stated she was a Karaite. They were not exterminated by the Germans. They are Semites, but do not accept the Talmud. There were quite a few of Karaites in Vilnius, they had their temples in Trakai and in Lukiškės Street in Vilnius.

I was taken to the office and my testimony was compared with Teresa's. When she saw me, Teresa froze with fear and kept mixing up her testimony, saying, for example, that I had known her before the war, which was not true. I knew she was in such a state that she did not know what

---

[45] Translation: This is a lie.

she was saying. Later I found out that she and her mother had been shot. Following that testimony cross-examination, the prison guards escorted me inside. I entered a large cell filled with a diverse group of people. There were intelligent women there and simple women who worked in the stalls or on the farms.

There I met two of my former clients, thieves, who upon their return from the kitchen where they had been on 'peeling potatoes' duty, told all the weeping women that imprisonment in one cell with them should be regarded an honour. One of them, already well acquainted with prison practices, would 'justly divide' the parcels the inmates received from their families, while another, as far as I recall, tried to convince me that she was rightfully entitled to keep what she had stolen, because stealing in her opinion was a form of art. To take a wallet from the inside pocket of a jacket is something you had to learn from childhood.

The thieves were very fair when it came to dividing the food. There were so-called 'parcel days' in the prison, when a Lithuanian guard would bring a basket, which had to be unloaded and returned empty. The wrapping paper was taken away, as were the boxes. We came up with the idea of keeping some of the wrapping paper and returning it on the next parcel day, with letters written on it. The letters had to be written inconspicuously, as the guards did not inspect the wrapping paper. There were also letters written on newspapers we received, which were hardly noticeable. As Christmas approached, I was transferred to a smaller cell where Miss Baniewiczówna became my companion. She was the daughter of a well-known merchant who had a clothes and coat shop opposite the Town Hall. Miss Baniewiczówna knew that Prokopowiczówna had been executed and, as she belonged to the same organisation, she assumed that she would share her fate. Nevertheless, she remained very calm and composed. She knelt on a bench with her elbows on the table and prayed quietly. In cases such as hers, the sentences were passed in absentia. She used to say that she was prepared for death, as if it was just a matter of turning the doorknob and going into another room. My situation was frighteningly similar, except that I kept believing that the Germans would come to the conclusion that I really considered 'Mademoiselle' to be French. I still had a glimmer of hope that I would survive. While I was still in that cell, Baniewiczówna was sentenced to one year in prison. My joy was great!

In Lukiškės Prison there was a little person who called herself a dwarf. She had great artistic skills, noticed by the prison authorities, and she was asked to make toys for the Christmas tree in the prison chapel. Because the dwarf liked me, she said she would not be able to do it without my help. So the authorities agreed to put me in the same cell as her. I glued paper chains and helped cut coloured paper, while she drew stars, angels, dolls, etc. The dolls came in handy for correspondence with home. The prison guards – Lithuanian women – would bring us scraps of various materials and we would make dolls, ballerinas or gnomes. The gnomes' tall hats served as ideal hiding places for our secret messages. When returning the basket that the guards used for the parcels, we would put letters there with messages about people and things. I still have the dolls my son used to get from me when I was in prison. I also have a letter written by the dwarf to my Pumpkin, in which she described the history of her case in a veiled way.

On the ground floor there was a Catholic priest, also an inmate. I witnessed confession and absolution taking place without direct contact with the priest, but at a distance. All forms of communication happened there. Prisoners tapped to each other on the radiators. The prisoners knew who had been brought in, who had been taken away, or who had been taken early in the morning for a beating.

In prison I came down with influenza. At first, I remained in my cell. Later I was transferred to the prison infirmary, where I met Halina, a woman I had never met personally before but who had been involved in my first case alongside Olo Bormann. Halina was a cheerful person who did not seem bothered by the matter of smuggling my money to Warsaw. She wrote a poem which I have kept to this day. I also kept some angels cut out of thick paper, made in prison by the dwarf. I was still in hospital when she turned up, explaining that although she was not ill, she felt an absolute need to be there with me, so she feigned some kind of illness or pain to be transferred to infirmary. Unfortunately, as I found out later, she was executed by the Germans, because she was deeply involved in the resistance movement.

When I think back to Lukiškės Prison, I remember the solidarity between fellow prisoners. We did not talk about our cases, but at every step you could feel the kindness between fellow inmates. We shared parcels, gave each other advice and did everything we could to keep from breaking down. Sitting around doing nothing is extremely depressing, whether the particular case was serious or trivial. So to pass the time, we invented various activities. I taught my fellow inmates several poems by heart. I remember young girls repeating the poem *Człowiek* (Human) recited by Sempoliński; it was written during my work as a prompter at the theatre in Vilnius[46].

After three months in prison, I was released on 11 February 1942. I was still ill. However, I had the opportunity to notify my mother that I was leaving the next day. After gathering my belongings, I found myself at the gate, extremely happy. I asked the prison guard to check whether my mother had arrived with a carriage. There was no one. I asked him to let me wait inside, but he refused, opened the gate and pushed me out into the street. It was cold and snowing. I could barely stand on my feet, I had a fever and was very weak. What was I to do? With no strength to walk, should I stand and wait? With a fever? I decided to walk in the direction of Lukiškės Square, heading for the apartment and reading room of my Aunt Elżbieta Żukowska[47] in Mickiewicza Street, near the court houses. I dragged myself there rather than walked, resting every now and then, stopping at a friend's house on Montwiłowski Alley, which was on the way. Finally, I made it to my aunt's, where I found my mother and Pumpkin, who was seven years old at the time.

That was the second time I was imprisoned, but as fate would have it, nine years later, in Poland, I was imprisoned for a third time for seven months and that was probably the hardest time ...

Why was I locked up for the third time? My niece, Wanda Falewiczówna, called Tuta in the family, lived with me at that time. Her mother and my sister-in-law lived first in Legnica, then in Morąg, and relations between mother and daughter were strained. One day Tuta called from Legnica and said she wanted to visit me in Toruń. Of course I was happy to have her and so she came and enrolled to school. In this early period of Stalinism, in 1949–1951, in almost every secondary school in Poland

---

[46] During my stay in Lukiškės Prison, I made a rosary from bread, which I gave to my cousin Andrzej Falewicz. Today, this rosary is in a large glass cabinet containing the most valuable orders and distinctions of the Falewicz family, in the collection of my nephew J. K. Falewicz.

[47] Sisters Elżbieta and Antonina Żukowski, both members of the Polish Military Organisation (POW), close associates and friends (still from the Vilnius times) of Marshal Piłsudski, ran the well-known Tomasz Zan Reading Room in Vilnius.

SWEDEN

Bornholm
(Denmark)

Baltic Sea

Klaipeda

Lithuanian SSR
Taurage

Panevezys

Utena

Daugavpils

Svenčioneliai

Russian SFSR
KALININGRAD

Kovno

Marijampole

VILNIUS

Słupsk   Gdynia

Kołobrzeg

Koszalin

Gdansk   Elbląg

Suwałki

Lida

MINSK

Grodno

Novogrudok

Szczecin   Szczecinek

Olsztyn

Białystok

Baranavichy

Slutsk

Gorzów

Bydgoszcz   Torun

Ostroleka

POLISH PEOPLE'S

Poznan   Plock

Zielona Gora

Leszno   Konin

Glogow

REPUBLIC

Siedlce

WARSAW

Lodz

Radom

Brest

Pinsk

Byelorussian SSR

Lublin

Kovel

Zgorzelec   Wroclaw

Jablonec   Kłodzko

Opole   Częstochowa

Kielce

Zamosc

Lutsk

Rivne

Shepetivka

PRAGUE

Bytom

Katowice

Opava

Cieszyn   Krakow

Jihlava   Olomouc

Nowy Sacz   Przemysl

Rzeszow

Jaroslaw

Lviv

Ternopil

Sanok

Drohobych

Boryslav

Stanislawow

Kamianets-
Podilskyi

C Z E C H O S L O V A K I A

Brno   Ruzomberok

Trencin   Banska
Bystrica

Presov   Kosice

Mukachevo

Chernivtsi

VIENA

AUSTRIA   Bratislava

Gyor   BUDAPEST

H U N G A R Y

Debrecen

Satu Mare

R O M A N I A

Suceava

Ukrainian SSR

S O V I E T   U N I O N

POLISH LANDS IN THE YEAR 1945

0   250   500 km

Map creation: Marcin J. Sobiech, www.exgeo.pl

———— State boundaries   ○   Cities

– – – – Voivodship boundaries   WARSAW Name of state capitals

·········· Soviet republic boundaries   MINSK Name of soviet republic capitals

⇄ Polish-Soviet territorial exchange (1951)   Kielce Name of voivodship capitals

groups of young people were organising, talking about fighting the Bolsheviks, regaining independence. Secret youth organisations were formed. I know of such organisations in Olsztyn, Grudziądz, Inowrocław and many other towns. Such an organisation was also present in the secondary school Tuta attended, of which I was completely unaware, and I considered it perfectly natural that friends visited Tuta in her room. When I left to Warsaw on business, I received a phone call that Tuta had been arrested. There were four security officers in the apartment waiting for me and they were arresting anyone who came there.

Although I knew that I could be arrested, I returned to Toruń immediately after the phone call. One of the security officers let me in and informed me that the apartment was 'sealed' so no one was allowed to leave. What followed was, at times, downright ridiculous. The security officers would run to buy groceries, and whenever they opened the door for some visitor, they immediately informed them that they could not leave the apartment. One day a neighbour from Balinpol came, Mrs Szaniawska, the owner of Tautuliškės estate, an elderly lady who was truly in despair because she had left a bedridden person at home. She tried to persuade the security officers that her presence at home was essential, but to no avail; they did not release her. Then Janek's English teacher turned up, and was also held there. When he did not come home in the evening, his worried wife came to us to find out what had happened, and was detained as well. The women worried that due to their long absence from homes their children would come looking for them, so they decided to pray. They sat on the sofa and, looking out of the window of the ground-floor flat, they prayed. And their prayer went more or less like this: *Our father who art in heaven – maybe we should open the window and let them know not to come here – Hallowed be Thy name – they will certainly not let us open the window – Thy kingdom come – maybe they will not come – Thy will be done – but they will be very concerned – On earth as it is in heaven – damn them all!*

People not only occupied sofas and couches, but also slept in armchairs. Even my antique dealer, from whom I bought collectibles, was detained with us. As he didn't come home, his wife came to find out why her husband had not returned for so long, and tragically, she could not leave my apartment either. But the brave and loud-mouthed woman started shouting that there were three children sleeping at home and announced that if they did not let her out, she would break a window and shout to the street that people were being murdered here. Finally she achieved her goal and was allowed to go home. (This was not the first time I had learnt that shouting was a good weapon against security officers.)

This went on for several days and nights. My Janek remained emotionally stable and played chess with the security officers, and when they were leaving, he said: 'What a pity that they are leaving so soon ...'

Some time after Tuta's arrest and after the apartment situation the doorbell rang at night and two uniformed officers stood in the doorway, showing me a written pre-trial detention order against me; I was told to get ready to leave the house. I began to pack as they waited. I put various things into the 'Petersburg-type tote bag'[48] and it took quite a long time. The impatient security officers asked me what I was doing and I replied that I was taking the most necessary things. To which they replied: 'How do you know what you need?' I said: 'I've been detained twice already, so I have an idea what is necessary and what is not.' I put on my winter clothes (it was 28 February 1951) and was escorted by these two officers to the Security Office. It was two in the morning, but the place was busy even at night. The first interrogation took place in the warden's office. I was told the grounds for the detention: under Article 18 of the Minor Criminal Code, I was charged with failing to report what had happened a few days before.

And a few days earlier Wiącek, my niece's school friend, showed up at my place in the afternoon and asked me to let him into Tuta's room. He explained that Tuta had sent him to take care of something. Surprised, I let him into the room, and from the doorway I saw him go up to the bed and take out some papers from under the blanket, which he then threw into the stove that stood in the hall. This, of course, gave me reason to believe that Tuta was also involved in some underground activity. I felt reassured by the thought that something that could be used as evidence against her had been burnt. Later it turned out that burnt materials were anti-Soviet leaflets that young people had distributed in the trams. Wiącek told the security officers about his visit and hence the arrest for 'knowing and not reporting'. I spent the night in part in the warden's office and in part in a detention cell. Wiącek was in the neighbouring one.

---

[48] The same I used at the front in 1920 and in the German prisons in Vilnius.

While I was there I could hear other detainees talking. I found out that my niece Tuta was put in a cell above us, on the first floor. I heard them calling out to her: 'Tuta, confess, because we have already confessed. Don't get yourself killed.' I had no contact with her, but later she and her friends told me that she had been badly beaten and that her face was bruised. I had no idea what happened to her after that. I only found out much later, when she was serving a six-year prison sentence, first for a year in Toruń, then for a year in Fordon and finally in Bojanowo. Then an amnesty was announced and she was released from Bojanowo.

I stayed awake all night in the cell, listening to the conversations and thinking hard. At one point a guard came and told me to go to the toilet, where there was nothing but the toilet seat. This did not last long and I went back to my cell again. Listening to the young people's conversation, I knew for sure that the charges against me during the preliminary inter- rogation were correct, that I would be held criminally responsible, because Wiącek's visit to my apartment and the burning of the leaflets would be sufficient grounds for the authorities to convict me under Article 18 of the Minor Criminal Code.

My stay in Toruń detention was very short, soon they drove me to Bydgoszcz. I was alone in a cold cell. The bed was primitive, a bench with a hard straw mattress and a blanket. You slept with your clothes on, but without your shoes. I was immediately summoned for questioning. It was night. There was a small chair with a backrest opposite the interrogator's desk. The interrogations went on and on, and that first night in Bydgoszcz was really unbearable. Once the interrogators left the room, I was left under the 'care' of a young security officer who sat at a desk. They replaced my chair, which had a backrest, with a stool without one. The bulb shone directly in my face. I knew about their interrogation methods and as soon as I was left with this young security officer, I told him that I would not sit on the stool at night and that I would lie down on the floor, which I did. The floor was red brick. My 'carer' leaned over the desk and fell asleep. Then I got up and, right in front of him, I wrote kite messages, hoping to find an opportunity to send them out later. When I got up the next morning from that hard floor, I noticed that my navy blue suit was covered in red brick powder.

The interrogations were often held at night; that was their method. The guard would open the cell door at night and call out: 'Get ready for interrogation.' Then, dressed in the same suit all the time, I would get off the hard bed, put on my shoes and wait for the door to open. When the door opened, I was led up the winding iron stairs to the first floor. But sometimes I would wait a couple of hours and then the guard would open the door and say that the interrogation was cancelled. This was one of the ways of oppressing prisoners. I was still alone in the cell, but I managed to contact the person in the cell next door, Mr Foss, a professor of German studies from Nicolaus Copernicus University in Toruń. We established our own way of communicating. His and my bench were set on a common iron rail that had some clearance, so if you lay down on this bench and lowered your head towards the rail, you could hear a voice from the neighbouring cell.

He was tortured with sleep deprivation; the situation went on for a fortnight. The interrogators changed and he had to sit on a stool 24 hours a day, blinded by the glaring light of a bulb, answering the same questions over and over again. He was completely broken and exhausted. He was then released without trial and died two weeks later. They accused him of espionage in Królewiec before the war, where he studied German literature. Once I was caught talking to Professor Foss and the guard ordered punishment. He opened the door and led me towards a seclusion room for solitary confinement. I did not know what was going to happen to me, but I was terrified, as I knew from other people that the seclusion rooms were horrible. As the guard guided me towards this room, I braced myself for the worst, but I was in for an unexpected surprise. He took me to another cell, not the seclusion room. Most importantly, however, there was a woman there with whom I had served time until I was transferred to the main prison in Wały Jagiellońskie Street.

This woman came from a farm near Świecie. Entering the cell and seeing her, I shouted with joy: 'Praise the Lord – another human being at last!' Talking to her I found out that she was charged with espionage. A simple woman with two little children! She was desperate and frightened because the interrogator had told her seven months earlier that there was only one punishment for espionage – the death penalty. She did not wash, did not eat and when the children's voices came through the small window under the ceiling she cried out: 'Close it, close it!'

She told me that she had a brother who lived in Switzerland and who was sending her parcels of stockings or tights, asking her to send them to different places. But generally the investigating authorities were not interested in her, she had already been detained for seven months or more. No one called her in for further questioning, and she kept repeating that she was innocent, that she knew nothing of any espionage, while as for me, she thought that I was not the person I claimed to be, but Wanda Wasilewska, put in that cell on purpose so that I could learn everything from her and later write a book about her. After a while, however, she began to trust me and I tried to explain to her that her fears were unwarranted because they would certainly let her out soon. I tried to bring up the subject of her life in the country. I inquired about her farm, how many cows she had, what kind of cows they were, what they sowed, etc. I avoided the subject of her young children, as that would drive her to utter despair.

I urged her to eat and showed her how to make a rosary out of bread. We were given military bread, dark, quite tasty. You could make a rosary out of it. I used to make such rosaries in Lukiškės Prison. You squeezed the bread for a couple of days, spat on it to mould it into small beads, dry and pierced the beads with a needle and a thin thread. I already had such a rosary. When I left the cell, I left it behind the radiator, out of sight, but I thought that if a desperate person ended up in the cell, finding the rosary might lift their spirits.

After a while a young woman came to our cell. She was a nurse from a hospital on the outskirts of Katowice. She confided in me that she ran a contact place where she received illegal papers. She was very brave and did not tell the authorities who she was supplying it with. Her husband managed to leave Poland. Both of them served in the Home Army during the occupation. This new fellow prisoner also had a lot to tell. This girl had been in the Kedyw (Directorate of Sabotage) unit of the Home Army during the occupation, had been trained to lay mines and had taken part in blowing up bridges. Trusting me, she told me about her adventures during the occupation. She was in the Lublin area. The Home Army had their informers in the Gestapo. One of the informers reported that on a certain day the Germans were planning to escort prisoners to be shot by a firing squad. The execution was to take place in the woods, at a place reached by crossing a bridge. She had participated in mining this bridge. A group of Home Army soldiers were waiting for the Germans and prisoners to cross. A German car was in front, followed by the prisoners' van and another car with German guards. The soldiers let the first two cars pass and blew up the third car along with the bridge. There was a commotion and the main attack of the partisans targeted the first car, killing all the Germans. The prisoners were so frightened that they clustered together so that the Home Army soldiers had to force them to flee as the Germans were only five kilometres away and it was essential to act quickly, disperse and escape from the explosion site fast.

She told an interesting story about how she was once riding a bicycle, carrying guns, and fell over. Her briefcase fell on the road. A German who was passing by stopped and in a courteous manner helped her pick up the briefcase ...

Once a Home Army partisan unit stationed in a village was informed that Germans were coming to the village. They had to disperse and hide their weapons. They put the guns in a briefcase and she was told to hide them. There was a grave in the cemetery which the Home Army used as a hiding place. The cemetery was surrounded by a wall and as the gate was close to the street, in plain sight, she could not use it. With great difficulty she climbed over the fence and located the grave, which was brick walled and had a heavy gravestone. She managed to move the gravestone and prop it up somehow. She climbed down the ladder into the grave and hid the weapons deep inside, but as she climbed back up the ladder to make a slightly larger gap, the supports under the gravestone slipped and it fell down. The poor girl was unable to lift it. She was trapped in a stone grave! She sat on the ladder, gripped with terrible fear. She hoped someone would find her, but who and when? What would happen to the Home Army people? They might not have expected something like that! They will be looking for her, but will they guess where she was trapped? Half dead, she waited for mercy and time dragged on immeasurably. After a while she heard voices. She was afraid to call for help because she did not know who was coming. The voices grew closer and turned out to be her people. Eventually she was found and brought out of the grave half alive.

She also told me that once she was riding a horse carrying some reports and it was already dark. There were two roads leading to the village, diverging at the cross by the side. Upon reaching the cross, she wondered which way to go. To the left was a wider, busier road, to the right – a path.

She wanted to go left, but when she turned her horse to go down that road, the animal refused to move. She tried to force it, but the horse would not go. In a hurry she went right, and when she arrived, her friends immediately inquired which way she had come, because on the wide road she would have met German patrols. She believed it was no accident, that God was watching over her and had saved her ...

She also told me about a mission she had not been on, but her friends had been there and told her all about it later. It was a mission of rescuing political prisoners from a district prison (I do not remember the name). When the Home Army soldiers dressed in German uniforms opened the prison gates, the partisans ordered the German guards to face the wall and they freed the prisoners, who were to be executed, from their cells and from the basement of the prison.

These are just some of the stories this girl told about the activities of the Home Army in the Lublin region. It has now been documented in detail, but I quote the story told by my fellow prisoner in order to better show the character of this wonderful girl. One day they called her in for interrogation. We were all afraid that they would torture her into revealing who had given her the papers. A little later we found out that she had been moved to another cell in the Security Office detention block and that she was holding up well. I do not know what happened to her after that, but I am convinced that she did not give anyone up.

Another episode from the prison in Chodkiewicza Street: once the cell door opened and a guard came in to search the prisoners for any forbidden objects. A Semitic-looking officer with the rank of lieutenant stood in the doorway and watched as the guard searched us. I had a holy pendant in my shirt pocket. The guard took it away, saying that prisoners were not allowed any metal objects. I told him that for me it was not a metal object but a respected and important symbol. The guard stood his ground: forbidden. I then turned to the Jewish officer and, referring to the decree on freedom of religion and conscience, asked for the religious symbol to be returned to me. The officer froze in surprise. Totally caught off guard, he said abruptly to the guard: 'Give it back.'

After a month of detention in the basement of the Security Office, I was told that I would be transferred to a large prison, which I knew well, having been a defence attorney for clients imprisoned there. I was overjoyed that finally I would be out of a basement. In the main prison living conditions would be completely different and perhaps the constant fear of nightly interrogations would end.

My first companion was left alone in the cell. I found out later that she had committed suicide after my departure, hanging herself with a rope made from strands of torn panties. When times changed somewhat and the thaw began after Stalin's death, the family of the deceased filed a complaint with the Prosecutor's Office demanding an investigation into the death of this prisoner, martyred for a crime she had not committed. I was summoned as a witness to the Voivodship Prosecutor's Office in Bydgoszcz to explain the circumstances leading to her suicide, because the family claimed that she had been murdered. My testimony took several hours. I did not suspect murder or torture, in my opinion the deceased's mental state was so terrible that she apparently decided to do what interrogators suggested, which was to be hanged for espionage. No one questioned or summoned her for six or eight months. This woman left behind two young children. A simple woman from the countryside waiting to be hanged – so she did it herself, seeing no hope of saving her life. I told the prosecutor who questioned me that the authorities were to blame for her death because they had ignored her case; they were the ones who had caused her such distress, that she had taken her own life! I knew her case and it seemed simple. She would certainly not have been found guilty of receiving parcels from her brother who lived abroad.

I was escorted from the cell in Chodkiewicz Street, where the Security Office headquarters were located, to Wały Jagiellońskie Street, to a large prison next to the courthouse. I knew this prison well, because as an attorney I used to see my clients there. Of course, I only knew the waiting rooms and the visiting room. Now I was to become more familiar with the entire establishment. The first thing after crossing the prison threshold was a visit to a doctor. This doctor was also a political prisoner, sentenced to ten years. (Another doctor would come to the prison from outside). The doctor asked me about my health and possible illnesses. I told him that I was not suffering from any illness, but that my nerves were terribly shattered. When he asked me to close my eyes and stretch my arms out in front of me, my hands shook terribly. At that point the doctor said he would refer me to the women's ward of the prison hospital.

It was a large room with six or eight beds, I cannot remember exactly. In prisons it was forbidden to use the beds during the day, but this did not apply to the hospital, where you could spend whole day in bed if you wished. Not all the beds were occupied. Among the prisoners was a woman, Wodecka, who had tried to kill herself five times. She ate needles, broke windows and cut her veins with glass. She was so aggressive that the guards were afraid to enter her hospital room alone. I remember that she had beautiful red hair, which she took special care of. Once she noticed that the other prisoner had lice in her hair; she made a terrible scene: the other prisoner refused to be examined and the women began to fight. I banged on the door and told the guards about the lice in the hospital. The lice-ridden prisoner was taken away. I do not know what happened to her.

Wodecka told me her life story. She had been sentenced before. 'Actually, all my sentences are justified,' she said. 'Five years for forging dollars – that's justified, eight months for attempting to cross the border – also just, for trying to escape from prison ...' The guards were bribed by her husband when, as a prisoner, she was working with silkworms in the gardens by the Vistula in Fordon. Her husband, who was Jewish, managed to escape to the West, while she was captured.

There was no strict prison regime in the hospital and the company was mixed. The guard knew that I was a lawyer and approached me with a strange request: the women detained in this unit were mostly under investigation, not sentenced yet. Some of them wanted to apply to the Public Prosecutor's Office to have their detention lifted, but they did not know how to do it. The guard asked me to go out into the corridor and write these petitions for the prisoners; I did so willingly. My writs of relief had a very good effect because the prisoners were released. Word spread through the women's ward that a lawyer was writing effective petitions and complaints, and so the guard opened the cells to let me out into the corridor, where a table, two chairs, paper, etc. had been prepared.

When Wodecka saw me in the corridor, she began to suspect that I had some kind of suspicious relations with the prison authorities. As a result she began to harass me so often that I requested to be transferred from the hospital to a regular cell. They agreed, and after I had gathered my modest belongings, I was put in a cell with three girls who had already been convicted and were serving their sentences: Władzia Czerepak, Inka and Hania. One of them had been sentenced to five years, the second and the third to eight years, for their involvement in an illegal youth organisation.

The atmosphere was very different there. The girls welcomed me warmly and I have stayed in touch with Władzia Czerepak ever since, we've been friends for thirty years now. Władzia Czerepak now works at the rubber factory in Grudziądz, I do not know the fate of the other girls.

They were 'idealists', tough yet nice. Once a so-called 'political' security officer, a prison employee, came to our cell and asked them what their sentences were and why they were imprisoned. Władzia replied defiantly 'Only five years', and Inka said in the same tone: 'Only eight years'. And the reason? 'Involvement in an organisation.'

At that time there were such more or less formal associations or organisations in schools all over Pomerania. I know of those in Inowrocław, Grudziądz, Olsztyn, Kcynia, Szubin and, of course, Toruń.

Once, Hanka was sent to solitary confinement for violating prison regulations, or perhaps for talking back. After three days she returned to our cell completely broken, dirty and dishevelled. I explained to her that it was pointless to be offensive towards the guards, that you only hurt yourself by doing so. But her attitude was indicative of the courage of the young people and the political convictions they had formed.

When the amnesty was announced, I went to Bojanowo near Poznań to pick up my niece, Wanda Falewiczówna, who had served just over three years of her six-year sentence. It was probably a kilometre, maybe more, from the railway station to the women's juvenile detention centre. I made a phone call and went to the prison board, asking for a pass. I met with the warden, who said that Falewicz was leaving the prison unreformed. I knew that she had misbehaved while serving her sentence and spent twenty-one days in solitary confinement. Hanka was broken after three days, while Tuta, when the prison warden who visited her asked how she felt replied: 'Just like in prison. How am I supposed to feel?' When he repeated his question, she said 'When you do time, you will know ...'

It was a camp for 2,000 girls. Political prisoners were serving their time together with thieves, prostitutes and the like. The language they used, the noisy behaviour and the aggressiveness of these girls added to the hardships of political prisoners. When Tuta was still in prison, I was thinking of ways to get her released, and I suggested in a letter that she should go to the prison doctor and obtain a certificate confirming an ailment of a feminine nature. She understood my intentions and suggestions, and later, as we were walking from the prison to the train station, she said: 'Yes Auntie, I tried, but he was really surprised, as other women were tough ...'

She left Bojanowo looking good, cheerful and brave, and on the way she told me how one of the female prisoners, when she misbehaved, was taken by a guard to the warden, who shouted at her and threatened to beat her ... She was so terrified that she climbed up the bars in the corridor and the guard could not get her into her cell. When she finally came down, he took her back to the warden, and when asked the reason for her behaviour, she replied that it was because of the warden's threat. She was afraid that they would immediately proceed to beating her.

The three wasted years of my niece's life had thwarted her plans. She now works as a surgical nurse at the hospital in Banacha Street in Warsaw.

The women's ward of the Bydgoszcz prison was clean. The guards would often check whether the windowsills had been dusted properly, the floor clean, etc. We would wear shoes when going to the yard, but upon return to the cell, we put on slippers. The food was acceptable. Dark bread, grain coffee in the morning and evening, a litre of soup for dinner. This was too much for me, so I used to give half my portion to Władzia, whose appetite was insatiable. But I found it hard to finish even this half-litre portion of the soup. The guards were rather helpful, except for one older woman who would yell a lot and was unpleasant. I asked to be assigned to some work and after a while they allowed me to join a group of women who were mending the prison undergarments in the attic; time passed more quickly.

We were not allowed to look through the peepholes into other cells. Once, when I was in the corridor, I peeped into some cells, curious to see what kind of people were there. The guard noticed and punished me by making me stand facing the wall.

In the Bydgoszcz prison Morse code was widely used for communication, and I admired those smart girls who knew who was doing time, where and under what charges. The girls here did not tap through the wall, but on the radiators.

How did you bathe?

You went to the bathhouse in the basement, where there were many showers. When your underwear and prison uniform needed washing, you left it in the changing room. Naked, in an unheated room, we stood under the showers waiting for the guard to come and open the taps. It was very cold in there. After showering, we often had to wait a long time to get clean underwear. Then we walked through cold corridors back to our cells.

174

Every fortnight you could buy something in the canteen if you had money in your prison account. Smokers could buy cigarettes. You could buy sausages, sugar, bread rolls and onions. The food was kept on the high windowsill, but it spoilt very quickly. In this respect the Lukiškės and Bydgoszcz prisons were much alike.

The prison libraries were frequented by many readers. Once in Lukiškės Prison, when I asked for a book, they gave me a book in English, just out of spite. They thought I would not be able to read it, but the book turned out to be very interesting. It was entitled *Borstal Institutions*, and covered the subject of the organisation of youth detention centres. It also discussed methods of their rehabilitation and re-education. That is how my interest in this field was born. The preface to the book was sixty pages long and concerned the age of adolescence. After my release I found extensive literature on the subject (Kryjski, Teresa Büler and others). It helped me a lot in my work as a defence attorney in juvenile criminal cases. Borstal institutions looked after prisoners when they served their sentence and after release, finding them jobs, enabling them to learn a trade. In England there were five or six such homes for juvenile offenders for boys and one for girls. From then on my colleagues considered me a youth specialist. The Lithuanian guard who, with a malicious smile, brought me an English book did not realise the favour he did me ...[49]

After a few months of imprisonment in Bydgoszcz, I was informed that my trial by court of assize would be held at the Military Court in Toruń. I started to get ready. I washed my prison clothes. The ironing was a bit unusual: you had to spread evenly the skirt and jacket made of grey fabric under the mattress for the whole night. In the morning a police officer came to escort me to the police detention centre in 1 Maja Street in Bydgoszcz. There the police officer handed me over to the MO (Milicja Obywatelska, Citizens' Militia) and I learnt that I had to wait until the next morning, when a police officer would come to take me to Toruń for the trial. The manager of this custody was very kind to me and gave me a new and clean blanket for the night. But at eight o'clock in the evening shifts changed and my next 'guardian', seeing a new blanket, took it away

---

[49] Interest in social policy and resocialisation runs in our family. My grandfather Karol Falewicz (1830–1914) worked on (and wrote a lot about) this issue. I have been involved in it, and now my nephew Jan Karol Falewicz is involved in it; he has written quite a few publications on the topic.

and gave me an old and dirty one. It turned out that this custody was a detention centre for various drunkards, so I might say that the night was unforgettable.

The detention centre consisted of a large room with rows of 'pens' where the drunks, brawling terribly, were put. I admired the patience of the militia guards (!?), who talked to the drunks calmly and politely, explaining that they would let them go the next day to go to work. The shouting and arguing with the detainees went on all night! Some of the detainees attacked the policemen, but the next morning they were surprised to find themselves in custody, politely explained themselves, apologised and wandered off to work.

Back in prison I was visited by my defence attorney, Barrister Mitkiewicz from Bydgoszcz, but in Toruń I was defended by a very well-known Warsaw barrister, Mieczysław Maślanko[50].

What was that day like?

In the morning a policeman showed up to escort me to Toruń. We travelled by train. We still had some time, so I asked him to let me see Janek and my husband's sister Zosia Malewska, who was looking after my house in Toruń. The policeman agreed and I met them in a park, opposite my flat in Bydgoska Street[51]. I heard that he faced disciplinary action for allowing me to speak with Zosia and Janek. After the sentence was delivered, he took me back to the prison in Bydgoszcz. When we were very close to the prison gate, he stopped and said that he would not be able to say goodbye to me in prison, but he wanted to and kissed my hand.

The court hearing was a sensation in Toruń. The courtroom was full, many people were standing against the walls, my colleagues, judges, were also present.

The charge of 'knowing and not reporting' was upheld and the military court sentenced me to one year's imprisonment for not reporting to the authorities that Wiącek had burned those leaflets. So when I returned to Bydgoszcz, my status changed to that of a criminal prisoner. The attitude towards such prisoners was much stricter, because in the case of detained on remand, the authorities understood that the prisoner might be acquitted and detention might be ruled unjustified. However, we need to

---

[50] The most famous barrister who defended before the military courts in the Stalinist period.

[51] Opposite my lovely apartment with a garden at 48 Bydgoska Street, there was a beautiful Toruń park stretching all the way to the Vistula river.

remember that during this period the authorities imprisoned large numbers of innocent people who, after serving their sentences, were found to have been wrongly imprisoned and even received compensation for wrongful conviction.

I was released after seven months, i.e. halfway through my sentence. However, my case led to further problems, because a lawyer with a criminal record cannot appear in court and practise law. So I requested a review hearing, which resulted in my acquittal. In that hearing the notorious *Minor Criminal Code* was not applied; instead, I was charged under Article 148 of the Criminal Code: 'Anyone who helps to cover up traces of a crime is liable to punishment.' I was acquitted under another section of the same article, which states that anyone who covers up the traces of a crime that may incriminate themselves or their family is not liable to punishment.

I was acquitted. I was able to return home and resumed my legal practice and, after some time, the Voivodship Court in Bydgoszcz even awarded me damages for unjustified imprisonment of seven months, paying me a total of 14,000 zloty!

That was the end of my third and (hopefully) last imprisonment in my life.

Carlota Thorkildsen in Świnoujście

CHAPTER X

Disciplinary Actions

In my long career as a lawyer, I have been the subject of two disciplinary proceedings. The first took place in Vilnius, the other was conducted after the war in Łódź and Warsaw.

I would like to describe them.

In Vilnius, I was approached by my colleague, Barrister Witold Jankowski, who asked me to replace him at the assizes of the District Court in Lida in the case of a Lithuanian accused of secretly teaching the Lithuanian language[52]. He told me not to worry about the verdict, as his client would certainly be convicted. I went to Lida. During the trial, a prosecution witness – an undercover agent – testified that my client had already been convicted of similar crimes. As the accused had no previous criminal record, I protested. In response, the undercover officer said that indeed the defendant had not been convicted because he had acquaintances in the court and had been acquitted. To this, I retorted: 'There, some snot standing before the court dares to criticise the verdicts of the High Court.' After the trial, the agent complained to the Bar Council that I had publicly called him a 'snot'. The Bar Council made a case against me for insulting a witness and I was given a warning.

The second case took place after the war in Toruń. At that time, I was a disciplinary ombudswoman of the Toruń Bar Council, so as a member of the council, I could not be tried by the Toruń Council but by the Supreme Council.

My client, a well-known restaurateur and owner of a large house in Toruń, had been a reserve officer before the war, while during the occupation he signed the Category II Deutsche Volksliste (German people's list) and was tried for renunciation of nationality. He was tried under the so-called 'June Decree' and faced a severe punishment. The prosecutor

---

[52] Often, when glorifying pre-war times, we forget about darker side of this period. It's gloom is reflected today.

emphasised in his speech that the accused had betrayed his country, as he had been a Polish officer and became a German without having to do so.

I defended the accused by pointing out the forced situation in which he found himself. He had no family in the territory of the so-called General Government, to which the Polish intelligentsia had fled from Pomerania and he had a large family of four children, one of whom was crippled by polio. As a reserve officer, he was never seen in uniform, only in his restaurant, where he often worked as a waiter. He had to stay in Toruń, where it was forbidden to speak Polish, and finally he followed the advice of Germans living in his house and signed the Volksliste. I also said that at that time the courts of the General Government did not judge in the name of the Republic, as they were sworn to do, but 'in the name of the law'. 'And it was good,' I added, 'because Poles are judged differently by Poles and by Germans.' And in any case the situation was forced ...

I was accused of contempt of court and had to go to Warsaw for a disciplinary hearing. I took the defence upon myself. Among the judges was a lawyer, Mieczysław Maślanko, with whom I later became friends and who defended me in a criminal case in Toruń. Having a lot of experience in defence on the grounds of the 'June Decree' and the 'August Decree', I presented the situation of Poles in Pomerania, where people were put in camps for speaking Polish. I know the case of the wife of a tailor who sewed beautiful uniforms before the war and who then sewed them for the Germans during the occupation. There were students in his workshop who spoke Polish among themselves, and she, fearing for them, warned them not to expose their Polish. She was later accused of forbidding them to speak Polish ... I also know of the case of a woman who, in a shelter in Bydgoszcz, asked people not to speak Polish because she would later be held responsible as a house caretaker. She was tried and was sentenced to twelve years in prison! A friend of mine, the Supreme Court prosecutor Joachim Markowicz, racked his brains over how to overturn this terrible sentence. He himself told me about it!

Förster in Gdańsk said in one of his speeches that if anyone in Pomerania did not accept the Volksliste, they would be 'wiped off the face of the earth'. I submitted to the court a pamphlet by Bishop Adamski, in which he described the situation of Poles in the territories annexed to the Reich and who turned to Bishop Gawlina in London, asking him for advice on how to behave and save face. Bishop Gawlina replied: 'Don't let yourself be expelled from these lands; if there is no other way, accept the Volskliste.'

Then a new law came out, which considerably reduced the penalties, and Article 4 of this law provided for an acquittal for a person who had served in the Polish army (even with Category II), had lived alone or had been in danger of being expelled; the article provided for two more reasons for acquittal that I no longer remember.

The situation was completely different in the General Government, where no one was persecuted for using the Polish language, and it was different in Pomerania. The concentration camps on the other side of the Vistula were full of Poles ...

Despite my arguments, I was given a reprimand. With such a punishment I could no longer be a member of the Bar Council, so I appealed to the Supreme Court, which was then residing in Łódź. In the end my punishment was just a warning – the lowest punishment in disciplinary proceedings and I was convicted not for 'contempt of court' but for using an inappropriate comparison. I was tried by Judge Mieczysław Szerer, whom I had met before the war, when both of us acted as defence attorneys for communist youth in Vilnius.

As neither case discredited me, I regret that there were only two of such disciplinary actions. For there were situations, both before and after the war, that determined defence and criticising the authorities could end very unpleasantly for a lawyer who spoke the truth and asserted it firmly and courageously.

Take, for example, the sentencing of farmers failing to pay their quotas. Tens of thousands of completely innocent farmers were imprisoned. That very year, snow fell on 9 May, severely damaging the young crops. The farmers were completely unable to meet the quotas. But – interestingly and sadly at the same time – the Bar Council at that time gave written instructions not to raise in the defence the issue of unreasonably high quotas demanded by the authorities. I had a case in Aleksandrów Kujawski just then, where I addressed this problem, but at that time I did not know about the Bar Council's recommendations. Fortunately, I signed the acknowledgement note only after I returned to Toruń; while a colleague of mine, a senior barrister[53], suffered unpleasant consequences for raising the issue of the quota in his defence. I got away with it!

---

[53] Toruń barrister Przysiecki.

I remember another case of a forester from near Toruń, whom I defended in court. He was accused of collaborating with the Germans and being malicious towards the Polish population. He faced at least three years in prison. More than a dozen witnesses appeared in court and testified that the forester was extremely strict and did not allow anyone to take anything from the forest. In other words: he collaborated with the Germans and hurt local people.

It was obvious that the judge of the Special Court, Bukowski, looked at the accused with contempt, but fortunately to the end of the trial one last witness was summoned, a forest inspector who knew the defendant from before the war. The inspector testified that the accused was a man who cared for the state welfare as if it were his own, he described the accused as a very honest and exemplary forestry worker, who took care of the forest, did not allow theft nor bribery, in short – he was a man of value and high morals.

I based my entire defence speech on the testimony of this last witness. The verdict was acquittal, despite a dozen prosecution witnesses. The testimony of these dozen witnesses, who defamed the accused, was the revenge of the people who had illegally cut down the trees.

The inspector explained to the court that the accused was an exemplary worker both before the war, and now. It is improbable that he would become demoralised during the few years of occupation.

The cases during the Stalinist period were interesting and painful. Military courts, special courts and common courts of law had their hands full. Most of the cases arose from false accusations and many people were wrongly convicted. This was especially true of the Home Army. Great people were put in the dock – ardent patriots, idealistic and courageous people. Their sentences were very harsh. After Stalin's death, at a time when Gomułka took over the government in Poland, these people were partially rehabilitated. Some of them received small compensation.

I remember an incident in Toruń when the Security Office ordered those who had served in the Home Army to reveal themselves. The head of the Security Office (with one eye, I think his name was Sadokierski) gave his word of honour that no one would be persecuted, but everyone should come forward. However, it was just a ruse. People who fought during the war in the underground admitted their affiliation with the Home Army, naively thinking that there would be no consequences, maybe even hoping for medals and triumphal procession under a white and red banner! What a poor memory they had! As if they did not remember the Trial of the Sixteen or the old Soviet tried-and-tested ways of operating. It turned out that they were accused of collaboration with the occupying forces, of actions to the detriment of the Red Army and the Polish People's Republic. Their sentences were severe, including the death penalty. In the case of Sylwan Stankiewicz, a ten-year prison sentence was passed, and in case of his son, tried in another group trial, heavy sentences were also handed down. Terrible things happened in the Polish judiciary at that time; even if some people endured eight to twelve years in prison, they came out with their health destroyed, often to die immediately after their release. But how many died: General Fieldorf, a heroic commander of the Kedyw unit of the Home Army, a great figure (about whom a friend of my nephew's, Dr Rybicki, commander of the Warsaw Kedyw Department, plans to write a book), General Krzyżanowski 'Wilk' – commander of the Vilnius District of the Home Army, Colonel Pilot Juszyrat, a hero of the Battle of Britain, who returned to Poland, and many, many great patriots, great Poles.

I am sure that there will be people who will describe this period much better than me. In her book about the trial of Kazimierz Moczarski, Barrister Aniela Steinsbergowa described the technique of murdering people who were subjected to torture and as a result confessed to everything they were accused of. And the methods of torture, as Moczarski listed in his famous memorial, were over forty. Kangaroo courts were held, without possibility of defence, in a small room of the prison in Rakowiecka Street, a place I got to know while waiting for a criminal prisoner who was to be released the following day and my role was to inform him about it.

I am writing these few remarks aware that others, younger ones, will do it better than me. But I cannot remain silent, I cannot fail to mention it, because I was a witness, often an eyewitness, of what happened in the Polish justice system during those terrible years, years of contempt …

Professor Antoni Bohdziewicz and Helena as film co-director of The Reality; atelier in Lodz, 1960

SWEDEN

Bornholm (Denmark)

Klaipeda

LITHUANIA Utena Daugavpils

Panevezys

Taurage

Kovno

Baltic Sea

RUSSIA
Kaliningrad

VILNIUS

Marijampole

Svencioneliai

Słupsk Gdynia

Kołobrzeg

Koszalin Gdansk Elbląg

Suwałki

Grodno

Lida

MINSK

Szczecinek

Olsztyn

EAST GERMANY

Szczecin

Bydgoszcz Torun

Ostroleka

Białystok

Baranavichy

Novogrudok

Slutsk

Gorzów

R E P U B L I C   O F

Płock

BELARUS

Poznan

WARSAW

Zielona Góra

Leszno Konin

Lodz

Siedlce

Brest

Pinsk

Głogów

P O L A N D

Zgorzelec

Wrocław

Radom

Lublin

Kovel

Opole Częstochowa

Kielce

Zamosc

Lutsk

Rivne

Jabloneč

Kłodzko

Bytom

Shepetivka

PRAGUE

Katowice

Krakow

Rzeszow

Jaroslaw

U K R A I N E

Opava

CZECH REPUBLIC

Olomouc

Cieszyn

Nowy Sacz

Przemysl

Lviv

Jihlava

Sanok

Drohobych

Ternopil

Brno

Ruzomberok

Borysław

Stanislawow

Kamianets-Podilskyi

S L O V A K I A

Trenčin

Banská Bystrica

Košice

MOLDOVA

VIENA

BRATISLAVA

Mukachevo

Chernivtsi

AUSTRIA

Győr BUDAPEST

H U N G A R Y

Debrecen

Satu Mare

R O M A N I A

Suceava

POLISH LANDS IN THE YEAR 2024

0   250   500 km

Map creation: Marcin J. Sobiech, www.exgeo.pl

—————— State boundaries   ○   Cities

- - - - - - Voivodship boundaries   WARSAW Name of state capitals

Kielce Name of voivodship capitals

184

CHAPTER XI
Animal Welfare Society

༈

The Animal Welfare Society was founded in Toruń on the initiative of Mr Chrzanowski, and I immediately signed up. This was an obvious step, as in my memoirs I have repeatedly demonstrated my love for animals. As I was a lawyer, I was given the position of legal adviser to the society.

We held meetings from time to time to discuss current affairs, and each of us had a big badge and the right to intervene in cases when animals were mistreated. A member of the society had the right to refer cases of animal abuse to the Administrative Arbitration Court to have the guilty party fines. I myself once saw a horse-drawn cart on a street in Toruń, in which three Soviet soldiers were riding and a cow was tied with a rope to the cart. The cow could not keep up with the cart and the rope was taut to the point that the poor beast was choking.

I approached the cart and asked them to stop. I presented the badge on my lapel and said in Russian: *U nas nie lzia izdiewatsa nad żywotnymi* (In our country, it is forbidden to abuse animals). Surprisingly, the intervention turned out to be effective. One of the soldiers got off the cart without a word and led the cow in the back, behind the cart …

The cases we dealt with were varied. For example, in a village near Toruń, a dog contracted rabies and was shot. The district vet ordered the police to shoot all the dogs in the village, apparently thinking that this would be the easiest solution to the problem. He assumed that potentially they could all have been bitten by this rabid dog, which was absolutely impossible. At the behest of this mad vet, the order was carried out. The dogs were tied to the kennels and killed by the police in front of the despairing children.

To make matters worse, the society was sued by this veterinarian, who filed a complaint that the society had insulted him (we did alarm the press about it). I stood up for the society, defending its good intentions. The society was of the opinion that the matter could have been handled in a different way, rather than allowing all the animals in the whole village to be slaughtered. Every animal owner would have willingly agreed to isolate and observe their dog, which would certainly not have led to the killing of all the poor creatures. The case ended in favour of the society and its doctors were acquitted.

It was a sign of the times that it was not the irresponsible veterinarian who was held responsible by his superiors or by the Medical Chamber, but those who had acted in the name of reason, elementary principles of humanism and professional integrity. This is what began to happen in our country at that time ...

The second case was high-profile.

There was an article in the *Express Wieczorny* (Evening Express) newspaper in Warsaw entitled: *Pigs Swimming in Boiling Water at the Toruń Meat Processing Plant*. The article described the practices at the Toruń abattoir. Pigs that were supposed to be killed by electrocution and then thrown into pools of hot water in order to remove the hair, were not killed beforehand, but died swimming in a pool of very hot, almost boiling water. The article was reprinted by *Gazeta Bydgoska* (Bydgoszcz Paper). Of course, both mentions were commented on by the people as evidence of inhumane practices at the abattoir. But the meat processing plant was very large enterprise under the authority of the Toruń City Council, and felt deeply affected by the articles. Both magazines were sued for slander and spreading false news. *Express Wieczorny* sent its lawyer from Warsaw, *Gazeta Bydgoska* sent its lawyer from Bydgoszcz, while Maciej Bajraszewski, my colleague from Vilnius, was to act as a prosecutor on behalf of the city council. I was to act as the defender of the Animal Welfare Society, because the society had also spoken out against the city council and the abattoir, accusing them of inadequate supervision and animal abuse.

We were all waiting in the hall, trying to convince Bajraszewski that he was going to lose the case because these things had actually happened and we had many eyewitnesses to prove that the articles were true. We explained that Bajraszewski, by supporting the accusation, would only expose the city council to losses due to coverage of court and legal costs of the defendants and we urged him to withdraw the case, promising on behalf of the defendants not to claim any costs. And this is what happened.

I still have a souvenir from those days, as I received a book from the Animal Welfare Society entitled *Psychologia Zwierząt* (Animal Psychology)[54] with a very nice dedication from President Chrzanowski, in recognition of my contribution to the Animal Welfare Society in Toruń.

Cambridge

---

[54] Written by the eminent academic, the first president of the Polish Academy of Sciences, Jan Dembowski.

Lovely dogs

Helena with her beloved dogs

CHAPTER XII
Yad Vashem

⊚⌒⌒⊚

L ying before me is a statement written in Łódź on 14 December 1951 by Ludwik Sempoliński. Here is what it says.

I hereby declare that I met Citizen Helena Sztukowska in Vilnius September 1939, when I was there as a refugee with my mother, staying in Citizen Helena Sztukowska's apartment. At that time, Citizen H.S.'s apartment became a safe haven for a number of refugees from Warsaw, to whom she selflessly offered her hospitality, sharing what she had at a time of great difficulty in obtaining food. Apart from me, she also helped Ed. Michał Orlicz, Feliks Parnell, Świerczewska and Dziewoński (famous actors). Citizen Orlicz, whose situation was dire, lived and received full subsistence for a year, which he recalled with gratitude when he met me today, on 14 December 1951. In 1940–1941 (until the outbreak of the German–Soviet war), Citizen Sztukowska worked as a prompter in the Teatr Miniatur, of which I was one of the directors. In 1940, Citizen Sztukowska was evicted from her apartment, so we all moved into Citizen H.S. flat in Jezuicka Street, without any conveniences or water in the kitchen, while Citizen Sztukowska lived there throughout the occupation. At the outbreak of the German–Soviet war, when Vilnius was bombed, we left the city on foot in a larger group towards the countryside and found shelter in the modest farmhouse of Citizen H.S.'s mother, called Balinpol, where we stayed for a year and a half. Said group included Józef Edelsztein, the props master at the theatre and the engineer Horwicz, both Jews. Since I was also hiding with them at the same time under the name of Kalina, as I was wanted by the Nazis for imitating Hitler's character, the two citizens, i.e. Helena Sztukowska and her mother, put themselves in great danger, and yet they never let it show and welcomed us very warmly and selflessly. In connection with my stay at Citizen Helena Sztukowska's, I gave an interview to the Express Wieczorny

(Evening Express) newspaper in the winter of 1947, in which I thanked Citizen H.S. for saving my life. At the same time, I declare the selfless-ness of Citizen H.S. towards everyone she hid. I witnessed that when Citizen Józef Edelsztein, who was a poor man and lost his only blanket when he visited his family in Warsaw, she provided him with a warm coat, clothes and food. I met him again near Lida, at the modest farm-house of Hawinowicze, where I was hiding after the arrest of Citizen Helena Sztukowska, when I had to leave Balinpol. From there I helped him to get through Pińsk to Warsaw, where he went to the theatre run by Michał Znicz, where he was probably killed. Engineer Horwicz also left Warsaw and visited the family of Helena Sztukowska. Apart from us, Citizen Helena Sztukowska hid in Balinpol for five months a Jewish woman pretending to be French, called 'Mademoiselle'. When the military police discovered her presence, she hid her in the neigh-bourhood. For hiding her, Citizen Helena Sztukowska was sent to a German prison. Apart from that, Citizen Helena Sztukowska hid another Jewish woman, her secretary's sister and her son in her apart-ment in Vilnius in Jezuicka Street, where she settled permanently after the liberation of Vilnius and where she remained after Citizen H.S. left the town. The group of people who were hidden in Balinpol by Citizen Helena Sztukowska also included Citizen Sukiennicka with her son, who hid for five months under the name Topolska from the Gestapo, who were after her as a communist. After the liberation, in 1944, she returned to the theatre and worked as a prompter, first in the Teatr Miniatur, and then in the drama theatre under the direction of Stefan Martyka. With this theatre and the Lutnia theatre she was evacuated to Toruń in May 1945, where she worked as a prompter for another two months and then resigned after returning to her career as a lawyer.

In giving this information about the people and facts that I remember, I am leaving out other facts that I have heard about and people whom Citizen Helena Sztukowska helped, but whom I did not know personally.

In a word, Citizen Helena Sztukowska maintained an excellent attitude as a human being throughout the occupation, she showed a lot of courage and self-sacrifice; as a citizen she was a role model and an example during the occupation. I declare this with full awareness as

one of those who are still alive and owe their lives precisely to the self-less generosity of Citizen Helena Sztukowska.
   Ludwik Sempoliński

Sempoliński's statement, written in 1951 in the middle of the Stalinism period, when I was released from prison and filed my appeal, full of euphemisms and expressions characteristic of 'those years' ('citizen' instead of 'lady', 'modest farmhouse' instead of 'estate' etc.), reminded me of a huge number of minor and sometimes very serious events from the Second World War. I have already written about some of them (like the story of 'Mademoiselle') in my memoirs, but there were so many such incidents, sometimes so dangerous and threatening, that my memoirs would be incomplete if I did not mention them.

It seems to me that I should present my work during the occupation against the background of what was happening in Vilnius before the war. I spent my university years and many years of my life afterwards in this, as Piłsudski said, pleasant city, where one could hear many different languages everywhere. Almost 40 percent of the inhabitants were Jews. They were numerous in the city. Some lived in the ghetto – completely isolated from Polish life – but others, especially the intelligentsia, mixed with the cultural life of the country. Vilnius, like all border cities where there were numerous national minorities (Jews, Lithuanians, Russians, Belarussians, Tatars and Karaites), was a welcoming and tolerant place. I had many Jewish colleagues at the university and later at work. Our relationships were excellent and I do not recall any nationality-related conflicts.

After the war, my friend Halina Sukiennicka, who lived in London, sent me a photograph showing the Vilnius Bar Chamber 'in corpore'. At least half of the faces in the photograph had distinctive Semitic features. Most of these people died tragically during the years of German occupation, many of them shot in the Ponary forests near Vilnius ...

Before the war it was said that 'Every nobleman has his Jew'. If this is true, then I was an exceptional noblewoman, for I had not one but a hundred Jews, with whom I fought side by side at the front, studied, worked, made friends, and, during the occupation, I tried as much as I could to help them in their terrible fate. There were many of them in the Vilnius area. In Balinpol, my parents' estate, where my mother ran a boarding house in the 1930s, the meat supplier was a Jew from a nearby town. All the towns in eastern Poland were full of Jews. In some they made up the vast majority of the population and often did not speak Polish well. The poor Jews, but also the Jewish intelligentsia, spoke to each other in jargon or Russian. This was also the case in Vilnius.

How did they end up in the Vilnius region? Apart from the Jewish population that had settled there centuries ago, they were mostly the so-called Litvaks, whom the Tsar had forcibly moved from Russia by establishing the so-called 'settlement lines'. Expelled from Russia, they settled in the Vilnius area, creating a real 'state within a state'. What this state looked like can be seen in a book published in the United States in 1974. This book, consisting of two huge volumes (with a small appendix) is entitled *Jerusalem of Lithuania*. There I found many friends, colleagues from the University of Vilnius and from my legal career. There is also (on p. 470) a photograph of me with captions in three languages: English, Hebrew and Russian. The caption reads: Lawyer Helena Sztukowska saved the Blumenthal-Shapiro family. The albums include a photograph of Professor Czeżowski with his wife and daughter. This photo was taken in Jerusalem, where Czeżowski was invited by the twelve people whose lives he saved during those terrible days of the extermination of the Jewish people. Professor Tadeusz Czeżowski was a very good friend of mine. There are many other Poles mentioned in this book who saved people of Jewish origin, risking and often sacrificing their own lives.

At the same time, after reading this book, it becomes clear how well organised the Jews were in the Vilnius region. They had their own schools, their own trade unions, which brought together representatives of different professions. There were unions for doctors, engineers, merchants, teachers, etc. There were two Jewish societies at the university[55]. There were also many at the bar. This can be seen in a photograph I received from London, which shows almost the entire Vilnius district – that is, Vilnius and other cities such as Białystok and Grodno, or those where there were municipal courts.

Relations with lawyers of Jewish origin were good in Vilnius, unlike in other districts where there was a ruthless struggle for participation in the

---

[55] It is interesting that this unheard-of in other countries autonomy and freedom of organisation is not reflected in the book. Only the anti-Semitic sentiments are mentioned! There is something unfair about this book!

governing bodies, as in Galicia, for example, where there was a large Jewish dominance in the bar. In Vilnius and the Vilnius province, we decided by mutual agreement that Jews would be allocated a certain number of seats. The idea was that all delegates would be treated equally, like Polish candidates. Therefore, if the Poles had any reservations about a candidate, the Jews would change him. The opposite also happened. Everyone then voted for the jointly chosen candidates. This is how it was arranged in Vilnius; I do not know how it was arranged in Warsaw.

Why was I so involved in hiding Jews during the German occupation?

Before the war, almost every day when I walked down Mickiewicza Street, where the court was, I passed a small Jewish shop where you could buy food until late at night. The owner's wife was very energetic and it was she who actually ran the shop. Her husband could not even speak Polish. He usually brought in the crates and stocked the goods. That was the extent of his work in the shop.

The shopkeeper had three daughters: Ethel, Masha and a third whose name I cannot remember. Once, when I was buying something, I asked what Ethel was doing. I was told that she was ill and in bed. 'What is wrong with her?' I asked. 'She is talking nonsense, moonstruck!' I decided to go and see her. She was indeed talking nonsense, as if she had been out of her senses. I told the mother that lying in bed would not help, that she needed to be taken to a university hospital, to the psychiatric ward. After some time, when Ethel was already in hospital, I met two female doctors, psychiatrists, with whom I talked about her. I remember that one of the doctors was Jakubiańcówna, famous for having examined Marshal Piłsudski's brain. I do not remember the name of the other, but she was known for claiming that the mentally ill should not be kept in hospitals, but treated in the countryside among the healthy. She was a pioneer of modern concepts in psychiatry. They both knew Ethel and predicted that she would recover. She was treated with baths but also with medication. The doctors claimed that the cause of the illness was the trauma she had experienced: after graduating from primary school Ethel wished to continue her education, but her mother told her to stop thinking 'about such foolishness' and prompted her to work in the shop ...

After leaving the hospital, Ethel returned home. After a while, her mother came to see me and asked me to find a typing job for Ethel. *She is so fond of typing; if she might come see you and do some typing for you, it would be her pleasure.*

So Ethel started coming to me and typing. After a while, as I got to know her better, I suggested that instead of writing unnecessary letters, she could write for me and I would dictate to her. She showed considerable skill in writing and I then suggested that she become my secretary. She made rapid progress. There were times when I did not have time to read a file myself because I had to appear in another case, and the court made the files available only till noon. In such cases Ethel would go in my stead to read them, and then in the afternoon she would summarise the case for me so well and thoroughly that I knew exactly how to construct my defence.

We changed her name from Ethel to Edwarda. Edwarda was promoted so quickly that other well-known barristers, such as Łuczywek or Kowalski, wanted to employ her in their offices.

This continued until the outbreak of the Second World War and the beginning of the occupation. There was no more work, no more Polish courts. Edwarda escaped from the Germans and headed east. There she joined the Polish army being formed by General Anders, and after the war she ended up in London. She worked as a telephone operator in schools for Polish children in England (housed in barracks in Cambridge). She enrolled in a number of courses that provided her with the opportunity to develop her career. She spent past years working in radio. She is now retired.

Meanwhile, in Vilnius, Ethel's parents and her younger sister were killed by the Germans during the liquidation of the ghetto. The Germans intensified the terror. Some of my friends, wonderful Poles, were also killed: Barrister Engiel, Professor Pelczar, Professor Gutkowski. The Germans threw me out of my large apartment into a flat without any comforts, with a dark kitchen. The house was close to the Vilnius ghetto, just opposite the barracks where drunk Lithuanian soldiers returned from places of execution.

I am still in Vilnius, but longing for Balinpol.

One day someone rang the doorbell and I opened it. In the door Edwarda's sister, Masha, was standing in the hall, holding her two-year-old son: 'Save me for the sake of my child.' I took her in, of course. For three years I hid her in various places, but the main base was my flat in Jezuicka Street. Masha still worked in the ghetto for some time, but somehow she would sneak out and come to me in Jezuicka Street (which ran very close to the ghetto walls). My flat was constantly busy with hiding Polish conspirators wanted by the Gestapo and meetings of the higher authorities of the Home Army. My mother and I were hiding Sempoliński. We were also hiding barrister Sukiennicka with her twelve-year-old son, the props master of the Teatr Miniatur, a young Jew from Warsaw. There was also engineer Horwicz, a Jew who had forged documents that I provided; he claimed that these papers saved his life at least five times. I remember when I found out that Masha and her child were in danger. At night I hitched a horse to a sledge, took Masha, her child and the maid, a Polish woman, and drove them through the forest, along narrow snow-covered roads to our empty summer house. I returned from there alone at night, unharnessing the horses so that no one would know of my night escapade. I was constantly travelling between Balinpol and Vilnius. My son Janek was so used to the conspiracy that he often asked me secretly if it was fine to say 'something' in front of a certain man.

The Jews I hid told me of their terrible, chilling experiences.

Once Magdalena (Masha) hid in the cellar of the janitor's house when he went to Kowno to trade. A hole had been dug in the cellar and the opening was covered with a screen so that it was not visible from the front door. While Masha and her son Szymek were hiding there, thieves came to steal coal. Fortunately, they were so busy stealing that they did not look behind the screen. Another time Magdalena and her son were hidden in the attic. Szymek had to whisper so as not to reveal their presence. The poor boy was so used to whispering that when he came to see me with his mother, he also spoke in a whisper.

Barrister Izraelitówna told me the following shocking story. A group of Jews were hiding in a house on the first floor. When they heard that the Gestapo were looking for them, they climbed up the ladder to the attic of that house, pulled the ladder up and closed the entrance to the attic. Among them was a woman who with an infant. The runaways from the ghetto feared that the baby would cry and thus reveal their presence. So they agreed that if the child cried, it would be suffocated. So they stood over the child with their hands outstretched, ready to grip the child's throat. Poor, desperate people driven to madness. Fortunately, the child slept peacefully and everyone was saved this time. The Gestapo did not enter the attic ...

It was very difficult to get out of the ghetto because the Jewish guards guarded the walls loyally and were remembered for their wrongdoings. When talking about the Judenpolizei, Masha was outright shaking with indignation. There were incidents when young Jewish women trying to get out of the ghetto were met with the proposition: 'Either you give yourself to me or you won't get out.' Desperate, weeping, humiliated women would give themselves up standing against the wall in order to go out into the city and get a piece of bread for their starving children.

Quite a few people knew that I was hiding Jews. My flat in Jezuicka Street was close to the ghetto and I was often visited by complete strangers, Jews, who would leave suitcases with me for safekeeping until they decided to escape from the ghetto. They would soon reappear, take their possessions and leave ... The fact that Sztukowska was not only storing things, but also returned them afterwards was widely known. It was all very dangerous, but unavoidable in view of the enormous misfortune and the sheer number of people at risk.

The following anecdote may serve as an example of this 'fame'. One room in my Aunt Janina Niewodniczańska-Falewicz apartment was requisitioned for a German engineer, who lived there and who employed a couple of Jews possessing permits to work in the city (outside the ghetto borders) at certain times. My aunt, who spoke several languages including German, befriended this German engineer and used this contact for various conspiratorial purposes. They visited each other and I took every arising opportunity to leave compromising papers in the pocket of the overcoat without worrying that someone might find them. The German was a Bavarian, from near Munich. He was a Catholic and his car was a real laboratory for the study of propellants. The German spoke fluent French. It was obvious that he was a well-mannered man and well educated. It later turned out that he was acquainted with our neighbour Biler, who had a house on the Vilija River, a few kilometres from Balinpol.

Once, on his way to Biler, Schmidt (for that was the name of that tenant of my aunt) stopped in Balinpol, introduced himself and asked to exchange something of his for groceries. His driver was Viennese and, judging by demeanour, rather harmless, as later events confirmed. A Jewish couple working for Schmidt had not been granted the permit to work outside the ghetto walls and should have returned there. The poor Jews knelt before

Schmidt, begging to be allowed to stay with him. Schmidt then ordered the driver to take them to ... Balinpol. In Balinpol the house was full of people in hiding. My advice was to transfer them to Belarus, where the extermination of Jews had not yet begun as it had in the Vilnius area. The border with Belarus was fourteen kilometres from Balinpol. The driver agreed on condition that I would go with him and show him exactly where the Jews were to be taken. We drove to the border, to the place where there was the possibility of crossing the border unspotted, as the land was covered by a dense forest. The Jews left.

The driver took me back to Balinpol and returned to Vilnius. The next morning when I came out on the balcony, I saw this unfortunate Jewish couple entering our estate ... There was no room for them in the house, so they were accommodated in a quadrangle with our stablemen. I had to leave for Vilnius. I do not know if they managed to save themselves.

When the Soviet offensive began and the Russian army arrived, it was a great joy for the Jews, who were leaving Vilnius en masse, going primarily to Israel. Magdalena stayed in my apartment in Vilnius after we left for the Polish People's Republic, but after a while she also left Vilnius and was in Warsaw for a few days, where she joined a group of Jewish emigrants heading for Israel. When I came from Toruń to see her, she was no longer in Warsaw. I was told that she had left the day before. Masha and her son were in Israel for a very short time because her husband's sister persuaded her to move to Mexico, where she was living. She offered to set them up there. This was because Masha had remarried, her new husband David Shapiro had come to Vilnius while being an officer in the Soviet army and, after demobilisation, had worked in the former Jabłkowski Brothers shop in Vilnius. Magdalena (Masha), her husband and son (whom her husband adopted and gave his surname to) initially worked in commerce. I exchanged letters with Magdalena when she left Israel for Mexico. Magdalena held various jobs; she baked cakes, she traded, while her husband had a shoe shop.

Her son Szymon matured quickly and started a successful career. He established the only pharmacy in Mexico that offered medicines for the poultry. Medicinal products were imported from the United States. Today he has a huge office employing secretaries and typists. He has also set up his own large chicken farm, where he employs eighty Mexicans, with a veterinarian in charge. He has this huge farm, a big apartment in Mexico and a nice flat in New York.

Karina Kaufer with her grandfather Simon Blumental and Jan standing in front of drawings she created depicting aspects of Helena's life.
San Diego 2024

Reunion in London 2023, Helena's son Jan, Simon's daughter Liza with children Ari and Karina. Next generation of survivors

Szymon married a lovely English girl, Ann, who converted to Judaism because it was important to Magdalena, who kept all the Jewish customs.

In 1968 Szymon invited me to Mexico, he even sent me a plane ticket. It was difficult to obtain a permission to visit Mexico: a lawyer had to help with my invitation and Szymon paid a deposit of 10,000 pesos as a guarantee that I would not stay in the country.

I stayed with them for two months. On my way back I stopped for five days in Montreal, Canada.

I arrived on a plane with only twenty-something passengers on board. In Montreal, a lot of passengers got off and not many got on. Thus, on the Montreal-Mexico leg of the flight, I had six seats at my disposal, six blankets and six pillows, and still I could not sleep! However, I managed to speak to the pilot of the plane. I told him that I used to be a pilot too, and he allowed me to sit in the other seat next to the pilot. When I did, he explained to me where we were, I observed the cities that, from the height of a few thousand metres, looked like little fireflies. I was greeted at the airport with flowers, the deposit was paid and I was driven to Magdalena and her husband's apartment. A huge bouquet of red roses welcomed me in my room.

I came to Mexico, to Magdalena's, before Passover, Easter, when we could not eat bread. We only ate matzah. I recall when I once came out of my room at night, I saw a candle burning. I thought Magdalena had forgotten to put it out, so I scrupulously blew out the candle. In the morning, Magdalena asked: 'Who did this?' Of course, I confessed. Everyone burst out laughing because it turned out that, according to the religious tradition, the candle had to burn to the end.

During the holiday season we were invited to a Jewish home for what was called the Seder – a treat resembling our Easter feast. There were twenty or maybe more people sitting around the table. The main seat was occupied by three elderly gentlemen with yarmulkes on their heads, who had their books open. They were praying and swaying. They were 'wailing' and the rest of the company listened in silence. There were young people there as well. Even boys who went to English schools had to put on their yarmulkes and pray.

Only after these ceremonies did the feast begin. The party was extremely lavish, even though it was a potluck. As we were not able to eat all the delicacies served to us, we were also invited the next day. I was referred to as Shabbos goy.

I spent two months in Mexico, exploring the city and surrounding area with Magdalena. We visited churches, the famous Our Lady of Guadalupe, I was shown synagogues, monuments of the Maya civilisation, the magnificent pyramids.

When we visited the miraculous image of Our Lady, we saw women walking on their knees across the entire square leading to the church, with their knees bare, as they did not want to tear their stockings, sometimes leaning on the arm of the man who accompanied them.

There is an entrance fee to the pyramids and it is difficult to climb them because the steps are very high. Magdalena sat on the first step and I climbed a little higher to have a photo taken.

When I visited the synagogues, I noticed that in some of them the objects of worship were tied six times over with barbed wire. There were arrays of six candles burning everywhere. There were even six reciters in the magnificent academy building of the Museum of Jewish Martyrdom. All this in memory of the six million Jews murdered during the Holocaust. The walls of the great concert hall in Mexico City were covered with polychrome depicting the suffering faces of people in striped uniforms.

After my trip to Mexico, I flew to Montreal. I stayed with my friend Mrs Sawczyńska, who worked as a newsagent at the airport. Information about my visit to Montreal reached General Szylling's wife, who was the sister of cavalry master Dobrowolski, an acquaintance of Tadeusz and Andrzej Falewicz. Dobrowolski was a military attaché of the Polish Legation in Mexico, and I had met him earlier at Magdalena's. In Montreal, the general's wife introduced me to an extremely interesting man, Rabbi Stern, a philosopher and thinker, highly respected not only by the Jewish community. She called him and asked him to see me, saying that I had rescued many Jews during the occupation and that I was now just returning from Mexico, where I was visiting some of those who had been rescued.

I recall the meeting with Rabbi Stern with profound emotion. In a huge synagogue with a stage and a dining hall next to it, several hundred people had gathered after the service, seated at tables like in a restaurant. Rabbi Stern led me up to the stage, asked the diners to be quiet and, holding a microphone, made a speech. He enumerated my merits and contribution to saving the Jews, spoke of my attitude towards the Jews, etc. Afterwards, without any notice, he handed me the microphone saying, 'Now please

Helena with Simon Blumental, Mexico, 1968

finish my speech.' Unprepared, not knowing what to say, I just asked the Rabbi if I could speak in French. When I got permission, I thanked Rabbi Stern very kindly for his speech. I also said what I knew about the fate of the Jews of Vilnius and the help that Polish society had offered them in those terrible times of occupation. The whole hall applauded! As a token of that day, I received an *Old Testament* from Rabbi Stern with a dedication: *God is One*. When the ceremony was over, various Jews from different parts of the world came up to me, speaking in different languages. They inquired about the details of my help to the Jews. I also met Mr and Mrs Kamras from Vilnius. Mrs Kamras is the daughter of the Vilnius lawyer Komgold, my colleague. When the ceremony was over, I was invited, together with my friend, General Szylling's wife, and a few other people, to dinner in a restaurant located on the thirty-seventh floor. High windows gave wonderful view of the entire of Montreal. There was no service in this restaurant. A variety of dishes were prepared, from appetisers to cakes and ice cream. The food was arranged in pyramids and the guests could choose whatever they wanted.

Since that meeting, Mr and Mrs Kamras have been sending me 10 or 13 dollars every Christmas. I remember how one of the Jews who said goodbye to me at the airport stuffed a dozen or so individual dollar bills into my pocket so that I could buy something on the plane that was to take me to Poland ...

The gratitude I felt from Magdalena was touching! When I went to England a few years ago, Magdalena flew there from Mexico. The first time she flew in when I was supposed to be there, but due to a delay in passport and visa formalities, my visit was postponed by a couple of months. She then came a second time and spent ten days with me at my son's place, always affectionate, warm and grateful. She gave me beautiful Astrakhan furs and, when I tried to refuse, she said: 'You have done much more for me ...'

While I was in Mexico, the editor of a Jewish newspaper came and interviewed me at length. I still have this newspaper; there is a photo of the three of us: Magdalena, Szymon and me.

I have written so much about Magdalena because, since we were in constant contact, she is the one I remember the most. But there were many Jews who passed through my flat in Jezuicka Street, through Balinpol, whom I took care of. I have mentioned a few of them. Sempoliński also writes about some of these people. Many names have escaped my memory.

During my stay in the UK in 1982, I received a letter from Jerusalem notifying me that I had been awarded the Medal of the Righteous Among the Nations by the Yad Vashem Organisation, and authorising me to plant a tree in the Garden of the Righteous Among the Nations.

On 30 May I received this medal and a diploma written in Hebrew and French from the Israeli ambassador in London. I quote the French text:

Diplome d' honneur

La present Diplome atteste qu'en sa seance du 18 fevrier 1982 La Commision d'Hommage aux Justes des Nations etablie par l'Institut Commemoratif des Martyrs et des Heros Yad Vashem, sur la foi des temoignages recueilles par elle, a rendu hommage a Sztukowska Helena, qui, au peril de sa vie a sauve des Juifs persecutes pendent la periode de l'holcauste en Europe, lui a decerne la Medaille des Justes parmi les Nations et l'a autorisee a planter un arbre en son nom dans l'Allee Justes sur le Mont du Souvenir a Jerusalem.

Fait a Jerusalem, le 23 mai 1982

(-) ....   *(-)..*
(-) pour l'Institut.............................   *(-) pour la Commision*
Yad Vashem ....   *des Justes*

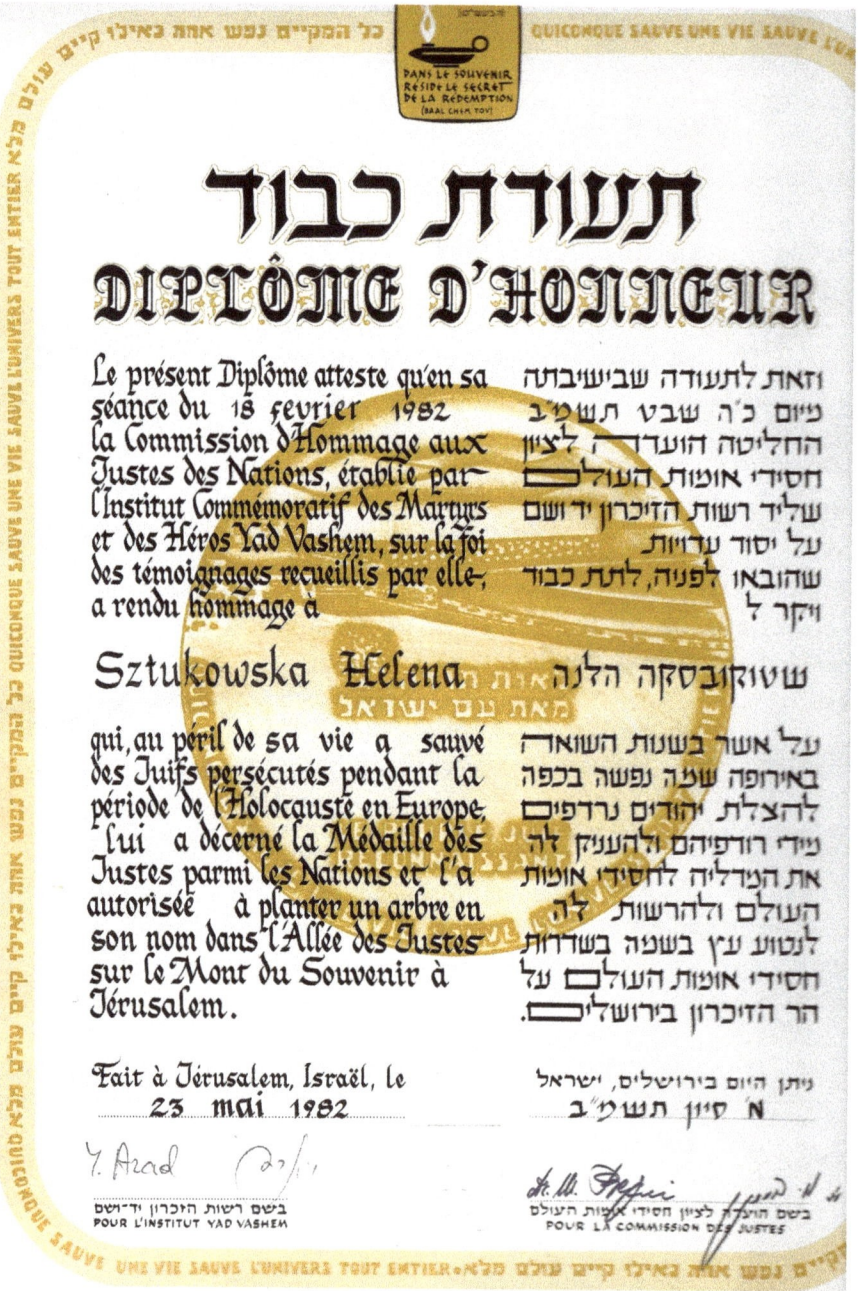

כל המקיים נפש אחה כאילו קיים עולם מלא QUICONQUE SAUVE UNE VIE SAUVE L

DANS LE SOUVENIR
RESIDE LE SECRET
DE LA RÉDEMPTION
(BAAL CHEM TOV)

תעודת כבוד
DIPLÔME D'HONNEUR

Le présent Diplôme atteste qu'en sa séance du 18 février 1982 la Commission d'Hommage aux Justes des Nations, établie par l'Institut Commémoratif des Martyrs et des Héros Yad Vashem, sur la foi des témoignages recueillis par elle, a rendu hommage à

Sztukowska Helena

qui, au péril de sa vie a sauvé des Juifs persécutés pendant la période de l'Holocauste en Europe, lui a décerné la Médaille des Justes parmi les Nations et l'a autorisée à planter un arbre en son nom dans l'Allée des Justes sur le Mont du Souvenir à Jérusalem.

Fait à Jérusalem, Israël, le
23 mai 1982

Y. Arad

בשם רשות הזכרון יד-ושם
POUR L'INSTITUT YAD VASHEM

POUR LA COMMISSION DES JUSTES

204

Remembrance is the secret of redemption

(Baal Chem Tov)

Certificate Of Honour

This is to certify that in its session of 18 February 1982 the Commission for the Designation of the Righteous, established by Yad Vashem, the Holocaust heroes and Martyrs Remembrance Authority, on the basis of evidence presented before it, has decided to honour Sztukowska Helena who, during the Holocaust period in Europe risked her life to save persecuted Jews. The Commission, therefore, has accorded her the Medal of the Righteous Among the Nations and authorised her to plant a tree in the Garden of the Righteous at Yad Vashem, Jerusalem.

Jerusalem, Israel

23 May 1982

Y. Arad

On behalf of the Yad Vashem
Institute

On behalf of the Commission for
the Designation of the Righteous

WHOEVER SAVES ONE LIFE IS AS THOUGH HE HAD SAVED THE ENTIRE WORlD

I would be lying if I said I was not proud of this distinction. After all, there are not many more than 3,000 people in the world who hold this title. In Poland such eminent people as Zofia Kossak-Szczucka and Władysław Bartoszewski. I did not plant a tree in the Garden of the Righteous Among the Nations on the Mount of Remembrance in Jerusalem. I did not have the strength to go there. That was done on my behalf by someone from the Yad Vashem Institute. But I like to look at the diploma, which reminds me that people do not forget.

During my recent stay in Nieborów, where my nephew Jan Falewicz and I were working on the final draft of my memoirs, I met the writer Julian Stryjkowski, who read the Hebrew text of the diploma to me. Stryjkowski is a very kind, quiet and modest man. He speaks quietly but his voice is warm and full of fire. Once, when we were sitting in the smoking room, he told us that he had never ever kissed women's hands, that it was a strange custom to him.

When I was leaving for Warsaw, he placed a kiss on my hand. He looked meaningfully at my nephew and whispered quietly: Yad Vashem! The righteous among the nations!

Nieborów, April 1984.

Epilogue

⌒⌒⌒

Helena finished her memoirs in April 1984. They were published in Polish and in an appendix to the above she had written of some of the 9,000 cases she had undertaken as a barrister.

Although her son Jan (nickname Pumpkin) had made a life in England, she resisted his entreaties to move there. She still believed that Poland was where she needed to be, she still believed she could continue to be of service to the Polish people.

She remained in Warsaw where she was looked after by her friends; she enjoyed conversation, bridge and company.

She died in her sleep on 4 August 1985 and was buried in the Powazki Cemetery in Warsaw, a worthy resting place for her alongside many of the most notable Poles of recent generations.

It was fitting that she should be remembered as her life had been devoted to Poland. Her courage, resilience and steadfast loyalty to the Polish people had been constant and unwavering throughout her life notwithstanding the tumultuous and dangerous times through which she had lived. Her memoirs take the reader into another age, one which should not be forgotten. Despite the ravages of war, invasion and occupation she remained optimistic of the determination of the Polish people to survive, indeed to prosper. Against the prejudices of the age she was able as a woman to qualify as a barrister, she defended those accused by hostile and repressive regimes, she undertook challenging work in the field of prison reform, she never lost her sense of what was right or the essential good in humanity.

The passages relating to her marriage to and love for Josef her husband remain touching and inspiring. He was a poet, diplomat and soldier. Tragically they were not together long. He perished in the Katyń Forest massacres along with many other notable and leading Polish figures whom the Russians under Stalin believed would hamper their ambitions to subjugate the Polish people.

The memoirs are a testament to the spirit of a woman who made the world a better place.

It was her son Jan who determined that they should be published in English. He wanted those who were related to Helena and others whose lives she touched but who are not Polish speaking to be able to read her remarkable story.

We are all inspired by reading about Helena.

www.ingramcontent.com/pod-product-compliance
Lightning Source LLC
Chambersburg PA
CBHW041930260326
41914CB00009B/1252